Everything an Organist Should Know

by Robert Leach
and Barry Williams

Barry Williams

ISBN no 0-9550749-0-8

Contents

Preface by Bishop of London

About the authors

Acknowledgments

Introduction

Preface by the Bishop of London

Ever since the installation of an organ, a gift from the Eastern Emperor, in Charlemagne's Chapel Royal in Aachen, the organist has been a notable figure in the culture and worship of the Western church.

I have personally had the good fortune to work with a succession of organists of high quality and imagination. Today, in the Diocese of London, the Church is fortunate, not only in high places of Christian worship like St Paul's and the Temple Church, but also in a host of parish churches to enjoy the services of organists who combine professional skill with Christian dedication. They should be seen as part of the ministerial team in the places where they serve and be regarded as a full partner in leading the worship of the people of God.

Unfortunately when things go wrong, both clergy, organists and other lay leaders can retreat into isolation when, of course, the offering of any liturgy requires the combination of talents and the creation of an integrated act of worship, rather than a fragmented series of "turns".

This useful volume provides the scaffolding for professional conduct and creative relationships for organists in our church. My gratitude for what organists can contribute to the life of the Church of England leads me on to thank Robert Leach and Barry Williams for so helpfully bringing together Everything Else an Organist Should Know.

+ Richard Londin
The Rt Revd and Rt Hon Richard Chartres DD FSA

About the authors

Robert Leach and Barry Williams

Robert Leach FCCA FIPPM ACertCM is a chartered certified accountant. He is the author of over 30 books, mainly on tax and payroll, including Payroll Factbook and Tax Factbook published by Sweet & Maxwell, and The Church Treasurer's Handbook published by SCM-Canterbury Press. He is a church organist and choirmaster, an undiscovered composer, and also plays for local orchestras and in a dance band. He is a member of council of the Royal School of Church Music, and chairman of the trustees of the Church of England Newspaper. He has been a member of General Synod for Guildford diocese since 1995, where he has served on the pensions board and Central Board of Finance.

Barry Williams MA LLM FTCL ARCM is a lawyer in the professional civil service, and Head of Her Majesty's Revenue and Customs Appeals Unit in London, where he advises on and conducts complex appeals for The Crown. He lectures on many subjects related to church music, including child protection, performer's rights, copyright and the legal aspects of organ building. He is an honorary adviser to the RSCM and has mediated in many organist disputes. He is Organ Adviser in the Diocese of Oxford and is the honorary legal adviser to the Cathedral Organists' Association and the Plainsong and Mediaeval Music Society. He is an honorary member of the Institute of British Organ building and is an organ recitalist and choir director.

Acknowledgments

We acknowledge the help of many individuals in providing information and reviewing chapters in this book. (Acknowledgment does not necessarily mean that the person agrees with all of the content that they reviewed.)

For reviewing the whole book:

Prof. Peter Aston DPhil, GBSM, FTCL, FCI, ARCM, FRSCM, Hon. RCM, Hon. FGCM, FRSA, composer and Chairman of the Academic Board of the Guild of Church Musicians

Prof. John Harper MA PhD FRCO(CHM), Director General of the Royal School of Church Music

Neil Hoyle, chief executive to the Incorporated Society of Musicians

Peter Wright MA FRCO, president of the Royal College of Organists (2005/06)

Canon Bob Baker BA, prolocutor of the lower house of the Convocation of Canterbury, member of the Archbishops' Council

Fr Gerard Bradley, priest, organist and professor at Wonersh Seminary

Ven Bob Reiss MA, Archdeacon of Surrey, now Canon at Westminster Abbey

For reviewing particular chapters:

Chapter 1: Good relationships

Alastair McKay, director of Bridge Builders, Menonite Church, London

Dr Michael O'Connor, (former) warden of the Royal School of Church Music

Chapter 4: Fees and budgets

Michael Chamberlain LLD FCA, organist, and chairman of Finance Committee, Archbishops' Council

Chapter 5: Copyright

Chris Williams, European sales manager of Christian Copyright Licensing Ltd

Chapter 6: Protecting our children

Simon Bass, Churches Child Protection Advisory Service

Simon Parton, organist and diocesan secretary for Southwark

Chapter 7: Tax

HM Revenue and Customs

Chapter 8: Health and safety

Andrew Dawson, Ecclesiastical Insurance Group

Cover: Specially commissioned cartoon by Mark Wood, cartoonist published in The Spectator, Private Eye, The Sun, The Times, Daily Mirror and many other publications.

Published by Organist Publications Ltd.

ISBN number 0-9550749-0-8

Production: Grove Business Services. Printed by Biddles Ltd.

Introduction

The need for the book

In September 2003, a course on Organist as Manager was held in London, sponsored by the Guild of Church Musicians, Royal College of Organists and Royal School of Church Music, all of whom attended. The course dealt with the main areas of an organist's work outside music and theology. It was clear from the reaction that there was a need to cover all these areas. It is often here that organists get into difficulty.

The result is this book of nine chapters comprising a dog's breakfast of law, accounts, science, theology, regulation and received wisdom. Chapters 3 to 8 mainly explain law, while chapters 1 and 2 largely give practical advice in difficult areas. Chapter 9 is a miscellany of topics which do not justify an entire chapter.

Our aim is to provide a single authoritative and complete reference book. Although intended for organists, there is much in this book which will also be of relevance to clergy, readers, music group leaders and non-church musicians. Inevitably, the book concentrates on the Church of England, as that is where most organists work. However we have endeavoured to cover other denominations.

For practical reasons, the book is produced by a company set up by the authors for the purpose. However we have worked closely with respected bodies, and are grateful to the many consultants and others who have provided us with information and commented on the draft chapters. We are always pleased to hear of topics or experiences which readers may wish to suggest for future editions.

For convenience, we have used the term "minister" to include deans, vicars, rectors, priests in charge and similar office holders. No slight or disrespect is intended by this. Similarly, we have used the term "organist" to include choirmasters, combined posts of organists and choirmasters, directors of music and similar office holders.

Also, we have adopted the legal practice of using "he" and "his" to mean "he or she" and "his or her" when inclusive language is not readily possible. We are sure our valued female ministers and sister organists will have the grace to accept that this is purely for ease of reading.

It is often observed that there is a shortage of organists in Britain. Our research indicates that is not so. The shortage is because two-thirds of qualified organists are not prepared to accept a regular church appointment. Many times the reason for this is because of a problem, such as clergy relations, which this book seeks to address.

This book is written in the hope that it will assist organists to perform their duties more easily and happily to the greater glory of God.

Robert Leach
Barry Williams

Note on legal sources

In the UK, there are two main sources of law: statutes and cases. Statutes include Acts of Parliament which have a name such as Licensing Act 2003. Statutory instruments, which are issued under the authority of an Act, have a name and number such as Copyright and Related Rights Regulations SI 2003 No 2498. Court cases give the names of the parties to the case and the year that it was heard, such as Hall v Lorimer [1993]. These legal sources have been quoted throughout.

---

1 Good relationships

Introduction

The organist is a key figure in the worshipping life of the church. Playing "the king of instruments" is a wonderful experience in itself. Doing so for the glory of God is a particular blessing.

The work of a church organist requires a knowledge of music and theology (both generally outside the scope of this book) plus practical skills and knowledge in many areas. While all church offices require particular mixes of knowledge and skills, the office of organist is unique in that:

- so few church members can play the organ, compared with the number capable of holding other church offices;
- the organist plays a key function in leading worship without having undertaken any formal training or licensing arranged by the church authorities;
- the organist must work with a minister who may have had little training in the organist's work; and
- as choirmaster, he is the only church officer whose regular duties include telling other church members (the choir) what they are doing wrong.

None of this need be a problem, provided the organist starts from a secure base. That base starts by having a good relationship with the minister.

In 1995, the Archbishops' Commission on Church Music report In Tune With Heaven found only 3% of clergy reporting a poor relationship with their organist. Unfortunately the report did not ask the equivalent question of organists. The authors' experience is that an organist is fortunate if he can manage a career without at least one serious run-in with the clergy.

The authors have witnessed and experienced horror stories of serious breakdowns in relationships, often with some of the most bizarre behaviour. These breakdowns cause huge hurt to individuals involved, create problems for church organisation and distress for other members. Perhaps worst of all, such breakdowns are dishonouring to God and set a poor witness of working together as one Christian body.

It is long overdue for these issues to be confronted. This section aims to tiptoe through this minefield with some guidance on how to prevent problems from arising, and what to do when they do arise. The separate issues of running a choir and enjoying good relations with the congregation are addressed in chapter 2.

An organist must use all reasonable efforts to maintain good relations with the clergy, understanding their position at all times, and should seek to remedy any problems as quickly and as amicably as possible.

Unlike many of the following chapters, there is little unequivocal law which may be quoted in this area. Instead, this chapter seeks to collect together received wisdom, common sense and experience in the form of recommendations to solve problems, or, better, to prevent them from happening.

What follows is intended to advise in situations most commonly encountered by organists. The advice may need amending in a church or community which has a significantly different culture.

Prevention

The elements

Prevention is better than cure. An organist should strive to prevent problems developing, even if you believe that others are not making similar efforts.

There are three elements to any relationship:

- your attitude;
- their attitude; and
- how you interact.

You have absolute control over your own attitude, significant influence over the interaction, and very little influence over the attitude of the other party. Indeed the comments below only address the first and third elements. Any influence you have over the minister will naturally flow from your attitude and how you interact.

So the first step for the organist is to have a positive attitude. Ask yourself these questions:

- am I committed to serving the objects of the church?
- can I work with the minister and other church officers?
- am I prepared to listen to what others want?
- am I prepared to explain myself?

- can I work with other people (whatever I think of them)?
- do I appear cheerful?
- do I appear self-confident?
- can I take criticism, however seemingly ignorant and unjustified?

This list is not exhaustive. It simply addresses some of the main elements in self-preparation to make you as effective an organist as is possible.

The second step is establishing a working relationship with the minister. You begin by simply getting to know each other. See if you can answer these questions about your minister:

- how long has he been at the church?
- where was he before?
- why did he move?
- how long has he been a minister?
- what job did he have before entering the ministry?
- is he married?
- how many children does he have?
- where did he grow up?
- what are his hobbies and interests?

Does he know similar information about you? How willing have you been to share this?

You should make opportunities simply to chat, such as by having lunch together occasionally. Learn to relax in each other's company, and to discuss subjects far removed from church music, while not allowing such discussion itself to become a difficulty. All this will help stop problems arising, and will create the right atmosphere in which to solve any that do arise. You will find out what values are important to each other, and what makes each other "tick".

The book *Weary and Ill at Ease* by Robin Rees (published by Gracewing Books) conducted a survey of attitudes by ministers and organists. This survey finds that a minister gets on better with an organist:

- who is younger;
- who has not been in post as long as the minister;
- when the minister enjoys the organist's solo playing;

- who is involved in other church life; and
- where there are regular discussions between them.

Factors that Rees surprisingly found did *not* affect the relationship include:

- whether the organist is a Christian;
- how long the minister spent in secular employment;
- whether the contract gives the organist a right of appeal.

The more pro-active elements of a good relationship are explained further below.

Two fundamentals

The two requirements for a good relationship between organist and minister (or any other relationship) are:

- common agenda; and
- mutual respect.

These two fundamentals are like railway lines. They do not guarantee that you will not hit problems, but they should ensure that you stay on track.

The requirement for **common agenda** means that the minister and organist are agreed on what they are trying to achieve.

The requirement for **mutual respect** means that both the organist and minister respect each other, including the skills and experience they each offer. This involves an appropriate attitude by both parties. From this comes the trust which should lie at the heart of any relationship.

One of the authors of this book was organist and choirmaster of Saint Stephen's Church, Norbury and Thornton Heath in the mid 1970s. The then vicar, the Revd Michael Alan Collis, without exception thanked the choir for their singing after every service and always made a point of thanking the organist for the music each Sunday. This appreciation generated an atmosphere of immense loyalty. The few but sincere words encouraged folk to give of their very best.

Common agenda

A common agenda means that you are both working towards the same goals. There should be clear boundaries, and no ambiguity about responsibilities and duties, or who does what.

In the Church some of these are general. It is the function of all churches to worship God, welcome visitors, pray for the world, help the needy, read scripture and preach the gospel. If a church fails to do any of these things, it has problems far more fundamental than its relationship with the organist.

Some issues arise in connection with the conduct of worship. Many of such issues are covered by the canons or rules of the denomination. Read them.

How any particular church implements those policies in its own situation is a matter for the church leadership. The structure of this leadership varies according to the denomination. These range from the centralised authority of Roman Catholics and some house churches, through to the totally congregational policies of the Baptist Church. Most churches in between have a mixed leadership of minister and council. The Church of England has a mixed government of clergy and parochial church councils (PCCs). Each provides a check on the other, allowing the church to have the advantages of both single leadership and collective responsibility.

At an individual church level, a parish may properly adopt such local policies as to link up with other churches, to concentrate on particular areas of ministry, or to engage in particular activities. It is not the function of an organist to second-guess the minister and church council on such matters. An organist is as entitled as anyone else to contribute to the discussion on local policy. Indeed, an organist has a particular training and expertise which should be made available to the church. However once a policy has been agreed, it is the organist's function to follow it and not question it, much less to obstruct it.

Examples of policies and how an organist can help deliver them include:

Link with other churches

Make contact with the organists or other musicians in those churches and consider opportunities for working together, such as joint services with other choirs or organ-swapping.

Reach-out to a particular group

Consider how the choir may be involved. If reaching out to children, you could tie in a campaign to recruit children to the choir, explaining the benefits and linking it to other initiatives. If reaching out to other groups, you could arrange for the choir to sing to them.

Undertake an event

Consider what music would be appropriate for this event. If a policy does not itself involve music, such as starting an Alpha course, consider choosing an anthem to perform when the policy is launched.

Fund-raising

Organise a concert for the purpose.

Any policy

Use your imagination to choose a voluntary which ties in with the theme. If the church is launching an appeal to repair the clock, play Haydn's Clock Symphony as the voluntary, and have this noted on the service sheet. Such things are appreciated.

Musical agenda

In addition to the church's overall agenda, it is good policy to have an agenda for the music. This may include:

- enlarging the choir;
- introducing a children's choir;
- introducing a training programme;
- producing a hymn book supplement;
- setting up a music group;
- planning a festival or performance of a major work;
- introducing some new forms of music.

It is good to have an over-arching music policy in a church, but this is outside the scope of this book.

A church with no **musical agenda** is unhealthy. Church life is like a down escalator: you need to keep moving forward to stop going backwards. The musical agenda need not be radical, but you should have one.

The organist should be at the forefront in advancing such ideas, but should ensure that the minister accepts it and "owns" the idea. The organist should always be ready to explain ideas. One unsubtle example was an organist who said, "Vicar, for the carol service we can do traditional carols with some modern items, or we can do modern carols with some traditional carols, or we can do a mixture of modern and traditional carols." The vicar chose the mixture, the organist praised his wisdom to the skies, and continued with the selection of music he had chosen two months earlier. Most discussions on musical agenda are more open-ended!

If the minister has a specific request for music, it is politic to accommodate him even if you consider it not the best music. Making clear that an item is included "just for you" demonstrates co-operation and buys goodwill. Hymns and songs can be traced through the Hymnquest Database (details in Appendix 1).

The organist's job, like any job, will inevitably include some parts you enjoy less than others. It may even include parts you do not enjoy at all, family services or youth services perhaps. Remember that if you accept the job, you accept the **whole package.** Do your job in every part of that package as well as you can.

Mutual respect

In a good relationship, the organist must respect the minister and the minister must respect the organist. You can deliver the first, and then expect the second.

There is a biblical principle that the church is like a single body where the members are like the parts of the body working together (1 Corinthians 12:12-31). This should be the basis of the relationship between minister and organist. A minister who has an experienced, trained organist capable of exercising a musical ministry should allow that organist to do so. If the minister sees such an organist as nothing more than a human juke box to play the numbers the minister chooses, you can count the days before there is a bust-up. According to *Weary and Ill at Ease*, over half of all clergy spend less than four hours of their training studying music in worship.

Many problems arise because of differing expectations, sometimes reflecting the different abilities of organists. It should be clearly understood what the organist's role is and where the boundaries are. It should be agreed whether there is a separate music group and, if so, who co-ordinates the music. Some sample questions for an organist to ask at interview are given on page 48.

It should be added that respect in itself means nothing unless it is demonstrated. **Respect** does not mean pretending that failings do not exist, but simply accepting a person despite those failings.

Some examples of how an organist can demonstrate respect for a minister include:

- **a friendly relationship**, such as inviting the minister to all choir social events, and seeking opportunities to socialise, such as the occasional drink at the pub or invitation to dinner. Food and drink is the currency of goodwill;

- words of **encouragement**, such as saying when you thought a sermon or leadership of a service was good;

- **sympathy** when he has problems.

You may be surprised at how much goodwill can be generated by a simple handwritten note of appreciation or sympathy.

Preachers sometimes mention hymns or other music in a sermon. Quietly playing a verse of the quoted hymn, or a snatch of other music, later in the service is usually very much appreciated. An ideal time is just before the final voluntary.

Avoid making **criticism**. It is probably better for an organist not to comment adversely on sermons or prayers. Do nothing unless it has a clear constructive purpose. It is difficult to see what purpose is served by telling the minister that his sermon was boring. Acts 20:7-12 records how Eutychus fell asleep when Paul was preaching, so the problem is not new.

Be careful of **jokes** about the minister. A verbal or practical joke on someone is only funny if the someone sees it that way. Lampooning leaders is a time-honoured custom in free democratic societies — children lampoon parents, pupils lampoon teachers, choristers lampoon the choirmaster, and everyone lampoons the prime minister. The British army once ran advertisements in which the right to lampoon leaders was seen as a fundamental freedom worth defending. However not everyone may see jokes in such an enlightened way, so be doubly careful. If a joke does backfire, simply apologise. Do not tell the minister that he is a humourless fool.

(One day you will be asked the joke: What is the difference between an organist and a terrorist? Answer: you can negotiate with a terrorist. It is a matter for your judgment whether you reply by asking what is the difference between a minister and a terrorist? Answer: the terrorist knows what he is doing!)

It is also worth sharing your own problems with the minister. This helps to build up trust and a sense of collaborative ministry. It can help protect your position if the problem is not resolved as you hoped.

Some practical issues

Organists are probably more vulnerable than other church officers for two main reasons:

- the choir can take on a life of its own; and

- the organist may have a strong personality.

A survey by Oxford clergy found that organists stayed in post longer than Anglican clergy, noting "the parson may have his freehold but the organist may have the stranglehold on the parish" (Parish and People 1986). Subsequent surveys indicate an average tenure of seven years for a vicar and ten years for an organist.

If you ask what are the hallmarks of an **independent body**, your list might include:

- its own name;
- its own leadership;
- a defined membership;
- regular meetings;
- its own premises;
- its own property.

All these probably apply to a choir. It may also have its own funds and produce its own newsletters, and even have its own rules and policies. Some of these apply to other groups, such as Sunday School and youth group, but they are unlikely to have them all. Also most other groups exist to "be", whereas a choir exists to "do", so a choir is usually the most disciplined of all church groups, and therefore the most coherent.

The choir may be the largest church group under a single leader. In some churches, the choir can represent a quarter or more of the entire congregation. All this can happen without any intention to set up a rival body. Some ministers see the organist as leader of the opposition. Sometimes the minister is right.

As organist, you direct the choir only in rehearsal and performance of music. You do not direct choir members in any other area of church policy or activity, and must accept that choir members will exercise their own judgment in such areas.

Strong personality can be seen as a problem in an organist, particularly if the minister is a weak personality. It should be understood that a certain strength of personality is a job requirement for an organist. **Self-confidence** is needed to perform week after week in front of hundreds of people, to direct a body of musicians and to inspire them to greater performance. However self-confidence is easily mistaken for arrogance.

There is a **vulnerability in performance** for both ministers and organists, which they can cope with differently. A sharing of that common experience can help improve the relationship.

One survey showed that 60% of musicians but only 8% of church ministers are extraverts. This highlights the significant extent to which a self-confident organist can appear out of place in the church.

A new minister

A change of minister can be a difficult time, as the new minister inevitably comes with his own ideas into a church with its own routines.

Normally, a wise minister will not immediately try to makes changes, but will largely follow the existing arrangements for a year or so. However, there will be changes simply because the minister is a different person. The organist should be sensitive to the fact that a new minister may not even be aware that he is doing things differently.

It is essential for the organist and new minister to get to know each other, as already outlined.

Choosing the music

A sometimes controversial area of the relationship is who should **choose the music**. The ideal arrangement is:

- the minister prepares a list of forthcoming services, noting any special themes, visiting preachers or other special arrangements or departures from the lectionary or church calendar;
- the organist prepares a draft list of hymns and other music which is sent to the minister, and possibly to others; and
- the minister checks that he is happy with the list, or suggests changes which the organist accepts.

Ideally the **music list** is prepared for a period of between one and three months, and is published before the start of that period.

Such an arrangement cannot be followed when the organist is not able to exercise such a ministry (such as a "reluctant organist" or stand-in organist), or where the culture of the church is that a single person plans the entire service, as in the Methodist Church. But in the latter case, the church should realise that it is compromising the quality of its music by excluding those trained to exercise a music ministry.

Once the music list is prepared, it should be followed but not inflexibly. There must be a balance between the two biblical principles of:

- not quenching the spirit of spontaneity (1 Thessalonians 5:19) and
- worship being done decently and in order (1 Corinthians 14:40).

For music lists, these two principles are met by allowing occasional departures from the published music list for good reason, such as to change the hymn near the sermon (which is usually written after the music list is compiled) to reflect the sermon's message, or to reflect a significant event such as the terrorist attack on 11 September 2001.

There are many useful guides to choosing music, particularly the Royal School of Church Music's excellent quarterly guide *Sunday by Sunday*.

Church councils

Where a church has a council, worship committee or similar, that body must clearly understand its role in the worship of the church.

In the Church of England, the PCC or worship committee has no control over the music whatsoever, which is solely a matter for the minister and organist. Most other denominations have similar policies. We have been aware of problems when church councils and worship committees interfere in the work of the organist.

It is good practice for there to be an occasional discussion at church council on music, but this should only be done with the organist present. The council should know that it has no authority to pass resolutions on music. It is useful if a member of the choir is also a member of the church council.

When things go wrong

Perspective

When problems arise, it is first necessary to identify the **underlying reason**. The minister changing the last hymn is not a problem. The minister is almost certainly entitled to change a hymn and may have good reason for doing so. It is more likely that the problem is not telling you in enough time, changing the hymn just to annoy you, or simply not appreciating that the choir spent an hour practising the descant. A wise minister will first ask the organist if he is happy to change the hymn, which will usually avoid the problem.

Similarly an organist changing a hymn or otherwise departing from what is expected can be unsettling to the minister. The organist must try to avoid wrong-footing the minister, and be ready to listen and explain if this happens.

Next, decide whether the problem goes to the **heart of the relationship** or is simply the result of normal human fallibility. Issues which arise because of forgetfulness, thoughtlessness or clumsiness may be very irritating at the time, but do not undermine the relationship. They should be addressed, particularly if they keep happening, but they should not be blown up into a fundamental problem.

Conversely, the same principle applies if you make a mistake from **fallibility**, such as forgetting to come in at the right part of the service, forgetting the last verse or playing a fistful of wrong notes. If you have made a mistake, simply admit it and apologise. Do not justify it.

Incidents based on fallibility must not be regarded as portents of the apocalypse. Not every slip-up is the tip of an iceberg. They should still be addressed, usually by making an effort to be more careful next time. Avoid imposing **new procedures** to deal with a single slip-up. Such new procedures often create more problems than they solve.

The serious issues are when the matter in contention indicates a **breakdown** in relationship. Examples include deliberate annoyance, non-communication, abuse, shouting, gossip and arbitrary behaviour. None of these are acceptable. They cannot be excused on the basis of pressure of work, divine nature or artistic temperament.

As a rough guide, consider overlooking the first instance if not too serious. Walk away and act as if it had not happened. It may be that the minister will realise what he has done, and there will be no recurrence. Only when something happens a second time is it usually worth addressing.

Next, ask yourself if this behaviour is **in character**. Suppose a person is normally happy to be teased about their weight. One day you make such a remark and get a mouthful of abuse. The natural reaction is to be equally abusive in reply, but that is almost certainly the worst option. An out-of-character remark often indicates that a person is under pressure in some way, for which a sympathetic response is usually more appropriate. Answering a cry for help is not only morally correct, but will help improve future relations.

Banter is a normal part of a healthy relationship. It demonstrates the trust and respect people have for each other, and keeps the relationship happy and open. It is noticeable that any musical ensemble from symphony orchestra to rock band has gelled when members tease each other about their performance. It is a fundamental mistake to see banter as a problem. However banter must never be used as a cover for expressing serious views, and banter should avoid known sensitivities. It is best to avoid banter based on race, sex or disability, even if the "victim" makes such comments.

Sometimes a minister may shout at you because he is having real problems elsewhere, and you happened to ask about a hymn tune just after the minister heard a harrowing tale of a family suicide. To see this as a fundamental problem when it isn't one could lead to an otherwise avoidable breakdown. You can test this simply by coming back later.

Never attempt to solve a problem when you or the other person has lost their **temper**. You will not resolve anything, and will possibly say things you regret. Say that you will address the matter when both of you are calm. Although postponements can be appropriate for unfortunate moments and lost temper, postponements should always be kept short, otherwise the wound will fester.

The body is designed to tell you when it is reaching its limit, such as if trying to lift a weight which is too heavy. You do not continue until you strain a muscle or damage your back. Similarly, learn to detect emotional limits so you know when to step back before the needle goes into the red zone and you explode in anger.

Identifying problems

There are some specific skills which can help in identifying where real problems lie.

One method is analysing what people say. When people speak, they convey their meaning in three ways:

- what they say — the content of the words;
- how they say it — tone of voice, intensity and
- what else they communicate — body language.

Some much-quoted research says that the impact of the spoken word is determined:

- 8% by what is said;
- 37% by how it is said; and
- 55% by body language.

To this, we can add a fourth element of what is not said.

How someone says something is indicative, as any comment expressed in anything less than a straightforward manner may be hiding something.

Body language is the range of mannerisms or physical expressions which can convey what a person is really feeling. For example, smiling or frowning when someone first sees you may indicate whether they really like you. Most people are honest in relating facts, unless in great difficulty. People, particularly in the church, may find it more difficult to articulate negative or contrary views. Body language can give clues about such views. However you should check your conclusions by asking open questions which allow such views to be expressed.

When **listening** to others, some basic principles are worth remembering:

- listening is about showing respect and seeking understanding, not about agreement;
- listen loosely to the words and tightly to the meaning;
- stay curious and open, and not assuming or judging;
- remember that the other person will usually listen to you, but sometimes only after you have listened to them.

"Listen loosely to the words" means trying to understand the message that the person is seeking to convey, and not becoming focused on any barbed words used.

How an argument is expressed is also telling. If the argument is emotional, "you don't understand what it is like...." or similar, this can mean that there is no logical basis to their view, because if there was, they would use it. If a person resorts to insults, they may not even have an emotional argument, or may feel very threatened.

What people do not say is sometimes called **dogs barking in the night** from this famous quote from the Sherlock Holmes story *The Silver Blaze*:

> *"Is there anything else to which you would wish to draw my attention?"*
>
> *"To the curious incident of the dog in the night-time."*
>
> *"The dog did nothing in the night-time."*
>
> *"That was the curious incident", remarked Sherlock Holmes.*

He was investigating a racehorse nobbled in the night and noted that the stable dog had not barked, indicating the dog knew the person.

Suppose you have just performed a magnificent carol service to a packed church, and the minister says nothing. Or suppose you tell the minister you are thinking of leaving and just get the reply, "you will be difficult to replace" without asking why are you leaving, or if there is a problem. There is a deafening silence from dogs not barking. Something is clearly wrong, and a further conversation is needed.

There is a problem

The previous sections are designed to prevent problems and to deal with any which still arise. Sometimes this will not deal with the matter, and the problem remains.

First, don't go it alone. Talk to a friend, preferably a fellow organist. However tough you are and however conclusive your eventual victory, any issue imposes some strain which may not be obvious to you at the time. A friend can also help you with encouragement, restraint, advice and strategy.

It can sometimes be helpful to write down what has happened as a story. This not only provides a contemporary record but can help you work out in your own mind what the real issues are, and what is not important. Breach of trust is important. Bad language and abuse usually are not. Writing something down can also be cathartic.

Second, stay calm. Avoid **dramatic gestures**, such as shouting, walking out, slamming doors or hanging up on the telephone. You may feel better for three seconds, but you may have made the problem worse and weakened your own position. It is easy to get into a difficult situation; it can be much harder to get out.

Third, make sure the minister is the first person to know of your concerns, not the last. Be honest and complete in expressing your concern. It is always appropriate to be as polite as possible, but not to the extent of being less than completely honest. If honesty and kindness become incompatible, honesty must prevail.

Sometimes when a problem arises with a minister, they may treat this as a **pastoral issue** for which you need help. This may be a ploy to distract attention from the real issue, or they may have picked up a real need. It is up to you whether to accept such an approach. Doing so means that you acknowledge the problem is largely on your side. Be humble enough to acknowledge that this may be so. If you conclude that you may need counselling or support, ensure you follow it up, although you are likely to seek this from someone else.

However, if you believe the problem is largely on the minister's side, the matter should be dealt with as a complaint. Once you know there is a problem with the minister, see if the problem is specific to you.

Clergy can find their work difficult and lonely. Listening to confidential tales of grief can be mentally draining, and the church has a poor record of supporting its ministers. Parishioners can be unreasonable in demands. Clergy are not immune to marital, financial, medical and practical problems, but may be less willing to admit them. It is possible that the organist is simply the first port of call during a stormy period for him. For a church organist, moving house, changing job and changing church are usually three separate decisions; for a minister, they are usually one.

If you are having such problems with the minister, so will other church officers, but remember organists may be the first to be affected. This is because both minister and organist are trained professionals, but each of whose training involves little overlap with the other. You can become a qualified organist with no theological or ministerial training whatsoever, and you can become a minister with no musical training. Other factors are that both minister and organist bear responsibility in the church, and both can be strong personalities.

After organists, youth leaders and lay readers are often next to be affected by a minister's problematic behaviour. The answer is to discuss a problem with other officers, particularly those who work closely with him. Don't be surprised if some officers say there is no problem out of loyalty to the minister.

If the problem is with the minister, sympathy and support can help address the matter. It will not only resolve the problem, but a supportive approach can create goodwill for the future.

If there is a problem with the minister, such as alcoholism, misconduct or a breakdown, it is the responsibility of other church officers to deal with it. In the Church of England, this duty falls to the churchwardens who legally *must* report it to the bishop. The churchwardens have no discretion not to report a serious problem. If necessary, do not hesitate to remind them of this duty.

Complaints

In life, people knock against each other and sometimes hurt each other. In any community, it is important that any response is proportionate.

There is a difference between a bruise and a wound. A **bruise** you leave to heal itself over time; whereas a **wound** must be treated or it will fester. Similarly, some knocks and hurts are best ignored while other issues must be addressed.

The seriousness of the hurt depends wholly on the reaction to it. It is entirely subjective. Just as a blow may bruise one person but wound another, so the seriousness of a problem depends on how it is received rather than on the nature of the problem itself. One person may laugh at a jibe while another is offended.

If something bothers a person, it is a problem. The problem may be that the person should grow up and not let these things bother them, but that is a different issue. The fact that someone takes offence at what you have said does not mean that you are necessarily in the wrong, as people can largely choose what offends them, but it does mean that there is a problem.

A **complaint** is like an order form. The complainant wants something: an apology, compensation, recognition, redress or whatever. The art of dealing with a complaint is to see what the person wants, and then decide whether to give it. All organisations which deal with complaints routinely report that an apology is usually sufficient, even for serious cases. Many personnel problems can be attributed simply to ignoring people. If you do not recognise any wrong, the matter may be resolved by a letter acknowledging the concern and saying it will be properly considered.

If you make a mistake, admit it. More people get into trouble for cover-ups than for the original failing, see page 64.

Sometimes there may be a **mutual complaint** — A complains about B who complains about A. In such cases, each complaint must be dealt with separately, usually in the order in which they arose. A second complaint should not be dismissed as retaliation (even when it is), and the two should not be addressed together.

Methods for dealing with problems

The first point to make about dealing with problems with the clergy is to show **restraint** and self-control yourself. You may wish to lash out, but a calm and considered response is more effective and has fewer negative consequences.

There are three basic ways to solve a problem:

- concession;
- conciliation; and
- confrontation;

and you should consider them in that order.

Concession is where you simply let the matter pass, perhaps just registering an objection, but otherwise doing nothing. This accords with the biblical principle of turning the other cheek (Luke 6:29). This is not an injunction for Christians to let anyone walk all over them, but to show restraint.

Conciliation is where you discuss the problem with the person. If two people want to solve a problem, they will; if one of them does not, they won't. It is as simple as that.

Conciliation should be discussed in a face-to-face meeting. Avoid setting out your grievances in a letter. Letters are hard and impersonal and can entrench positions. (Drafting a letter to clarify issues in your own mind can be helpful, but don't post it.) Telephone calls are not so bad, but they still lack the personal interaction that comes from a meeting and is so important in conciliation.

Be particularly careful about **e-mails** as they are so easy to send, particularly on impulse. If an issue becomes emotionally charged, stop e-mail traffic and seek a face-to-face meeting. Disputes are rarely resolved by e-mail exchanges.

Many breakdown problems are attributed to attitude. **Attitude** is the set of responses a person usually follows. Study has shown that attitude is a combination of belief values and group experience. For either clergy or organists, bad attitude can result from belief in self-importance compounded by group experience of other clergy or organists with similar belief.

Attitude problems can only be demonstrated by means of **examples**, but the problem with offering examples is that the other person can then argue each example and never address the real underlying issue of attitude. It is usually better to state your view about the other person's attitude and invite them to confirm or deny it.

In starting any conciliation, it is advisable to be honest about any failings on your part. Suppose you were abusive when the minister was being unreasonable. It is a good idea to apologise for your rudeness at the start of your meeting. This will create a suitable atmosphere of contrition which is more likely to lead to his willingness to admit his own failings. If not, you have at least cleared your record and removed his ammunition should the matter move to confrontation.

For serious problems, conciliation may start with what appears to be a very negative period of **recrimination** in which accusations fly freely. This is not as negative as it may seem. When things have got really bad, it is necessary for people to unload their burdens and for everyone to see what the issues are.

A conciliation meeting should usually be separate from meetings for any other purpose. Conduct it in private and in as relaxed a manner as possible. Every problem is an opportunity, and relationship breakdowns are no exception. A conciliation meeting is a wonderful opportunity to clear all the other baggage that has been bothering you both.

When there is no goodwill, there is no goodwill to lose. When a relationship is at rock bottom, it cannot fall any further.

The first step to conciliation is to try to see the matter from the other person's **point of view**. The second step is to help others to see it from yours. The focus should be on trying to agree on how you will behave in the future, as well as reaching reconciliation for the past. The time is often spent on establishing the working relationship that should have been there in the first place.

An element in successful conciliation may be to **draw a line** under the problems and move on. As in all dispute resolution, it is advisable to be gracious but honest. Do not concede failures you honestly believe you do not have, but neither conceal failures you do have.

Confrontation is only appropriate when concession and conciliation have not worked. When a matter can neither be ignored nor resolved amicably, it becomes necessary to force the issue.

If an issue remains unresolved but will not go away, it may be necessary to **"up the ante"**. This means that the problem must be made *worse* to start the process of making it better. This is needed when the other party will not co-operate in conciliation. As a problem becomes more serious, more attention is paid to addressing it, and others may become involved in finding a solution. A letter from a solicitor to the minister is an effective way of upping the ante.

If you decide that confrontation is inevitable, you should check your contract of employment to see what grievance or discipline procedure you have agreed. You should also note that there are statutory discipline and grievance procedures from 1 October 2004 (see page 91).

Good biblical advice on church disputes is given in 1 Corinthians 6:1-7. The main point of this passage is that resources for handling disputes should be found within the church. Church bodies should identify those in their midst who have listening, mediating and (finally) judging skills to resolve disputes between church members. Church bodies should also be prepared to provide training in this area.

Involving a third person whom you both respect can assist in resolution. Be clear whether you want mediation or arbitration.

Mediation is a voluntary process where the mediator or mediators structure face-to-face dialogue between parties who are seeking to resolve disputes and address broken relationships. The key principle of mediation is that the *parties themselves* decide the outcome. The mediators do not determine the outcome, as an arbitrator does.

The mediator's task is to provide a structure and safe environment for dialogue and negotiation. Sometimes mediators are called conciliators (as in Clergy Discipline Measure). Basically mediators are either:

- insider-partial; or
- outsider-neutral.

Insider-partial mediators have an informal and existing relationship with the parties. Outsider-neutral mediators have a formal role and no direct relationship with the parties.

The mediator's role normally includes:

- helping the parties to articulate their own needs and interests;
- clarifying the areas of disagreement;
- helping the parties generate options to address these issues; and
- documenting any agreements reached.

In a more transformative approach, the mediator's role is also to:

- help the parties to express their own feelings and experience;
- understand the other's feelings and experience;
- encourage the parties to take responsibility for their own contribution to the past; and
- assist healing and reconciliation in the relationship.

The use of a mediator moves us back from confrontation to conciliation. Such temperature-lowering moves can be achieved by a mediator, even when they have been already dismissed by the parties.

There is a Christian mediation service called Bridge Builders, run by the London Menonite Centre, address in appendix 1. They also run courses in mediation skills.

Arbitration is where the person hears the facts and makes a decision, regardless of whether the parties agree. It is a judgment. Arbitration works on the basis of a commitment by both sides to abide by the arbitrator's decision.

For arbitration, you need to consider the principles of natural justice, explained later.

Involving a third party to advise, mediate or arbitrate should not be used as an excuse to spread gossip or dissent. Avoid anything which can lead to factions being created in the church. Once formed, they are difficult to disband.

Complaints about you

The above explains what to do if you are the complainant. If someone complains about you, you should see how far they follow the process explained above, and seek to ensure compliance. Too frequently a complainant charges into confrontation without even considering concession or conciliation.

You should not be alarmed at having a complaint made against you. Members of professional bodies, such as doctors, lawyers and accountants, expect at least two complaints against them during a professional career. If the complaint proves unfounded, you have the benefit of having been cleared and affirmed in your conduct. But remember you are entitled to have any complaint considered properly.

If you are having difficulty in having a complaint against you handled properly, it is advisable to find a lawyer quickly. Using a lawyer and even starting legal proceedings does not commit you to suing someone, but it has two great advantages:

- it demonstrates that you are taking the matter seriously, which can itself have a powerful moderating effect; and
- it provides a sure basis should the problem end up in court.

Even if the dispute does end up in court, the judge will usually expect the parties to have made some effort to resolve the matter themselves. There are recognised forms of **alternative dispute resolution** (ADR), most notably mediation and arbitration, which the courts promote. In employment law hearings, an employer or employee who has failed to follow a discipline or grievance procedure or who has otherwise behaved unreasonably could find that prejudices their position and can be reflected in any compensation awarded.

Once it becomes apparent that you have a dispute which *could* end up in court:

- keep detailed contemporary records of what happened and when;
- note what efforts you made to resolve the matter amicably;
- avoid retaliation, rudeness or anything else which may prejudice you;

- apologise for any slip-up, however trivial and regardless of whether you receive any apologies in return;

- continue doing your job normally;

- avoid gossip about the matter. It is reasonable to discuss the matter with your partner and adviser, but not with everyone else.

If you wish to stay in post, it is worth building up a file of notes relating to everyday business. The minister may argue that relations have broken down to the point where working together is impossible. Producing a folder of routine notes about hymn lists and church trivia can be effective. How can a minister say he cannot work with you when he clearly *is* working with you?

It is worth noting that the quality of the worship and music need not suffer in a dispute. In the 1990s there was a long protracted and bitter dispute at Lincoln Cathedral, yet many who attended commented on the beautiful worship. God calls us to be obedient, not necessarily to be in the right mood. God blesses obedience, which can often sort out any bad mood.

A **contemporary record** while issues are fresh in your mind is given great reliance by the courts. Such a record should be free of opinions and record:

- date, time and place;

- who was present;

- what happened, in sequence;

- what was said by whom, quoting exact words or summarising their meaning;

- noting any explanations anyone offered for their conduct; and

- noting the consequences.

(If you doubt the value of making such records, make one record of a contentious incident and then recollect the incident six months later before re-reading your note.)

Natural justice

A disciplinary hearing must comply with the laws of natural justice. This not only requires that justice is done, but that it is seen to be done.

This is a principle which has developed over the years in court cases. Its main provisions are:

- the judge must act fairly, in good faith, without bias, and "in a judicial temper";

- each party must have opportunity of adequately stating his case in the presence of the other, and to correct or contradict evidence from the other;

- someone may not be a judge in his own cause, and must declare any personal interest in the matter before him;

- a person must know in advance of what he is accused;

- each side must have sight of all documents referred to.

The right to hear, comment and contradict the other side means that one party may cross-examine the other.

In addition, natural justice can demand that a person is entitled to legal representation. Tribunals have the right to permit or deny such representation, where denial is acceptable in disciplinary cases which need a quick decision.

Human rights

Quite separate from the principles of natural justice is the developing law of human rights. You must note that human rights and natural justice are separate sets of legal rights, though they can overlap.

The European Convention for the Protection of Human Rights is now given the force of British law by Human Rights Act 1998.

Article 6 of the convention starts: "in the determination of his civil rights and obligations or of any criminal charge against him, everyone is entitled to a fair and public hearing within a reasonable time by an independent and impartial tribunal established by law." The rest of the section largely relates to criminal matters.

Disciplinary matters

If faced with disciplinary proceedings, consider your rights as required by:

- employment law, contract law and canon law (see chapter 3);

- natural law;

- human rights;

- any disciplinary and grievance procedure in your contract.

Avoid letting the matter be decided by another minister. Ministers with regional responsibilities, such as **archdeacons**, may like to believe that they are unbiased, but we have yet to hear of an archdeacon supporting an organist against a vicar.

An archdeacon can be formally required by a bishop to resolve a parish dispute. In such cases, the archdeacon should be assisted by a lay person with knowledge of an organist's role. An organist should not attend a meeting with just the minister and archdeacon (or equivalent) present.

The ideal chairman is a lawyer or magistrate from another church who knows neither the minister nor the organist, and whose appointment as mediator is supported by them both. The Clergy Discipline Measure (set out later) sets up tribunals to hear complaints against clergy. A chairman of such a tribunal is an obvious person to approach. For a serious allegation, such as where a cathedral organist could lose his job, there should be at least two other members. Never allow clergy to be a majority in any panel. What must always be avoided is a tribunal where the employer is accuser, witness, judge, jury and executioner. This is bad law.

A chairman and any panel members may reasonably want payment for their services. It is advisable to agree the fee in advance. The chairman can decide who should pay that fee as part of his judgment.

If the rules of natural justice have not been followed, any decision may be declared void. An order of *certiorari* can be obtained from the High Court to quash or suspend the decision.

Court action

Legal action must always be absolutely the last resort when every other option has failed.

The court you use depends on the nature of the problem. There are likely to be three choices:

- employment tribunal, to claim unfair dismissal;
- County Court, for compensation as an amount of money; and
- High Court for an injunction.

You do not need to use lawyers in any tribunal or court, and their use at tribunals is discouraged. However you must know what you are doing. British justice is said to grind slow but exceedingly small. There are strict rules of evidence and procedure which must be followed. You can always use a lawyer to advise you rather than to act for you. If you are a member of the Incorporated Society of Musicians, they may be able to provide legal advice.

Although business people often use tribunals, courts and other procedures for resolving disputes and remain in a working relationship, you should not expect that degree of magnanimity in the church. If you go to court, the almost certain outcome is the ending of any working relationship, and one or both of you leaving.

Some notes about employment tribunals are given on page 104.

County court

This section gives an introduction to suing through the courts. This must always be the very last resort.

The county court is appropriate when you want compensation in money terms up to £15,000. It is fairly simple to fill in a form to initiate proceedings. Claims above £15,000 must be made in the High Court where proceedings are stricter, and where it is usually advisable to have legal help. A financial claim through the courts can also be made using the website www.moneyclaim.gov.uk. This service has a telephone helpline as well as on-line guidance.

You must identify who you are suing. This is usually the minister. You are the claimant. The minister is the defendant, though the court or tribunal is likely to join the PCC (or equivalent body which pays the organist) as co-defendant.

There is a fee to pay for issuing the summons. This is added to your claim, and is paid by the other side if you win. The latest fees apply from 1 April 2003, and depend on the amount for which you are suing.

Maximum claim	Court fee
£300	£30
£500	£50
£1,000	£80
£5,000	£120
£15,000	£250

The county courts provide useful explanatory leaflets, particularly leaflet EX301. Every court has an office which can provide free assistance in completing the forms. You find it by looking up "courts" in the telephone directory. The court cannot advise on the merits of your claim, for which you can get assistance from a solicitor, the Citizen's Advice Bureau and other sources.

The claim forms N1 are available free from the county court office. They can also be downloaded from the website www.courtservice.gov.uk. The claim form comes with guidance for completing the form. You must complete three forms (you may photocopy an original), one for the defendant, one for the court and one for yourself.

You may claim for:

- financial loss you have suffered;
- interest on that loss;
- compensation for distress and inconvenience;
- the court fee; and
- other costs reasonably incurred, such as legal advice.

You should calculate all figures, though it is acceptable to put in an estimated maximum.

You may start a claim in any county court in the country, though a case may be transferred to a more suitable court, such as when the defendant lives in another area.

There is no such thing as the "small claims court". There is a **small claims procedure** in the county court. This procedure is simpler but is limited to £5,000 claim. Otherwise claims are allocated to **tracks**. This outlines how the case is managed by the court.

A summons is served regardless of the merits of the case. The defendant has these options:

- pay the amount in full, which ends the case;
- admit the claim but dispute the amount; or
- dispute the claim.

If a partial offer is made, you may accept it, which ends the case. Otherwise the case is listed to be heard before a judge. This may be in some months time. This hearing is private and informal, usually round a table in a small room at the court building.

If you bring the case, you have the job of proving it. If there is no clear evidence either way, you lose. Evidence is decided on the **balance of probabilities**, such as when facts are disputed.

If you win, you get a **judgment**, which must be enforced. If you lose, you receive nothing and lose your court fee and other expenses. The defendant may claim costs from you.

Either party may appeal. This will usually be heard by a more senior judge in the county court. Further appeals against decisions may then be made to the High Court, Court of Appeal and House of Lords.

Scandal

Scandal and embarrassment can hit anyone, however innocent. You may be aware of an accusation about to be made against you which could reflect on your suitability. In such a situation, you should disclose the matter to the minister first. This applies regardless of whether the accusation is true or not. If the failing is one which does reflect on your suitability, such as an allegation of child abuse, there may be implications such as investigation or even suspension (see page 182), but these are lessened by voluntary disclosure. For other allegations, a minister who already knows the issue is in a better position to defend you. Such disclosure is also likely to improve your relationship with the minister.

In general, the best policy on scandal is "all or nothing". You and the minister either say nothing to anyone (and that does mean saying nothing, not revealing the juicy bits and blanking out other parts) or you tell people everything. Churches do not always have a good reputation for keeping confidences or even avoiding idle speculation. If you have a drink problem or your wife has left you, you may feel very embarrassed about anyone knowing. However probably no-one else will be. If you say you have retired "for personal reasons", don't be surprised if the parish gossip is that you are on drugs, abusing children, insolvent and about to be locked up.

Resignation and retirement

There are many situations when an organist may properly resign without there being any problem, such as retiring, moving house, moving to another church, or simply deciding that your time there has finished. Always give plenty of notice, tell the choir yourself, and fix a date as soon as possible.

Never agree to stay until a successor has been found. You may stay there for ever. Having a firm leaving date concentrates the mind and helps the choir and congregation mentally to adjust to your departure.

In other situations, be reluctant to resign or retire as a solution to a problem. There have been too many instances of organists resigning over disputes that should have been easily settled (or not have arisen in the first place). Sadly many of these organists are then lost to the church completely, which is a significant factor in the general shortage of organists.

The organist usually has a trump card in resignation, as there is such a shortage of organists. However this is not a card which should be played just to get your own way on a trivial issue. Threatening to resign is rarely constructive as, at best, it only means you are tolerated under sufferance with a poor working relationship. You either resign or you do not.

If you really must threaten resignation, be prepared to resign if required. Never make a promise or threat unless you intend to carry it out.

Resignation is probably appropriate if:

- you are having difficulties with the minister which no other church officer is having;
- there is a breakdown in relations between yourself and the choir; or
- there is a breakdown in relations between yourself on one side, and the minister and other church officers on the other.

Resignation is not appropriate if there is simply a problem between yourself and the minister. You should first attempt to resolve the problem as suggested earlier, involving others as appropriate.

Sometimes it may become obvious that the particular skills you have as organist are not what is needed at the church, without there being any fault in either you or the church. Sometimes it is necessary for two Christians to part to avoid conflict. The dispute between Paul and Barnabas (Acts 15:36-41) is widely seen as a biblical example of this.

If there is a breakdown in relations which justifies your resignation, the reason or blame for the breakdown is immaterial. Apportioning blame is futile for "square peg in a round hole" situations.

For **retirement**, there can be no set age limit. Many organists remain competent at 90 while others are incompetent at 30. As the years pass and turn to decades, it is easy to get stuck in a rut, not move with the times and be unaware of the gradual deterioration in your ability.

The loyal servant who simply plods on past his **sell-by date** creates huge problems for organisations. To sack someone is ungracious, yet to ignore the problem is to allow the music and worship to deteriorate. We recommend the **driving licence model** — at the age of 70, you offer resignation to the minister in a way which he can easily accept. If he declines, make similar offers at least once every three years.

If you feel constrained from doing this, at least seek advice from a trusted and knowledgeable friend. Have the grace to accept when your work is done and leave before you deteriorate too much. You will probably find plenty of work as a retired organist without the effort of a regular commitment.

Retirement should always be when you are still able to carry on.

Practicalities of leaving

Leaving as organist, for whatever reason, can be an emotional experience for the organist, minister, choir and congregation. Many organists may not realise how much their musical contribution has meant to people. Indeed it is almost certainly true that in life generally we do not realise how much we all mean to each other.

Accept any **farewell gift** with good grace, even if you throw it away afterwards. Attend any farewell function to which you are invited, and consider holding your own. A packet of crisps and bottle of wine after choir practice can suffice. A farewell helps people cope with the finality of your departure. It also helps people put aside any negative feelings, helps keep relationships sweet and allows everyone to move on.

If you leave in less than happy circumstances, resist the temptation to issue any statement, or otherwise to bad-mouth the minister, choir or church. Be gracious but not dishonest. Explaining that "I believe it is time for me to move on and wish you all well" is preferable to any statement of self-justification and attacking others. Saying that you believe you are not the right person for that church is better than attacking the church for not being the right place for you.

After you have left in unhappy circumstances, it is possible that you may be **scapegoated** or **demonised** in some way. The extent to which you have shown good grace will restrict this from happening. When two people face difficulty, blaming an absent third person is a convenient way of not blaming each other. Comments in private conversation should be ignored anyway. However you do not have to tolerate untrue or malicious comments made publicly, particularly if this will hurt your reputation. If necessary, write a letter (or ask a solicitor to) asking for such statements to be retracted or corrected.

Once you have left, in happy or unhappy circumstances, it may be advisable to have a **quarantine year** when you do not go back to the church. This helps you accept the break, helps those you leave behind to accept that you have gone, and helps your successor to become established.

Never criticise your successor. It is reasonable still to be interested in what happens to a choir or church after you leave, and how your successor gets on, but this must not be done in any way which undermines your successor. Contact from former choir members is no problem if purely social. However do not get involved in any advice or comment about the music or other current issue *unless your successor asks you*.

Clergy discipline

All the denominations have their own system of discipline over ministers.

In the Church of England, discipline is under:

- Clergy Discipline Measure 2003 for conduct; and
- Ecclesiastical Jurisdiction Measure 1963 for doctrine, ritual and ceremonial.

The latter measure has never been used for that purpose. Indeed the last "heresy trial" in the Church of England was in 1871. (This was the last of a long series of court cases between high and low churchmen. One earlier case was *Holy and Ward v Cotterill [1820]* in York Consistory Court which held that it was illegal to sing hymns of human composure such as *Hail to the Lord's Anointed*, which Cotterill had edited. The Archbishop of York intervened so that this low church un-Anglican practice of allowing the congregation to sing hymns has been legally tolerated from 1821.)

Any complaint an organist has against an Anglican minister will be dealt with under the 2003 Measure, which takes effect in 2005.

Clergy Discipline Measure 2003

This provides a tribunal system for dealing with allegation of misconduct by Church of England clergy.

The Measure is designed to assist both lay and ordained church members. Lay people have an efficient system of dealing with grievances against clergy. Clergy may use the Measure to deal with troublesome parishioners who can be told to "put up or shut up".

Scope

The Measure applies to all who are ordained and allowed to minister in the Church of England. It thus includes vicars, curates, chaplains, retired clergy, bishops and archbishops, deans and canons, clergy in secular employment, overseas clergy allowed to work in England, non-stipendiary ministers and even clergy barred from ministry. The Measure applies to the whole of the Church of England, except the Isle of Man, Channel Islands and Diocese in Europe.

Procedure

To start a complaint, the procedure under the Measure is as follows:

- the complainant writes to the relevant bishop;

- the registrar of the diocese checks that the complainant is allowed to make the complaint and that there appears to be substance in the complaint;

- the registrar passes his views to the bishop, who may dismiss the complaint or decide to proceed;

- the bishop's decision is passed to the complainant and the clergyman accused;

- if the complainant is dissatisfied with a bishop's dismissal of the complaint, the complainant may ask the president of the tribunals to review the matter. The president may uphold the bishop's decision, or reverse it if "plainly wrong" and direct the bishop to deal with the complaint;

- where the bishop decides that there is complaint (or is directed to do so), he has 28 days to decide what to do between these five options:

  - do nothing;

  - leave the complaint on file;

  - attempt a reconciliation;

  - agree a penalty with the clergyman; or

  - order a formal investigation;

- if a bishop decides to do nothing, he must notify the complainant, who, if dissatisfied, may request the president of the tribunals to review this. The president may overrule the bishop;

- if a complaint is left on file, no further action is taken, but if a further complaint is made within five years (or a shorter period decided by the bishop), the original matter is also considered.

The complaint may be made in an ordinary letter. There is no form to complete. A complaint which is frivolous, vexatious or malicious is rejected. The complaint should be made within 12 months of the alleged misconduct.

The Measure defines who may make a complaint. In general, this includes "any other person who has a proper interest in making the complaint".

Misconduct is defined in para 8(1) as:

    (a) doing any act in contravention of the laws ecclesiastical;

    (b) failing to do any act required by the laws ecclesiastical;

    (c) neglect or inefficiency in the performance of the duties of his office;

    (d) conduct unbecoming or inappropriate to the office and work of a clerk in Holy Orders.

Conciliation

One of the five options available to a bishop in dealing with a complaint is to direct a reconciliation between the clergyman and complainant. This is likely to be widely used, particularly when the complainant is the organist, so we give below the detailed provisions of the Measure as contained in para 15.

The bishop invites the complainant and clergyman to make representations on the matter. If the complainant and clergyman can agree who should be conciliator, that person is appointed. A bishop must be satisfied that the conciliator will be impartial.

A conciliator must make a report to the bishop within three months of his appointment. A conciliation may fail for any of these reasons:

- either the complainant or clergyman refuse to take part;
- the complainant and clergyman cannot agree on a conciliator;
- the conciliator fails to achieve conciliation.

If conciliation is achieved, that is the end of the matter. If it is not achieved, the matter is referred back to the bishop, who must choose one of the four remaining options.

Penalty by consent

In many cases, it is expected that the clergyman will agree that he has done wrong and be willing to accept a penalty. This avoids the delay, stress and possible embarrassment of a hearing.

If for any reason, penalty by consent fails, the bishop must order a formal investigation.

Formal investigation

A formal investigation may be ordered by the bishop or president of the tribunals, possibly after other attempts to address the concern have failed.

The bishop directs the "designated officer" to set up the investigation. The designated officer works in the legal office of the National Institutions of the Church of England. This designated officer tells the president of the tribunals whether he considers there is a case to answer. If he decides there is no case to answer, that is the end of the matter.

Any hearing is in private unless either:

- the clergyman requests that it be in public; or
- the tribunal decides that the interests of justice require it in public.

If held in public, the tribunal may exclude such people as it thinks fit from attending. The verdict is always given in public.

The disciplinary tribunal comprises five people, all of whom must be communicant members of the Church of England, namely a legally qualified chairman plus two clergy and two lay people.

There are six penalties which range from prohibition for life to a rebuke.

Summary of procedure for maintaining good relations with clergy

Avoiding problems:

- have an appropriate attitude yourself;
- get to know the clergy at a personal and social level;
- agree a common agenda;
- show respect to clergy and expect mutual respect;
- find ways in which you can deliver the church's agenda;
- be appreciative and supportive to clergy;
- avoid making criticism, however justified;
- always remember that the choir is part of the church;
- ensure that your self-confidence is not mistaken for arrogance.

When things go wrong:

- identify the underlying problem;
- distinguish between fallibility and fundamental problems;
- do not exaggerate the seriousness of problems;
- admit your own mistakes;
- be sympathetic for untypical conduct indicating stress;
- see banter as harmless fun, and ensure it is;
- never lose your temper — come back later if necessary;
- do not resign just because you have a problem with the minister;
- consider resignation if you have problems with the wider church.

When there is a fundamental problem:

- get support from a friend, preferably a fellow organist;
- avoid dramatic gestures like walking out;
- do not let a problem be treated as a pastoral issue;
- find out if other church officers have the same problem;
- if they do, press the churchwardens (or equivalent) to deal with it;
- if not, consider the points listed below.
- distinguish between "bruises" and "wounds", and ignore former;
- consider each complaint separately;
- ask what is wanted for each complaint.

When there is a fundamental problem between organist and minister:

- first consider **concession**, simply register a protest and then leave it;
- if concession is inappropriate, try **conciliation**, talking about it;
- be careful about giving examples in dealing with problems of attitude;
- concede your failings before addressing the minister's failings;
- for serious breakdowns, allow for recriminations to come out;
- keep conciliation meetings separate from other meetings;
- use a conciliation meeting to address *all* problems;
- start conciliation by trying to see things from the other person's perspective;
- conciliation ends when you both agree on what to do about the past, and how to go forward together;
- do not even consider **confrontation** until conciliation has failed.

If the problem moves to confrontation:

- if conciliation has failed and the issue is not being taken seriously, make the problem worse by "upping the ante";
- carefully read your contract, particularly on grievance procedures, and know your rights under the law;
- consider inviting a third person to assist you in resolving the matter;
- do not let that third person be a clergyman — find an independent person with appropriate mediation or legal skills;
- consider **mediation** first, then **arbitration**;
- mediation will move you back to conciliation;
- if going for arbitration, ensure terms of reference are clear and the principles of natural justice are followed;
- keep detailed contemporary records of everything that happens;
- avoid retaliation, rudeness, anger and anything else which undermines you;
- continue to do your job properly, regardless of how you feel;
- keep records to show that you are doing your job properly;
- avoid gossip;
- for clergy misconduct, consider the disciplinary proceedings;
- only use court action as a final resort when absolutely everything else has failed.

2 Running a choir

Introduction

Being a good organist does not necessarily mean that you are a good choirmaster.

Singing, conducting and choir training are skills that need to be learned separately from learning to play the organ. Moving both hands up and down in time to the music is not conducting. It is unlikely that an organist will be competent in singing, conducting and choir training unless he has had lessons in them. Such training may be complemented by reading books and watching experts, but there is no substitute for having personal lessons.

The musical skills for a singer, conductor and choir trainer are outside the scope of this book, beyond saying that someone with such skills will know:

- the correct body position when singing;
- how to sing from the diaphragm;
- what diphthongs are, and how to sing them;
- how vowel sounds affect perceived pitch;
- exactly where final consonants are sounded;
- how to give a clear up-beat and down-beat in conducting;
- how to conduct using each hand independently;
- when to change the vowel sound to improve tone;
- the different periods of music;

and much more.

In addition to musical skills, the good choirmaster needs to have the skills of a:

- teacher;
- administrator;
- counsellor; and
- bible scholar.

This chapter deals only with the personnel skills of a choirmaster.

Interviews and auditions

Auditions

To secure a good appointment, it is necessary to submit to an interview and other checking. You may reasonably be asked for references, to take a choir practice and to play a piece on the organ as well as being interviewed.

For the choir practice, you may assume that the choir has been packed for the occasion and that they have been told to behave. Always smile when introduced to the choir and begin by saying that you are pleased to be with them. You will probably be asked to direct them in an anthem. Remember that on this occasion your goal is not to produce a beautiful anthem, but to show them your skills.

Always thank the choir before you leave.

Preparation

An interview starts long before you attend. You should copy everything you send in, including the completed application form.

Write a CV about yourself and send it with the application form, regardless of whether requested. This gives:

- your name, address, date of birth, telephone number, e-mail and marital status;
- qualifications;
- achievements (such as published articles, major performances);
- list of positions, starting with the most recent;
- *brief note* on other work and interests.

For each position, you should give a start and finish date, job title, and note your main responsibilities. All this can be written on a single side of A4 paper.

Know the church. Visit a service before the interview, preferably before anyone realises who you are. Count the number of people in the choir and congregation. Take away any magazines or notices you can find. Look at any website.

If you know any organists who live near the area, ask them what they know. Don't contact the previous organist, even if you know him. It could prejudice your chances if that gets back.

Prepare a folder of documents to take to the interview including:

- copies of application form, CV, and job advert;
- any certificates of music qualifications;
- copies of any of your own arrangements or compositions;
- copies of choir newsletters;
- sample hymn lists you have compiled;
- any articles or reports you have prepared;

and any other documents which may seem relevant.

For the interview, dress smartly, however Bohemian your normal appearance is. You wish to convey that you are taking the interview seriously. Appear confident and polite. Smile as soon as you see the interviewers, and greet them with a firm but friendly "good afternoon". They have yet to ask you a single question, but will have already drawn some conclusions.

Make sure you know where the church is or wherever the interview is being held, and allow plenty of time to arrive there early. Appear at least ten minutes early.

Interview

An interview is ideally conducted by a small group, perhaps three people. Fewer can lead to prejudice while more becomes unwieldy. An interview is traditionally structured in this format:

- brief introductory remarks to relax everyone;
- general questions asked of all candidates;
- specific questions prompted by your form or CV;
- tougher questions;
- your turn to ask them questions.

However, organists are usually interviewed by church officials who do not always follow conventions used elsewhere, so do not be surprised if the format proves to be completely different.

Ideally, most interview questions should be **open questions**, such as "how" or "why" rather than "what". Keep your answers brief. Never comment that something is a daft question. Be relaxed but attentive, and smile.

Do not allow an interview to finish without asking your questions. A relationship is always a two-way street. Ask questions even if you already know the answers. Questions an organist may wish to ask include:

- why did the previous organist leave?
- (if he left some time ago) why was the vacancy not filled sooner?
- how many regular members of the choir are there?
- how many were in the choir last Sunday? [this may be significantly less than the previous answer]
- how many choir members are children?
- have there been any disagreements between the vicar and choir?
- were there disagreements between the previous organist and anyone?
- what hymn book do you use?
- which orders of service do you use?
- do you plan to change your hymn book or liturgy?
- at which services am I expected to play?
- how much pay is offered?
- who chooses the hymns?
- how many weddings and funerals do you have?
- what fee is provided for them?
- is there a worship committee?
- if so, what are its responsibilities and powers, and will I be expected to be on it?
- is there a music group?
- for which services do they play?
- what are the main issues facing your church?

Ask to see past music lists or hymn lists (even if you have already acquired one).

We recommend that you ask for contact details of the previous organist or organists to discuss the church with him, whatever reason for his leaving. The church takes up references on you; you are entitled to take up a reference on the church. Ask your predecessor:

- is the vicar co-operative?
- is the congregation appreciative?

- is the choir reliable?

- what problems did you have?

- how did you resolve them?

You should seek to have a conversation, possibly by meeting privately, rather than just get tick-box answers.

Watch out for the **halo effect**. This indicates the main bugbear of the previous organist. If he was late or rude or inconsiderate, you will be quizzed on that particular aspect, and your appointment will largely depend on how far you seem not to have his failings. This is poor interviewing, but it happens in the best-run organisations, and churches are not always the best-run organisations.

If the interview starts with a long speech about the church or what they are looking for, or they have difficulty of thinking of any questions, they are probably not certain of what they want or may be full of their own self-importance. Another failing by interviewer or candidate is spending far too long on your other interests.

A bad interview does not necessarily indicate a bad job, but you should know what you are up against. Similarly a difficult interview does not mean that you will not be appointed. You could be impressing them without realising it.

However if it becomes clear that the job is not worth a candle, stop the interview and make clear that you are withdrawing and say why. It may make them think about how to treat organists in the future.

Barry Rose was the first organist of Guildford Cathedral, appointed at 25 without formal qualifications. He created a choir from nothing and made it one of the finest in the country. However his interview was a disaster, as he recounts in *The Beat is Irrelevant* (Guildford Cathedral Old Choristers' Association, Guildford Cathedral). He had already argued about whether the post could be combined with school teacher and whether to have daily services, when Dr H K Andrews started to question him about how he would interpret a piece by Palestrina. "I got very cross and said, 'shouldn't we be talking about how you're going to get a choir going within a few months? You won't have anybody at Guildford until September, and the consecration is already fixed for May next year, and you've got to have the whole thing set up, the organ installed and everything.' In the end frustration took over. I said, 'we're wasting each other's time', and I went off and left them to it." Fortunately the cathedral provost had been impressed, and brought him back.

Selection choir?

You have now been appointed and must get on with running a choir. The first consideration is what type of choir you are expected to run.

There are two broad methods for admitting singers to a choir:

- selection; and
- non-selection.

Selection means that a person may only become a member of the choir if the person passes an audition or otherwise demonstrates sufficient talent or potential to be admitted.

Non-selection means that the choir admits almost anyone, and you train them up.

Generally cathedrals and the larger more traditional parish churches use selection, while many other churches use non-selection. Non-selection may be appropriate in churches with no choir or a poor choir. It will make the choir bigger sooner, but may not necessarily be better.

The distinction between the two approaches is not as great as may first appear. In a selection choir, members will still learn and be trained. It can be surprising how many talented and experienced singers have serious gaps in their musical knowledge. In a non-selection choir, it is usually necessary to spend some time with an individual before admitting them, even if just to find which part they should sing.

Nevertheless, you should be clear at the outset which sort of choir you are running. This is a policy which must be agreed with the minister, and understood by the choir itself and the wider church.

You should also be sure in yourself that you have the right aptitude to train and run a non-selection choir.

You should also remember that amateurs frequently have more **"attitude"** than professionals, and can be more likely to argue with you. Professional musicians turn up and just do what you ask.

Recruitment

Any guidance on running a choir presupposes that you have a choir to run. Recruiting people to join and stay is a problem with most choirs.

We are assuming that it is the church's wish that you have a choir. If the vicar and church council (or their equivalent) are in favour, you go ahead. There may be a few mutterings from Philistine malcontents, but we deal with that separately.

Before recruiting

Before recruiting members to the choir, you should ensure that you have a choir worth recruiting to. While some people may be persuaded to help set up a new choir, most recruits want to join something which is already successful. Even if you have just a hopeless handful, you can still:

- have choir practices;
- start and finish them on time;
- perform simple anthems (see below);
- be positive to the choir;
- create a social dimension;
- run the choir efficiently; and
- ensure it is properly resourced.

A choir is not sustained on a diet of hymns. There must be **anthems** also. These need not be difficult. Indeed they should not be difficult until you have adequate resources. The anthem may be in two parts or unison. It could be as simple as finding a hymn not in the repertoire, learning it, and singing it with the organ filling in any missing parts.

The point to emphasise is that *the choir must already be functioning before recruiting*.

Consider simple hymns and songs where you can provide an interesting accompaniment. Always keep the music within the limits of the choir's capabilities, but keep them performing.

Never tell a choir it is bad, however true that may be. Choristers are like plants: they bloom from sunshine not beatings with a big stick. Do not say, "this choir is hopeless, we must get in some decent singers before we can do some proper music". Instead say, "this choir is the basis for what I hope will be a larger choir".

Never criticise your **predecessor** (or successor for that matter). Acknowledge the work of those who have gone before you. There is nothing to be gained by attacking someone no longer there. Doing so will diminish your reputation and antagonise members who will have shown loyalty to your predecessor and be rightly annoyed by your uncharitable remarks.

At some point a chorister will say "but Fred told us to sing this differently". You point out that Fred is no longer running the choir, you are. There are different schools of singing just as there are different routes to the same place, and there are good reasons for your way. Never say that Fred was wrong.

Who should join a choir

This depends on whether you run a selection choir or non-selection choir, as explained on page 50.

It is still widely, but wrongly, believed that music is a "gift" bestowed on the privileged few, despite overwhelming evidence from educational research that anyone who can speak can be taught to sing.

You should not accept people into the choir unless they are prepared to attend both practices and services. This may seem blatantly obvious, but it is surprising how many choirmasters are asked if Johnny can attend Friday practices even though he is playing football on Sunday mornings. The answer is no. You are running a choir not a child-minding club. It is reasonable to allow a person to attend a few practices to get the feel of the choir or to overcome a crisis of confidence, but this should never start to become a permanent arrangement.

A question which frequently arises is whether choir members must be **Christians**. The answer is no. It is normally advisable that the person who leads the choir must be a Christian as he is exercising a Christian ministry, leading worship and representing the church. But that is not the position for a choir member. Someone who is anti-Christian is unlikely to want to join a church choir anyway, but such people are surprisingly few. Most people are tolerant or apathetic about the church.

There is no evidence that a non-believer sings sacred music less well than a believer. Atheists like Berlioz wrote beautiful church music. The issue is one of competence rather than spirituality. The church need be no more concerned on this matter than it should be about the spirituality of the man who checks the fire extinguishers or repairs the photocopier.

But there is another reason for including non-believers in church choirs. A choir is a powerful place to bring people to faith. Music breathes life into words of Jesus' salvation and of God's love. A choir brings singers into regular worship where scripture is read, prayers are said and the gospel proclaimed. They are in the regular company of believers. Hundreds of Christians have come to faith through choir membership. Indeed one of the authors of this book came to faith through involvement in church music.

Having climbed that ladder himself, he is not prepared to kick it away so that others cannot follow.

Disability

You should accommodate **disabled** people into the choir as far as possible. Indeed the church could be in breach of the Disability Discrimination Act 1995 if it fails to do so (see page 202.). The commonest example is excusing people with mobility problems, such as leg and joint problems, from processing or standing for long periods. Let them take their place before the service starts and sing while seated.

People with **sight problems** can be accommodated by producing enlarged photocopies of music, but note the copyright implications (see page 150). Our experience is that publishers are very co-operative in allowing enlarged copies for these purposes.

You should be reluctant to let people with **serious learning difficulties** join a choir as they are so time-demanding that they will bring choir practices to a grinding halt. Sometimes they may wish to join a choir so that they can wear robes, process, stand at the front, and generally "be someone". This is a pastoral problem rather than a musical one, and you may need pastoral assistance. A possible solution is to designate them as an associate chorister who "sings nicely" in the congregation. You can give them a badge to wear and possibly provide music and talk to them. That meets their pastoral need without compromising your choir. But do not patronise and do not be dishonest.

Other than for a specific disability, you should be reluctant to make special provisions for choir members. They are either choir members who attend practices and services and do what you say, or they are not.

Many people are discouraged from joining a choir because they are **tone deaf**. It cannot be said too strongly that *tone deafness is not a medical condition*. Research shows that anyone who can talk normally can be taught to sing in tune.

Recruiting methods

People join a choir because they are attracted to what it offers. They may be reluctant to join because of the commitment. Successful recruitment therefore involves promoting the attractions and addressing the reluctance. In short, recruitment is about relationships.

The most successful way to promote success is to be successful already, or at least to appear to be. That is why you should get the choir singing anthems and having practices, however small and weak the choir is. People will join something which is successful, not something which is falling apart. A choir which is already large, performing a wide range of beautiful music, performing it well, enjoying happy practices, and having a good social life will attract new members.

Simply putting a notice in the notice sheet or church magazine advertising for members is unlikely to have much response. The best recruiting method is to **approach** people personally. Identify good singers in the congregation and ask them. They may not say yes immediately as many church members will need to think about it and get used to the idea of fulfilling a new church role. Do not force the issue, as sometimes people say no, and then come back many months or even years later to say yes. You have planted the seed of the idea, and not all seed falls on the rocks (though it may sometimes seem that way).

It can be effective to invite others to join the choir just for a carol service or major work and then be free to leave. Not only do you have an augmented choir for these significant occasions, but some will stay as permanent members.

For **children**, it is productive to go into schools and promote the idea of singing in a choir. The church has much to offer in this field, and we should not be afraid of promoting the church in an area where the church is a recognised leader.

In 1994, educationalists recognised the **Mozart effect**: that the skills needed by children in learning singing or playing music has a significant effect on other learning. It is believed that this is by music's stimulation of memory and expression, and the reasoning in intervals and chords. The name is taken from the observable phenomenon that listening to Mozart stimulates the brain in tackling puzzles. Research by Agnes Chan at the Chinese University of Hong Kong found that children who learn music before the age of 12 have a higher IQ, better memory, and better grasp of science, mathematics and language, and better reasoning faculties. Subsequent research by Prof Glenn Schellenberg of Toronto University found that 6-year old children who study music improve their IQ by 2.7 points over other children.

It can be profitable to know the local music teachers. You can recruit from local scouts and guide groups, and from the Sunday school and youth group. Liaise with their leaders, and get them on side. Make contact with local singing teachers who may be able to refer pupils to you. Invite the teachers to visit a choir practice, or even to take one. Most schools will be happy to let you come in to talk about music and play the piano for them, particularly if you do so in a way which has general educational benefits rather than being just an advert for your choir.

It is worth noting how many pop stars started their musical careers in church choirs. They include Paul McCartney, Elvis Presley, Britney Spears, Whitney Houston, Aretha Franklin, Norah Jones, Brian Jones (of Rolling Stones), Harry Secombe, Sting, Will Yates, Pete Doherty (of Libertines), Peter Gabriel, Marvin Gaye, Ace of Base, P P Arnold, Ashford and Simpson, Randy Crawford, Patsy Cline, Dudley Moore, Gene Autry and Anita Baker.

Your minister and church council must also be supportive and provide help, such as contacts with **local schools**. You should never arrange to visit a school, scout group or similar without first discussing the matter with your minister. You are an ambassador for the church, and its relations with outside bodies is a matter broader than the choir. The church exists to reach out into the community. A choir is a wonderful way of delivering the church's ministry.

Scouts and guides both offer badges to members. These include music badges where choir activities qualify.

Always remember that existing choir members are the best recruiters. They know people who could be good choir members. Choir members have husbands, wives, sons, daughters, neighbours and friends, all of whom are potential choristers.

Organists are often involved with other musical activities where you meet singers who could be good choir members. Invite them to join the choir. In the first instance, it may be to augment the choir for a particular anthem on one occasion such as when you know you are short of tenors that day.

Never **poach** members from another church choir; that is unfair and unethical. However if someone has already decided to leave their church choir, there is no reason to refuse them.

The biggest hurdle to recruitment is **commitment**. Potential choristers are discouraged from joining because of the burden of being regularly committed to a weekly practice and weekly service, and its impact on their life. The easiest way to overcome this is to limit their initial commitment to a specific period, perhaps two months, or (better) to a particular event, such as until the carol service. It is easy to invite people to join the choir for a special event, and you can keep on having special events. Having attended a few practices, some of your guest singers will almost certainly want to join you permanently.

Retaining members

Recruitment is only half the story of building up a choir. The other half is to retain members once you have recruited them.

You must avoid shouting, hectoring, humiliating and mockery. Never lose your temper, however provoked. Count to five before replying, or excuse yourself and step outside for a minute if you really have difficulty controlling your temper.

As a choirmaster you must say whatever you need to say to your choir, but be careful how you say it. One method is to congratulate them on whatever the choir got right, and then to comment on up to three things which they did not, and say "let us now work on the phrasing" or "that was good, but we can make it better". If they don't get anything right, congratulate them for trying. Always be positive.

The choir practice must be enjoyable. If it is, choristers will stay. It's as simple as that.

Choir practice must be business-like. Members must go away knowing that they have achieved something, that they are better able to sing the anthems. The practice must not be so full of notices, discussions, jokes, prayers and speeches that no singing work is done. There is a place for discussion groups and prayer meetings within the church, but it is not choir practice.

Your style must always be one of **encouragement**, however discouraged you may feel. Much of a choirmaster's work is not so much teaching the choir skills as simply enabling choir members to use the skills they already have. Most people have more talent than they realise.

Always comment encouragingly about an anthem sung the previous week, but do not be deceitful. If it was a dreadful performance, thank them for their noble effort and explain that no-one always succeeds. Re-schedule the anthem, so that the efforts in learning it are not wasted. Always congratulate soloists at choir practice.

Another ingredient is the **sense of belonging**. Always welcome new members at choir practice. When someone leaves, always thank them at choir practice for their contribution and wish them well for the future. Make sure that the new member has a pigeon hole, robes, hymn book and other items as appropriate. Make sure that their name is written up somewhere in the vestry. They must feel that they belong with you.

Children may receive a surplice after a short introductory period, and should receive ribbons as they progress through their training. Persuade the minister to award these during the church service, perhaps at the end of the notices.

Part of being businesslike is that choir members always know what is happening. Music lists should be prepared in advance and pinned up in the choir vestry. It is useful for a vestry to have a blackboard or whiteboard on which you write up what books are needed for each practice and service. Copies of special music should be put out ready on a table. People like to belong to something which is well-run.

Allow people to make feedback to you, and preferably only to you. This is best done privately. People are easily discouraged if they feel no-one listens to them.

Get to know all the choir members personally, at least by name.

Maintain a **social life** for the choir. It is good to have events such as a choir dinner once a year, or a choir party. It is also good to have refreshments after choir practice, such as coffee. An electric kettle, coffee jar, cartons of long life milk and mugs can be hidden in most music cupboards. Celebrate everything you can think of — birthdays, wedding anniversaries, successful performances, end of term — with cake and wine. Give children Easter eggs and Christmas presents. Go out together occasionally.

For children, it is possible to build up the choir with social activities such as a youth group or football team. (Several football teams such as Bolton Wanderers and Aston Villa started from churches.) Normally such activities should only be run by someone able to give it the time, which is not likely to be you. It may be an adult in the choir.

Children and Sunday School

There is no reason why the children's choir and the Sunday School should see each other as competitors. On the contrary, as parts of the body of the church, they have a moral duty to work together and help each other. Ideally, each should help recruit members to the other. Sunday Schools provide basic Christian teaching while church choirs provide Christain training. Bringing up children does not just mean filling their heads with facts; it also requires involvement and participation. Our children are not the church of tomorrow; they are part of the church today.

An ideal arrangement is as follows:

- all children in the choir are automatically members of the church's Sunday School;

- choir children robe up before the service and attend Sunday School in robes;

- the church authorities determine which parts of the service the children attend. For Communion services, they may come in at the start or end of the Eucharistic prayer;

- children come in or out of a service during a hymn, or while music is played for the purpose;

- children are supervised coming in and out of a service;

- anthems are only performed when the choir children are present.

Choir children can normally have as much Sunday School time as other children. If not, having 20 minutes rather than 30 minutes will not make much difference. If there are sufficient numbers of choir children of a similar age, it may be possible to engage a Sunday School teacher for a choir class.

Choir practices

Preparation

You must prepare for choir practice. Know exactly what music you will rehearse, and make sure it is readily available.

You should have a fair idea of how many weeks it will take to prepare an anthem to performance standard. Do not try to get everything right at the first rehearsal.

Always have a watch or clock in ready sight. The most experienced choirmaster will find that he has spent 40 minutes when he intended to spend 15. The opposite sometimes happens. It is easy to lose track of time when engrossed in music.

It is usually a matter of established practice whether a choir robes for practices, though this is now quite rare. Robing is usually confined to a cassock without the surplice. If you do robe, allow time for robing and disrobing.

Time

You should have a weekly choir practice, usually with breaks during summer and short breaks (typically two weeks) after Easter and Christmas. Publish dates of choir practice well in advance.

Choir practices are traditionally held early on a Friday evening. The optimum duration is from 1¼ hours to 1½ hours. That is normally long enough to do the work while not so long that members tire and get bored. A new choirmaster should maintain whatever arrangement he inherits. If the choir has children, it is advisable to have a separate children's practice, preferably overlapping with the adult's practice.

You should be resistant to changing the times of choir practice. A day and time has become established, and choir members can organise the rest of their lives round that. In particular, you should not put back the time of choir practice because members "have difficulty getting here on time". Members who are ten minutes late at 7pm, will be ten minutes late at 7.30pm or 8pm. The problem is discipline not timing.

If it is necessary to change the day or time, have a clear and very good reason for doing so, put the matter up for discussion, and allow a long lead time before making the change.

Choir practices should start and finish **on time**. Breaks for children leaving and adults arriving should be on time and clearly indicated to allow for people to arrive and depart. (See page 171 for collecting children.) Avoid the disruption of people walking throughout the practice.

Pre-service practices of anthems are particularly beneficial. A choir anthem which sounds perfect at the end of a rehearsal on Friday night may not sound so good when approached cold on Sunday. A pre-service practice is best undertaken in the choir vestry and should be finished at least five minutes before the service starts. A pre-service practice should simply be a reminder and warm-up. It is far too late to start teaching notes and rhythms.

Ad hoc rehearsals are additional practices usually for specific events, such as the carol service or a major work. You must give plenty of notice, typically a month, for additional rehearsals. It is unreasonable to expect choristers to rearrange their entire life to attend extra rehearsals, particularly if the need for them is your lack of preparation.

For major works and anthems, it can be beneficial preparing **practice tapes**. You simply sit at a piano and record the relevant part. You must announce the title of each part and count in the beats where the part is not singing. It does not take long to do. Producing copies can be done yourself or delegated to a choir member. There are machines which copy tapes at double speed. Practice tapes are often much appreciated and will greatly help bring choir members up to standard.

Teaching sessions can also be a useful adjunct to choir practices. Choir members can often have a poor understanding of musical notation and singing technique but be reluctant to admit this. There are various schemes run by the RSCM as well as its *Voice* *for Life* scheme which provide an ideal opportunity to learn or revise basic musicianship skills.

If arranging additional rehearsals or teaching sessions, always remember to check with the church authorities that the vestry or church is available. It is not unknown for a choirmaster to arrange a rehearsal at a time convenient for himself and the choir, only to find a baptism or wedding rehearsal in progress, or that the churchwardens have arranged that time for the floor to be resanded.

Attendance

The Royal School of Church Music laid down a standard of 85% attendance for a chorister to be eligible for its Bronze Award. This excludes annual holiday, and equals about six times out of seven. This is the level of attendance you should reasonably expect from committed choristers.

It is disheartening for a choirmaster to prepare for a practice, only to find half the choir does not turn up. This is demotivating for you, but you must rise above it. The one thing not to do is to berate those who have turned up for poor attendance. After all, they are the ones who *have* attended.

Some choir members may miss practices for proper reasons, such as holidays, work commitments or illness. There is nothing you can do about that. What you are trying to stamp out is absence because the chorister is "too busy". This means that the chorister gives choir practice a low priority. If you have rehearsed on a Friday evening for the last 150 years, why did the chorister arrange a dinner party for that evening?

Confronting a "too busy" chorister is rarely likely to be productive. You should work towards making the choir practice enjoyable. In the meantime, plan music which does not rely on fringe members who turn up when they feel like it. As the choir sees practices being well run, with competent training of a good variety of interesting music in a pleasant atmosphere with a good social side, attendance will improve.

The dates of anthems should be announced in advance, and you should check that sufficient members will be present for the performance and final rehearsals. The longer notice you give, the more members will attend.

Some choirs have a **signing-out sheet** where choristers can indicate absences in advance. The disadvantage is that this can create the impression that attendance is optional. However a **holiday sheet** is useful to know in advance how many can attend during summer.

Sickness and last-minute business trips will always disturb the most careful plans. If someone in the choir telephones you to say they cannot attend because of sickness, do not rant about the problems that creates. Doing so achieves nothing and discourages them from letting you know next time and thus being able to address any problem. Instead, thank the person for letting you know and wish them a speedy recovery. That creates goodwill. If a choir is of a reasonable size, a last minute absence should not usually be a problem. Otherwise consider:

    (a) bringing in a singer to replace the part;

    (b) redeploying a singer from another voice;

    (c) covering the part on the organ; or

    (d) cancelling or postponing the anthem.

Ultimately exhortations and quiet words will not secure good attendance. Good attendance comes from properly run choirs with well conducted practices.

Time-keeping

It is disruptive to have members turn up after the practice has started. It is even worse when most of the choir turns up late.

The most effective way of dealing with lateness is to start on time regardless, even if only two people are there. Do not stop for latecomers, but ignore them until the next natural stop. Start and finish the choir practice on time.

Always remind the choir when the clocks go forward and back for **summer time** (the last Sundays in March and October).

Place

The best place for a choir practice is a separate room with plenty of air and light, chairs either in place or easily moved to place, and a piano in tune. Modern electric pianos are good enough now and have the advantage of staying in tune and allowing you to look at the choir while seated.

The final rehearsal for an anthem must always be in the place where it is performed. This allows you to check sight lines, acoustics and seating. This is particularly important on special occasions and when you have additional singers or instruments. Someone should stand in the body of the church while rehearsing to check that there is a proper balance between the singers and organ (and any soloists and other instruments). The organ console is often not the best place to judge balance, so the organist should note what registration provides the best balance even if it sounds too loud or quiet from the console.

Structure

A choir practice must always start with a **warm-up**. There are books of singing exercises provided, such as the *Voiceworks* books by Peter Hunt (Oxford University Press). However adults can resent time spent that way. It may be more expedient to use the hymns as warm-up material.

The choir practice must be paced so that people are not singing all the time.

A choir practice should not become a source for endless discussion, notices, prayers, anecdotes, jokes, gossip or digests of television programmes. A small amount of such stuff can leaven the practice, but otherwise concentrate on the job in hand.

Choir practice should end with a short **prayer**. The choristers' prayer is:

> *Bless, O Lord, us thy servants who minister in thy temple. Grant that what we sing with our lips, we may believe in our hearts, and what we believe in our hearts we may show forth in our lives. Through Jesus Christ our Lord. Amen.*

You may prefer to say "The Grace" or another prayer. You may wish to make up a prayer, particularly before a major performance like a carol service. If not happy about doing this yourself, invite someone else to do it for you or even encourage extemporary prayer. However remember that the prayer is simply to consecrate your efforts to God. A choir practice is not a prayer meeting. Jesus said that people should not go "babbling on like the heathen who imagine that the more they say the more God listens. God already knows your needs" (Matthew 6:7-8). Please note.

Donkeywork

There is always an amount of donkeywork in a practice, such as collecting up and putting away music, putting away chairs, switching off lights and locking up.

There is no law which says the choirmaster must do it all. Arrange for choir members to help.

Leadership

Some basic principles

A choir should be run as a benevolent dictatorship. You should not attempt to run a choir either as a democracy nor as a tyranny.

Leadership is a function, not a status. The conductor is the "baton part" of the ensemble and he should play his part and only his part in the same way that a flute player plays the flute part and only the flute part.

Your personality is an important factor.

Winning respect

Successful leadership only arises when you have won the respect of those you lead. You do this by showing an acceptable level of competence, combined with a pleasant personality. This is particularly important for a volunteer body, such as most church choirs, where a disenchanted member can easily leave or not attend.

This does not mean that you must seek popularity. If you do your job well, popularity automatically follows. A choirmaster who "delivers the goods" is a good leader.

A new choirmaster is always given a **honeymoon period** where you have the provisional goodwill of your new choir, and will probably be forgiven mistakes more readily. The new choirmaster must win the respect of the choir before this honeymoon period expires.

Leadership role

Musicians expect to be told what to do, and tend to regard discussion as time wasted. It may be diplomatic to ask the choir for an occasional opinion, particularly where you are planning something significantly different, but do not seek opinions on every last detail.

The ideal leadership style is one where members are neither browbeaten nor argumentative, but follow your direction while feeling relaxed about matters which concern them. It is quite reasonable for someone in the choir to point out that they are having difficulty singing a phrase and ask if you could sing it again, providing they do not do it so often that they take over the choir practice. If that does happen, simply reassure the person that you will look at all the notes in all parts in due course. Occasionally it may be necessary conspicuously to disregard a request from a chorister just to show who is boss.

An interesting perspective on leadership is provided in *John Wimber: the Way It Was* (Hodder & Stoughton), when his wife Carol Wimber writes about her late husband, the church leader and musician John Wimber:

> *He wasn't very sensitive, in the way of an awareness of what others were feeling or thinking, and I think that was good. He didn't struggle with fears about his own ability or the ability of others, and part of what made him a powerful leader was his ignorance of any other perspective. He wasn't even aware of the fears most of us have about ourselves, and we were glad to give up our thoughts on the subject, in exchange for his, anyhow.*

Admitting mistakes

No choirmaster is perfect. You should accept your fallibility with good grace.

It is a curious fact of human nature that admitting mistakes can score you more points for honesty than you lost through fallibility. President Clinton was not impeached for his hanky-panky with Monica Lewinsky, but for his attempts to cover it up. If you study any scandal, you will usually find that the cover-up caused far more approbation than the original misconduct.

If you keep making silly mistakes, you will appear incompetent. However the occasional mistake, readily admitted, will make you look both human and gracious, without affecting your reputation for competence. Also, admitting occasional mistakes makes it easier for choir members to admit their mistakes.

Setting dates for anthems

Anthems should be planned for at least one month ahead, and ideally about three months ahead.

This allows choir members to put the dates in their diaries to make a particular effort to attend. It allows them to tell you in advance if they cannot be there, and lets you decide if those who can attend are sufficient for the performance. It avoids the nightmare of a beautiful rehearsal on Friday evening, wrecked by finding that all the altos are away for the performance on Sunday. Advice on what to do in such situations is given on page 61.

Once a date has been fixed, every effort should be made to ensure that you perform it on that date. An occasional cancellation is probably inevitable, but frequent cancellations or postponements (perhaps more than one per year) quickly undermines confidence, and will anger choir members who made a particular effort to attend.

Dealing with choir members

Introduction

Running a choir would be much easier if it did not contain people, but as it does, you must learn to work with them.

It is essential that there is opportunity for the choir to chat with you. This rarely requires formal meetings. Conversations after choir, down at the pub or while clearing away the music, provide enough opportunity.

If some significant change is proposed, such as changes to the structure of services, it may be advisable to call a meeting of the choir to discuss the matter, or ask the choir to stay after a choir practice.

Any group of people will contain some colourful characters, some who argue, some who have strong personalities and those with firm opinions. That the church should have its share can be attributed to statistical random sampling. Why such people always end up in the choir is less easily explained.

The key is **discipline**. Discipline in rehearsing leads to a disciplined performance. You should never be reluctant to impose discipline, though you must be careful how you do it. The two basic principles are:

> (a) have a workmanlike approach from the outset; and

> (b) err on the side of being too tough and then perhaps ease up a little.

If you need to administer discipline, consider a stern look rather than saying anything. Sometimes ignoring a person can be effective. If you do say anything, be careful what you say.

Never criticise the minister or any other member of the church in front of the choir, however justified your observations may be. As choirmaster you hold a position of responsibility and trust. If you are seen as being disloyal to the minister, you are establishing disloyalty as an acceptable code. Do not expect the choir to be loyal to you.

Problem choristers

The foghorn

Reginald Frary begins his delightful book *It'll Be All Wrong on the Night* (Canterbury Press) thus:

> In the choir of the village church where my bachelor cousin Charlie is
> organist they've got a man affectionately known as Bodger, who has
> been there for fifty years and in all that time has never been late for a
> service, never missed a choir practice and never had the faintest idea
> how to sing.

The skill in teaching someone to sing here is probably outweighed by the skill in persuading him that he needs to learn.

Asking someone to keep the volume down "because you have a powerful voice" is diplomatic. Playing back a tape-recording can be effective.

The arguer

It is reasonable for a choir member to point out that he or she is having difficulty with a part, particularly if you have not noticed this. However it is not reasonable for anyone to tell you how to run the choir practice.

If someone does try to take over, just say firmly and gently that you will be dealing with those points in a minute, and continue with whatever you were about to do. If someone persists in being quarrelsome, avoid a slanging match. You can say, "please let me run this choir practice". Plain insults are usually best ignored, as other choir members will see them for what they are.

If someone persists in awkward behaviour, speak to them privately, explaining why they are such a nuisance. It is surprising how many times people think they are being helpful or funny. Do so on the basis of "I would appreciate your help at choir practices".

If there is a personal problem with the person, you may consider asking the minister or someone with pastoral skills to help. However this should be an exceptional case. You are the choirmaster and you must be able to work with every choir member. Any problem you have with an individual must be settled between you.

If you do decide that a chorister needs to be rebuked at a practice, say your words and then immediately return to the practice so that the chorister cannot reply without interrupting you. Ignore any attempt at interruptions.

If none of this deals with the problem, deal harshly with the awkward member. As a result, the chorister will either mend their ways or leave the choir. Whatever they do is almost certainly the desired result.

Past sell-by date

A difficult situation in all forms of church life is the person who is no longer capable of doing his job, whether through age or infirmity. The church is in the invidious position of choosing between tolerating incompetence dragging down the body, or of upsetting a long-serving and loyal member.

This problem should be addressed in two stages:

> (a) the decision must consider the choir;
>
> (b) the implementation must consider the individual.

If a singer really drags down the choir, the singer must go. A choir must never be compromised by a duff member who ruins performances, impedes practices and generally obstructs the efficient operation of the choir. But making the decision is the easy part. The difficult part is implementing it. Singers tend to think they are better than they really are at the best of times.

You can try breaking the news in two stages. First, try to explain that their singing voice has deteriorated significantly. Let the person digest that sad truth first before the second stage of discussing its implications. The person may come to terms with the fact and then discuss with you what their future role should be.

An elderly or lonely choir member may find the choir practice a highlight of the week's social life. There is no need to take that away from them. Allow a member to continue attending and find something for them to do. They can be your librarian. They can walk round the church during the final rehearsals to see if the balance is right (see page 74). You can give them a title of choir assistant and keep them involved. Sometimes it is possible to allow someone to remain in the choir and sing the hymns and simply sit out the anthems.

Always mark a chorister's leaving with at least some words of thanks, and possibly a certificate of long service.

Sweet eating

You must never tolerate any sweet eating, mint sucking or gum chewing. This prevents the mouth from being able to form the sounds properly. It is also dangerous as the sweet can slip down the open throat and cause suffocation. A sweet must be swallowed or spat out immediately. There is no objection to singers sipping water during a practice.

No-one need suck a **cough sweet** at choir practice. They can swig linctus before the practice and then sip water. Medically, this is much more effective.

Feuds and arguments

A choir is no different from any other organisation in that clashes between members sometimes arise, often for trivial reasons. These may have nothing to do with the choir. It can be a broken friendship, a finished romance or a dispute outside the choir or even outside the church.

An argument at a choir practice must never be tolerated. The people should be told firmly that this is unacceptable. You must not become argumentative yourself, but be firm and patient. Never order someone to leave but, in extremis, you may suggest that a person might like to withdraw to calm down. Saying "quiet" and getting straight on with the music can also be effective.

Where there are personality problems, they must be addressed. This should normally be done privately and individually asking people to co-operate for the greater good of the choir and church. The choirmaster should be quick to listen and slow to advise. Often merely listening can solve the problem.

Allocating solos

The task of allocating solos is entirely within the gift of the choirmaster. A solo must never be allocated solely because someone has "always" done it.

It is good to have a policy of encouraging all choristers to consider solos, and to be willing to allow someone to sing a solo for a first time, even in preference to a better established soloist. If this policy is well-known the established soloist is much less likely to feel put out.

There is no reason why one person must sing all the solos for their voice. It is reasonable to share it between people, and for a newcomer first to sing a small part.

Practical issues

Choir robes

There is nothing in canon law covering the robes a choir may or may not wear. Traditionally, choir robes have followed the robes of the clergy.

In the Church of England, rules for clergy robes are contained in Canon B8. The same canon states that the Church "does not attach any particular doctrinal significance to the diversities of vesture permitted by this Canon". Despite that, a minister needs the permission of the parochial church council to change his form of vesture.

For choirs, there is no law but plenty of custom. Church vestments largely derive from Rome in the third and fourth centuries. Greek pottery from 425 BC shows a choir singing in long flowing robes draped over the left shoulder. The original robes were like a monk's habit, of a loose gown tied round the waist with a piece of rope-like cord. Some choirs still wear this style.

In the Middle Ages, the **cassock** developed as an ankle-length black gown with long sleeves which completely covered other clothing. The **surplice** is a white garment stopping somewhere between the chest and knees, and originally with lace, and with large bell sleeves. The cassock and surplice are sometimes referred to as liturgical robes. An organist sometimes wears a special surplice with split sleeves so that they do not drape over the manuals.

As the clergy adopted this dress, so did the choir. The original reason was not to make the choir appear special, but for the more egalitarian purpose of showing that all are equal in the service of God. The humble farmhand looks the same as the lord of the manor when singing to their creator.

In time, other colours of cassock, particularly blue, were introduced. There are also many subtle variations in style and in choice of textile. There is no truth in the myth that royal sponsorship is needed to wear scarlet cassocks.

At the Reformation, the Geneva gown became the favoured robe of Protestant preachers. This is similar to the academic gown as worn with a mortar board. It is still widely favoured in certain denominations, such as black gospel choirs.

There are some accessories which have been subsequently added. White ruffs (pleated collars) date from the 16th century, and are now commonly worn by choir children. An alternative is the 19th-century Eton collar (large starched white collar) which is sometimes favoured in Catholic churches. A recent alternative is the white cravat which tidies up the neckline for choir men. A man who finds that a cravat irritates his skin should try a silk cravat.

It is also common to wear a medal on a ribbon. This may be part of the uniform, or may be awarded as part of a training scheme. The Royal School of Church Music offers such a scheme, where the colour of the ribbon indicates the level attained in *Voice for Life*.

There is a separate style of **ladies' robe**, though there is no reason why ladies cannot wear cassocks and surplices. The traditional ladies' robe is of the same colour as the men's cassock, with ribbing on the back and front, and is worn with white sleevelets and jabot. There is a more modern style which is a plainer garment more tailored to the female form, such as with a waist, and worn without a surplice. All robes are worn at full length regardless of current fashions; there were no mini-cassocks in the 1960s. Girls in choirs wear the same robes as boys.

Hoods are part of the normal wear of the clergy and are often worn by choristers. It is advisable to sew a button to the front of the cassock near the top for this purpose.

Choir dress is when all choir members who hold an academic qualification wear a hood over their robes, regardless of the subject. There is no theological or legal reason against wearing hoods for Communion services. The arguments about humility in approaching the Lord's table would equally serve to exclude RSCM ribbons, medals and badges.

Developments in modern liturgy mean that sometimes the choir appears in normal clothing of a common design, such as all wearing an ordinary shirt in a particular colour with black trousers or a black skirt.

Robes should be acquired in various **sizes**. These sizes do not need to be too accurate as robes are loose fitting garments which cover several sizes of normal clothes. Particular attention needs to be paid to children's robes as children tend to stay in the choir for a shorter period and tend to grow while there, see page 204. Arrangements should be made for the regular laundering of robes.

Another aspect of choir dress relates to clothes worn underneath which may be partly visible. It is normal to require choristers to wear black, brown or dark shoes, and not to wear trainers, sandals or plimsolls. The requirements of Anglican clergy dress were considerably relaxed during the 20th century, when it abolished the rule banning vicars from sleeping in embroidered night-caps. Canon C27 now states that a minister must wear "suitable" clothing at all times, except for recreation and other justifiable purposes. These days, it is difficult to see what clothing would be regarded as unsuitable.

Being equipped

Pencils should be provided by the church, as choristers will never remember. Always keep a stock; they do not cost much. If you have pencils, you also need erasers and pencil sharpeners. It is advisable also to keep mending tape. Invisible Sellotape or Scotch tape on a dispenser is ideal. Ordinary Sellotape dries out and falls off after a while, and can attract dirt which obliterates the music. It can also be useful to keep paper clips for marking the pages in anthem books or choral scores.

Some theory

Human resources management

The day-to-day running of a choir requires skills now known as **human resources management (HRM)**. This is now recognised as a separate business management skill, which goes beyond personnel and payroll functions.

The two main elements of HRM are:

- motivation; and
- leadership.

Motivation

Motivation is the psychology to make a person perform better.

The psychology involves identifying both motivators and hygiene factors. Both of these take the form of meeting a need.

Motivators are those factors which encourage better performance, such as recognition and sense of achievement. These are sometimes called **positive motivators**.

Hygiene factors are those factors whose presence does not promote better performance, but whose absence leads to worse performance, such as pay and working conditions. The term is an analogy from the world of medicine. Good hygiene will not make you healthier, but poor hygiene will make you less healthy.

Conflicts of needs should be avoided as it will inevitably lead to at least one need remaining unsatisfied. For example, asking someone to lie for you leads to a conflict between loyalty and honesty. Frustration of needs is when a need cannot be met for reasons outside your control.

For business, Frederick Herzberg identified these positive motivators:

- achievement;
- recognition;
- responsibility;
- promotion prospects; and
- the work itself;

and these hygiene factors:

- pay;
- relationships;
- quality of supervision;
- company policy;
- working conditions; and
- fringe benefits.

Maslow

Most HRM commentators have adopted **Maslow's Hierarchy of Needs**, which depicts five levels of human need:

(a) self-actualisation;

(b) esteem;

(c) social;

(d) safety;

(e) physiological.

This hierarchy is named after A H Maslow, an American psychologist. There are other models, sometimes with a different number of levels, but the principles behind them all are similar.

The theory behind Maslow is that needs must be met from the lowest level upwards.

The main **physiological needs** are warmth, food and shelter. Until these are met, the individual is not interested in any higher need. In other words, if someone is hungry and cold, they are not easily motivated to do anything except find food and warmth. They are not interested in any of the higher needs, the meeting of which provides motivation. So don't rehearse in a freezing church, and allow for meal breaks and comfort breaks.

Once physiological needs are met, the next need is **safety**. Once people are fed, clothed, sheltered and warm, they need to feel safe that this will continue. Any threat to what someone values becomes at least a hygiene factor. For a choir, this can include the slightest threat to disband the choir.

The third level up is **social** needs. These include love and friendship. Assuming that your choir is neither freezing nor threatened with disbandment, this is the level where most choirmasters start considering motivation.

The second highest level is **esteem**. This includes self-confidence, sense of achievement, recognition and respect. Many choirs wear robes and sit in a special place in the church. This in itself can meet the esteem needs of members.

If a choir performs an anthem well, all members of it should share the sense of achievement. Never tell a choir that a good performance was solely or primarily down to you, the composer, the accompanist, the soloist or someone else. Always tell a choir that a good performance is always a team effort and they should take pride in being part of that winning team.

Saying "thank you" is a cost-effective motivator. It meets this high level of personal need while costing nothing. Ensure that you always say thank you to the choir for a good performance. Thank them for a good effort for a bad performance. (Never pretend a bad performance was good. The choir will know when they have performed badly, and will not respect you for saying otherwise.)

Self-actualisation is the highest level of human need. This is the need to realise one's potential for continued self-development. This highest level can only be achieved when all four lower levels have been met.

For a choir, self-actualisation is when you have no serious problems with absenteeism, new members join without being recruited, and members ask you about courses to attend. At this point, you can motivate yourself by the knowledge that you have reached the top of Maslow. All you need do is stay there.

This happy state does not mean that you will have no problems, just that you have exchanged the problems of failure for the problems of success. These include finding enough music, robes and seating, and dealing with congregational grumbles that the choir is taking over the church. At least you will be sufficiently motivated to deal with such problems.

Children have a different perspective on life from adults. Their needs must be met from the bottom upwards as for adults, but sometimes these needs are addressed differently. Their safety needs include not being overlooked, particularly when the children rehearse with the adults. They get bored if most of what you say goes over their heads.

Esteem needs can be met by ribbons, badges, prizes, certificates and the suchlike. It can be effective to make a big fuss about such matters, such as the vicar presenting a ribbon at the service and notifying the parents in advance. Prizes need not be of any great intrinsic value. What matters is the achievement in winning a prize, not the increase in their personal wealth as a consequence. Expensive awards are usually a waste of money, as the expense adds nothing to the sense of achievement.

Self-actualisation is demonstrated when they enjoy the choir so much that they bring their friends and stay in the choir when their voice breaks. You should be so lucky.

Dealing with the congregation

Education

An organist should educate the congregation. Brief introductions to anthems should be complemented by articles in the magazine giving more details. Be willing to talk to church groups.

Feedback

In Tune With Heaven recommends that an organist receives feedback on church music. This is fine in theory, but in practice the average worshipper will only tell you what he likes or doesn't like, where the former is simply what he has got used to. Feedback can encourage criticism and lead to consumer religion.

It is best if feedback comes from someone who has good hearing and some musical knowledge. They can tell you if the sound was balanced, the words audible and the introduction appropriate. A former chorister is ideal, see page 67.

Choir v music group

An organist should not fear music groups. A properly constituted body of competent musicians playing a proper arrangement adds to worship. As with choirs, the standard must always be the best we can offer, and should be at least of a standard that the public would pay to hear.

The problem is that many groups come nowhere near the standard of competence taken for granted among organists. Guitarists and bass guitarists are not usually the problem as these are simple instruments. Players should be at least Associated Board grade 6 or equivalent. One or two people learning their instrument up to grade 5 can be "carried" by other more competent players. The biggest problem is often the drummer who cannot be "carried" and should be of a standard of a semi-professional player.

Another problem with music groups is that they do not **play the word**s. Tunes are banged out without the phrasing and dynamics which organists use to make words come alive.

An innovative though rarely-used option is for the organist to be the music group using a modern programmable **synthesiser**. Advances since the early 1990s mean that these produce CD-quality sounds and have sophisticated rhythm patterns which provide competent drumming. The pedals can be programmed to put in drum breaks. This requires the organist to learn some new skills, particularly on rhythm. The result is far better than most music groups.

Modern music

Organists should welcome modern music in its various different styles. Traditional hymn books are themselves collections of different music styles over several centuries. There is no reason to stop the canon of church music arbitrarily at 1920.

However, much greater care is needed in selecting modern music as its repertoire has yet to be filtered through time. A look through a 19th-century hymn book will reveal hundreds of banal or sentimental words to instantly forgettable tunes which died in the generation of their birth. Those 19th-century hymns we sing today are the best few percent. So comparisons between old and new tend to be between the best of the old and everything of the new; there is no like-for-like comparison.

Charles Wesley has 39 hymns in *Common Praise* and perhaps 10,000 not in, yet no-one would argue that he was a poor hymnwriter because of this high attrition. We should show similar recognition to Graham Kendrick when he is remembered for three hymns.

Everything that we now regard as traditional was once modern. A cursory study of the history of church music reveals that the introduction of polyphony, harmony, counterpoint, hymns and organs all aroused as much passion in their day as any innovation in this day. An organist should not be dismissive of all modern music, but should be highly selective and ready to educate.

Outreach music

An organist must be ready to rebut arguments that music groups assist outreach better than choirs and organs.

Choirs and organs can be the music of evangelism and outreach. No-one outside the church is likely to be attracted in by a poor performance of worship songs, but they will be attracted by a proper choir, even an amateur choir singing simple choral music, as carol services routinely demonstrate.

A look in any large record store shows that choral music is by far the most popular form of Christian music. Next popular are country-and-western and black gospel.

There is value in having a form of music specially for worshipping God. This is indeed the whole concept of **holiness**, being set apart for God. This resonates with those outside the church. They expect to hear circus music at a circus, and military music at a military display. Similarly they expect to hear church music in a church.

The Church of England's General Synod gave a measure of recognition to this in *Mission-Shaped Church* (Church House Publishing) in 2004. Here are two quotes:

On fresh expressions in worship:

> *"There is some evidence of an increase in attendance at cathedral and other churches offering traditional styles of worship.... People now as always are looking for mystery, beauty, stability and a sense of God's presence."*

On youth services:

> *"A pattern of innovation in liturgical revision and musical variety has not (on the whole) been sustained. A generation of young people find Graham Kendrick old-fashioned and Common Worship outmoded."*

Another relevant observation is made by Philip North in *The Vicar's Guide* (Church House Publishing, 2005):

> *"It is notoriously difficult to define what it is that makes for good worship. It is easy to assume that worship that matches our own particular taste or spirituality is bound to be what works, but this simply isn't the case. I have seen growth in churches that offer spontaneous charismatic worship and also in parishes that offer a very traditional High Mass. One of my friends in the Diocese of Durham saw extraordinary growth*

in a very down-at-heel church where he served as priest, and by far the most popular service was Prayer Book Evensong.

"There are, however, some factors that can be identified, and the first seems to be that those leading worship have real confidence in what it is that they are offering. We do not need to explain or be embarrassed by the Church's worship. We just need to offer."

A church should always be wary of being **trendy**. Those who marry the spirit of one generation are widows in the next.

Even by the standards of pop charts, traditional church music fares better. The only "music group" songs which have made the charts (as far as we can find) are *Colours of Day/Light Up the Fire* (no 31 by Parchment in 1972) and *Let the Flame Burn Brighter* (no 55 by Graham Kendrick in 1989). In contrast, traditional hymns such as *Amazing Grace, Morning Has Broken* and even *Jerusalem* have made the charts, as have anthems such as *Panis Angelicus* and *Ave Maria*. In 1994, Gregorian chants sung by Benedictine Monks of Santo Domingo de Silas was the 30th best-selling "pop" album in USA, beating Eric Clapton, the Rolling Stones and Rod Stewart. It was number 1 in Italy for six weeks. Even an Anglican chant has made the UK top 30 (*Highway Code* by Master Singers reached 25 in 1966).

It should also be noted that modern popular music is not a single form liked by all young people, but a plethora of different forms each of which is a turn-off for some young people. Also, a glance at *Top of the Pops* or MTV will show you that current pop music is often as far removed from the music of a youth service as it is from choral evensong.

Adverse comments

For some inexplicable reason, some congregation members feel free to make rude comments about the music which they would not dream of making about the flower arrangements or Sunday School tableau.

An organist should be resistant to such comments until they start to gain currency. A person who seems to know all about church music may be asked on what authority or experience he speaks. Someone who wishes to "share" a derogatory opinion can be invited to share your opinions.

There are the unsubtle who come up after a service to tell you how good another service or concert was. Some will come back fired up by different worship (usually monastic singing or a rave-up) which they wish to transplant to your church. To do so would probably require a different congregation.

And do not be swayed by those who seek to get their own way by saying they have prayed about it, as though God has decreed that their favourite hymns must be sung on that day or no-one will go to heaven. This is simply spiritual blackmail. God works through appointed leaders. For music, that means the organist.

3 Employment law

Introduction

Why should an organist need to know about employment law? Surely we are all Christians working to the greater glory of God, and any problems we incur on the way can easily be settled by a quiet chat over a cup of tea at the vicarage. If only!

Chapter 1 gives advice on how to maintain good relations with clergy. This chapter provides the legal basis for such relations.

Employment law needs to be considered for two reasons:

- to ensure that everyone knows what is expected of them; and
- to provide a safety net if things go wrong.

However honest and well-meaning individuals are, it is possible for them to go away with different ideas of what they agreed. Putting the agreement in writing is a simple way of ensuring that the parties are agreed.

Employment law also provides a safety net so that if things go wrong, there is at least a minimum level of co-operation which is guaranteed. This provides a level below which the relationship cannot fall any further, and from which it is hoped a relationship may recover.

A manufacturer tests its products against the worst possible conditions to which it could be subjected, however unlikely. That way the manufacturer knows that the product will survive real conditions. Similarly a contract must be drafted to cope with the worst conditions which, theoretically, could exist. You must imagine that everyone hates everyone else and is being as awkward as they can; where no-one will do anything unless they legally must. If the contract can maintain a working relationship in those worst conditions, then it will support you in whatever does happen. The policy is prepare for the worst, work for the best.

It is also worth observing that a clearly worded contract setting out grievance and discipline procedures is itself an effective way of avoiding problems in the first place.

Sources of law

For the organist there are three possible sources of law:

- contract law;
- employment law; and
- canon law.

Each of these approaches the subject from a different perspective. Contract law is usually the most important.

Canon law is only applicable in the Church of England. As the established Church, its canon law has the force of law like any other branch of law. Other denominations and religions, and other provinces of the Anglican Communion (such as in Scotland, Wales and Ireland) are not bound by Church of England canon law. Such denominations and provinces often have their own canon law or equivalent system of law.

The Roman Catholic church has very detailed canon law. However, this is not directly enforceable in the UK courts, except perhaps if it has been incorporated into the contract, when it may be enforceable under contract law, provided the contracting parties have accepted it as applicable to them.

Contract Law

A contract is a legally enforceable agreement between two parties, where each provides a benefit to the other. That is not the strict legal definition, but it will suffice for our purposes.

There are many aspects of contract law which must be clearly understood.

1 Each side provides a benefit

For a contract to be valid, each party to the contract must provide a benefit, known as the **consideration**, to the other party.

Most commonly, one party provides money and the other party provides goods or services. This is a contract of sale for goods or services. Almost all purchases are contracts. However, it is not necessary for money to be one of the considerations. For example, if two organists exchanged music, that would be a contract even though no money changed hands.

It is not necessary for the consideration to be adequate. If I sell you my car for one penny, there is a contract even though my car is worth much more. You have full contractual rights against me on the same basis as if you paid its full worth. However, if I give you my car for nothing, that is a gift and you have no contractual rights.

Where an organist is engaged for a fee or honorarium, it is obvious that there is a contract. However, the issue is not so clear when an organist plays at church without payment. In practice, a consideration is easily established. In one court case, used chocolate wrappers (which were thrown away) were held to be adequate consideration. If you have the right to use the organ for private practice, that is enough to establish consideration. If you have the right to be paid fees for playing at weddings and funerals, that is enough to establish consideration. This is regarded as consideration even if you never use the organ for practice and never play at weddings or funerals — the right to do so is itself sufficient. It is the opinion of the authors that it is probably impossible to be a church organist without creating a contract.

2 Contract is made when offer is accepted.

A contract is made when one party makes an offer which the other person accepts. Until there is an acceptance, there is no contract, only negotiations.

It does not matter who makes the offer. It may be that a seller offers to sell goods which the buyer accepts, or a buyer offers to buy goods which the seller accepts. Either way a contract is made when the offer is accepted.

Suppose you are asked to play the organ at a concert for £50. You agree to play but ask for £100. There is no contract as neither has accepted an offer from the other. After some haggling, he offers you £75 which you accept. Your acceptance establishes the contract. Suppose the following day, you change your mind and decide that you should have insisted on £100. Tough. You have made a contract and can be held to it.

A musician is only entitled to the fee that has been agreed, not to the fee that the musician thinks he is worth. Authoritative bodies publish suggested rates (see page 114), but these are not contractually binding on anyone. They simply guide the parties as to what rates they should consider.

A contract to perform as a musician is a personal contract which cannot be discharged by someone else. In practice, many musicians wrongly believe that if offered a more lucrative engagement, they can take it and send a "dep" (deputy) to play the original one. Although many musicians seem to get away with "depping", it is clearly a breach of contract unless, exceptionally, it was agreed when the musician was booked.

3 Contract need not be in writing

A contract need not be in writing or even spoken. It is sufficient that the words or actions make clear what the parties have agreed.

Suppose you go into a shop, pick up a bar of chocolate, give a pound to the shopkeeper, he gives you 20p change and you walk out the shop. You have made a binding contract for the purchase of that chocolate. No words were written or spoken, but it is obvious what you were both doing. A spoken contract or one implied from conduct is just as binding as a written contract.

A written contract may be varied verbally or by the conduct of the parties. This can create a problem for an organist who may agree to do things not required by the contract.

For example, suppose an organist was engaged to play for a defined list of services which do not include any carol services for the local school. However, for ten years, the organist has been happy to play for this service. It is possible that this course of conduct has established a change in the contract through **custom and practice** that means the organist is required to play for this service. If in year 11, the organist wishes to accept an alternative engagement, there could be a problem.

There is no laid down time limit on when custom and practice amounts to a change in contract, beyond saying that it is probably at the point when the practice has become so well established that the parties reasonably regard it as part of the contract.

If you find that you are regularly undertaking additional duties, which are not in your contract, it is worth writing a note making clear that you are performing these additional duties as an act of goodwill and they are not intended to vary your contract. The note does not have to be legalistic nor awkward. It is sufficient to say something like: "Dear John, I am happy to play for the school carol service this year as an addition to my duties, though I cannot guarantee that I will be able to play for this service in any future years. Kind regards." That is sufficient to avoid its becoming a contractual duty.

4 Only enforceable terms should be included

A written contract contains recitals and conditions. (Recitals here has nothing to do with organ recitals!)

The recitals simply identify the parties, give the date and state what type of contract it is. The conditions state what each party must do. A draft contract is produced by the

Incorporated Society of Musicians, Royal College of Organists and Royal School of Church Music.

You and the church are free to put in whatever conditions you may agree. However, the conditions should only contain provisions which one party may wish to enforce against the other party's will. There is no need to include any condition which begins "if the parties agree". If you agree to play at the Sunday School party, you simply do it. If you do not agree, you do not do it. Either way, the contract is irrelevant.

One of the authors saw a contract which included the condition "the parties agree that they each believe it is the will of God that N should be the youth worker for X church". It is difficult to see the purpose of such a clause, let alone how it could be enforced.

5 A contract and changes to it must be agreed voluntarily

It is an essential element of any contract that the parties enter into the agreement voluntarily. Normal persuasion and even cajoling will not void a contract, but any greater pressure may have the effect of voiding a contract. No organist should ever agree or vary a contract with a gun to his head.

The exact legal consequences depend on whether the improper pressure is duress or undue influence.

Duress is actual violence or threats of violence to the person. Incidents of duress are extremely rare, so the courts also accept **undue influence** as a basis for voiding a contract. Undue influence is the improper use of power over the contracting mind of the other party. Such influence includes any threat to sue or prosecute the other person if he does not agree. A leading case is *Williams v Bayley [1866]* when a colliery owner managed to set aside a mortgage of his colliery to a bank when the bank had threatened to report the owner's son for a fraud if he did not.

The exact scope of undue influence depends on whether there is a fiduciary relationship between the parties.

A **fiduciary relationship** is a special relationship where one party is bound to exercise his rights and powers in good faith for the benefit of the other. Such relationships include parent and child, doctor and patient, lawyer and client, trustee and beneficiary, and priest and parishioner. In each case the former person is considered to have some **dominance** over the other.

When there is no fiduciary relationship, the party who complains of undue influence must prove that actual pressure was applied. Undue influence includes threats of being sued, reported for a crime, or similar threats against a husband or wife. It is for you to show that you were subject to such pressure.

When there is a fiduciary relationship, the burden of proof is reversed. The dominant person must show that he did not exercise undue influence.

Employer and employee is not a fiduciary relationship, but to the extent that an organist is a worshipper of the priest's church, there is a fiduciary relationship.

If duress or undue influence is shown, the contract is voidable. That means that one party may have the contract set aside, but does not have to do so.

6 The contract must be certain

The contract must be clear as to what has been agreed. If not, the contract fails for **uncertainty**. So a reference to "on hire purchase terms" was held by the courts to be too vague. *(Scammell v Ouston [1941])*.

This does not mean that every last detail must be spelled out. The word "reasonable" is quite acceptable in contractual clauses, such as "the organist will be allowed reasonable opportunity to use the organ for private practice". Also, the courts are reluctant to strike down a whole contract because of a single uncertain clause.

Employment Law

Contract law works well when there are plenty of possible people with whom either party could contract, and the parties have an equal capacity to contract. So if you wish to sell your car, you have thousands of potential buyers, each buyer has thousands of potential sellers, and the two of you stand eyeball to eyeball as equal parties to agree whatever you wish.

Contract law works less well when there are not many people with whom you may contract or where one party has considerably more power than the other. In such instances, the law can intervene to redress the balance by giving one party some rights *regardless* of what the parties may agree. Employment is one such area. Others include credit agreements, timeshares and doorstep selling.

Employment law gives statutory rights to employees *in addition* to rights in the contract of employment. It is not generally possible to avoid these rights, even if the employer and employee agree to disregard them.

Employment rights generally started in the mid 1960s. The first rights related to notice periods, right to redundancy pay and protection from racial and sexual discrimination. They have been progressively added to over the years, with new rights added annually. Some employment law has been a political football. For example, various laws regarding trade unions have been introduced by one government and then reversed by the next. There now appears to be consensus between the main political parties on most aspects of employment law.

Employment law has grown up in a hotchpot with new provisions piled on top of old ones, particularly recent laws based on European directives. Because of this, the UK does not have a coherent system of employment law, but rather a ragbag of miscellaneous provisions which can have different rules and sometimes do not fit well together.

Employment rights can be categorised according to objectives:

- protection from dismissal (eg law against unfair dismissal and redundancy pay);
- protection from discrimination (eg anti racial discrimination laws and equal pay for women);
- accommodating family life (eg maternity leave and time off for dependant relatives);
- protecting pay (eg no unauthorised deductions and national minimum wage);
- making workplace safe and fair (eg health and safety laws and ban on capricious acts by employer).

Workers and employees

A distinction is made in law between workers and employees. "Workers" is the wider term. It includes all employees, but also includes contractors, seconded staff, temporary staff from agencies and others who may not legally be employees.

Workers have some rights; employees have many more.

Workers have the right to:

- national minimum wage;
- limits on working hours; and
- protection from discrimination.

Many of these rights are newer ones which derive from European Community law.

All workers have rights which derive from contract law, such as protection from wrongful dismissal or non-payment of fees.

All organists are workers and entitled to workers' rights. An organist who has a contract of employment is clearly also an employee or office holder. Whether other organists are employees is not quite so clear.

Is the organist an employee?

Probably. The authors believe that almost all church organists are legally employees of their church. However, we cannot be certain until a court or employment tribunal has ruled on the matter. This nearly happened in the Wetherby Church case summarised on page 111.

There have been many cases on whether other workers are legally employees. The deciding factor is whether there is any **control**, whether the employer can dictate how the employee must do his job. However, this must be interpreted according to the nature of the work. Directors, lecturers and hospital doctors enjoy considerable autonomy in how they do their work, but are usually employees or office holders.

An organist is an employee of the minister if he must perform the duties personally and has no unfettered right to substitute another person. In the Church of England, that duty to perform personally is explicitly stated in Canon B20, so it is difficult to see how a Church of England organist could not be regarded as an employee.

It is irrelevant that the parties sign an agreement which states that there is no contract of employment. Whether there is a contract of employment depends on the facts not on what the parties have agreed (itself a departure from normal contract law).

Some court cases on these points are noted below.

A contract of employment exists if three conditions are met:

- the servant agrees that, for a wage, he will provide his own work and skill in the performance of some service;
- he agrees to be under the other person's control to a sufficient degree to make that other person the master; and
- other provisions of the contract are consistent with a contract of employment.

(Ready Mixed Concrete (South East) Ltd v Minister of Pensions and National Insurance [1968] QBD).

Employment law is very different from what it was in the 1960s. The control test may not be decisive. We may need to consider the American view of looking at the economic reality of the relationship *(Lane v Shire Roofing Co Ltd [1995] CA).*

No exhaustive list can be compiled of what constitutes a contract of employment, nor is it possible to say what weight can be attached to the various considerations. Control is always one factor, but is not the sole determining factor. *(Market Investigations v Minister of Social Security [1969] QBD).*

It is possible to be an employee for more than one person, ie have two jobs. It is also possible to be an employee and self-employed at the same time.

Engagement

An employer is generally free to engage whomsoever he wishes in whatever way he wishes. There is no obligation on an employer to advertise a vacancy nor to accept the best candidate. You have no redress in law for being passed over in favour of a hopeless crony of the vicar. This is an area where there is plenty of good practice but little law.

The only legal restrictions on engagement are rules on discrimination, some limits on employing children (explained on page 178) and some rules in the public sector.

End of contract

An organist who is sacked, asked to resign or forced to resign may have certain rights against his employer, such as for unfair dismissal or wrongful dismissal.

In employment law, there are various ways by which an employment may end:

(a) **voluntarily**, the employee retires or resigns, or the employee and employer agree that it should end;

(b) **dismissal**, the employee is sacked;

(c) **frustration**, the employment is prevented from continuing;

(d) **redundancy**, the employee is no longer needed.

It should be noted that an organist resigning may constitute constructive dismissal for employment law purposes, as explained later.

Frustration is when a contract is prevented for reasons which are not the fault of either party, such as the organist losing an arm. It is difficult to imagine a situation for the other side. Even if the church burnt down and the organ destroyed, the organist would still be employed, and probably expected to play the organ or piano in temporary accommodation.

Redundancy in employment law means much more than simply not needing an employee. Redundancy only exists when:

(a) the employer's activity has ceased; or

(b) the activity has ceased at that location and not resumed within a nearby location; or

(c) the requirement for the work done by the employee has ceased or diminished, or is expected to do so.

There is much case law on what exactly constitutes redundancy.

If a church is closed so that regular worship ceases there, the organist is redundant. There is no redundancy just because the church authorities wish to reorganise the church (such as a cathedral combining the organist and a canon post) nor because the church authorities wish to replace the organ and choir with a music group. In each case the activity of the employer continues and the requirement for music remains. In such cases, the church authorities should consider whether to dismiss the organist and risk an action for unfair dismissal.

Someone who has been employed for two years and is made redundant is entitled to statutory redundancy pay. This is calculated as so many weeks' pay to a legal maximum depending on your age and length of service. Your contract of employment may have provisions for additional redundancy pay.

A person is not legally redundant just because the employer says he is. If the real reason is not redundancy, the organist is actually dismissed and may have claims for wrongful dismissal and unfair dismissal.

Dismissal

Nature of dismissal

An employee is dismissed when:

- the employer terminates the employment, verbally or in writing; or
- a fixed-term contract is not renewed; or
- the employee resigns and is able to claim constructive dismissal.

Care should be exercised about accepting a verbal resignation or dismissal. Generally the courts and tribunals will ignore words said in the heat of a moment, such as "that's it, I'm resigning" or "get out, you are fired". Several cases have ruled that "**** off" does not constitute dismissal. In most cases, employment tribunals have found that these are just expressions of exasperation. It must be clear from other evidence that there was a clear intention to resign or dismiss.

Even though an employee resigns, this may be regarded as dismissal for employment law purposes in three circumstances:

- the employee is asked to resign under terms which make it clear that he will be dismissed if he does not; or
- the employee is tricked into resigning; or
- there is constructive dismissal.

(Employment Rights Act 1996 s95)

There is also deemed dismissal when an employee is denied his legal right to return to work after a period of maternity leave, paternity leave or adoption leave.

Constructive dismissal

Constructive dismissal arises in one of two circumstances:

- the employer commits a fundamental breach of the contract of employment; or
- the employer's conduct is such that an employee cannot reasonably be expected to continue.

The law on constructive dismissal means that an employer cannot avoid his legal responsibilities by forcing out an employee. Having established that an employee has suffered constructive dismissal, the matter is then considered as for any other dismissal. There is no constructive dismissal when an employee resigns rather than accept a verbal or written warning.

A **fundamental breach** of the contract to justify constructive dismissal requires three elements:

- there must be a term of the contract;
- that term must have been breached; and
- that breach must be fundamental.

The terms of the contract are not confined to what is written in the contract of employment. First, it is possible for the contract to be have been varied in writing, spoken words or by the conduct of the parties, as explained above. Second, some terms may be implied into all contracts of employment.

A term may be implied into a contract of employment if it:

- is necessary to give the contract "business efficacy"; or
- reflects custom and practice in that employment which is "reasonable, certain and notorious"; or
- arises from an inherent legal duty, such as providing a safe working environment.

The breach may be actual or anticipatory. An **actual breach** is one which has happened. An **anticipatory breach** is when one party makes clear that they will breach a term. Although you can bring an action for anticipatory breaches, this is difficult in practice. A proposal on changed working conditions is not an anticipatory breach as it is not definite. Unless the change is expressed in writing as what will definitely happen, it is usually inadvisable to act on an anticipatory breach.

Unfair and wrongful dismissal

Having established that there has been a dismissal, the next question is to determine whether it was:

(a) wrongful; or

(b) unfair

These are separate considerations. A dismissal can be wrongful and unfair, either wrongful or unfair, or neither.

Wrongful dismissal is when an employee is sacked in the wrong manner.

Unfair dismissal is when an employee is sacked for an unfair reason.

Wrongful dismissal is a breach of contract. It arises in such cases as when:

- a notice period has not been given; or
- a discipline and grievance procedure has not been followed.

The contract of employment will usually specify a **notice period**, typically one month or three months, but any period may be agreed. An employee cannot be required to give more notice than the employer. There is a minimum statutory notice period according to length of service, thus:

Length of service	Notice period
less than one month	none
1 month – 2 years	one week
2 years – 12 years	one week for each full year of service
more than 12 years	12 weeks.

So the notice period is the statutory period unless the contract gives a longer period.

The notice period may be disregarded by an employer for a **summary dismissal**. This is when an employee's conduct is such that an employer could not reasonably be expected to continue employing the person. This usually arises for serious offences such as damaging property, theft or violence.

Discipline and grievance procedure

From 1 October 2004 there are statutory discipline and grievance procedures which must be followed by employers of any size. An employee who is dismissed when this statutory procedure has not been followed may claim automatically unfair dismissal. The statutory procedure is contained in Employment Act 2002 Sch 2 and Employment Act 2002 (Dispute Resolution) Regulations SI 2004 No 752.

There are two disciplinary procedures:

- 3-step standard procedure, for most dismissals; and
- 2-step modified procedure for summary dismissals.

These statutory procedures are the minimum which must be followed in all cases. If the contract of employment imposes additional requirements, they must be followed in addition to the statutory procedure.

Many employers have followed the Advisory Conciliation and Arbitration Service (ACAS) guidelines for dismissal to be preceded by a verbal warning and written warning. Such warnings do not constitute discipline in themselves. An employee may refuse to accept a warning. This does not have any real consequence, except that it could make a claim for unfair dismissal easier to prove.

There are some exceptions when these procedures do not apply, such as when dismissal is because the employee has reached retirement age.

The three steps for the standard procedure are:

1 stating the grounds for action, and inviting to a meeting;
2 a meeting to discuss the matter;
3 an appeal.

Step 1 requires an employer to send a written statement to the employee about the employee's conduct, characteristics or other circumstances which lead the employer to consider dismissal. The employee must be given reasonable time to consider this, and be invited to a meeting to discuss the matter. Step 1 usually must be within three months of the basis for considering discipline.

Step 2 is the meeting. No disciplinary action other than suspension on full pay may take place before this meeting. The time and place must be "reasonable" and allow each side to present their case. An employee has the right to be accompanied by one **companion**. This may be a trade union official or colleague to any disciplinary meeting under Employment Act 1999 ss10-15. No colleague or trade union official can be compelled to attend. An employer may allow someone else, such as a friend or adviser, to attend.

The companion may address the meeting and confer with the employee during the meeting, but has no right to answer questions on behalf of the employee.

The employee must make reasonable efforts to attend. If unavoidably prevented, such as by illness, a second date must be arranged. If the employee does not attend, step 2 is complete. An employer is not required to arrange a third meeting. The employer must inform the employee of his decision after this meeting. Any dismissal or other disciplinary action may then be taken. The employee must be told of the right of appeal.

Step 3, an appeal, follows unless the employee decides otherwise. The appeal requires a further meeting, not necessarily with different people.

The modified procedure comprises steps 1 and 3 of the standard procedure.

The grievance procedures are identical to the discipline procedure but with the parties reversed. Step 1 involves the employee sending the employer a statement of grievance. A grievance may only be made about action which an employer has taken or is contemplating taking. The employer must send a written response. A two-step modified grievance procedure applies when the employment has already ended.

Unfair dismissal arises from an Act of Parliament. It was first introduced under Industrial Relations Act 1971 and is now found in Employment Rights Act 1996 s94(1). The right to claim unfair dismissal therefore derives from the law and not from the contract of employment.

In general, an employee may only bring a claim for unfair dismissal if the employee:

(a) has worked for a qualifying period;

(b) is below retirement age;

(c) works in Great Britain; and

(d) was not involved in industrial action at the time.

From 1 June 1999, the **qualifying period** is one year, except for medical suspensions, when the period is one month, and for automatically unfair dismissals when there is no qualifying period.

Normal **retirement age** is 65 for a man. For a woman, it is 60 until 2010 when it gradually rises, reaching 65 in 2020. There are hundreds of regular organists over this age. They are not lacking in protection, however, as they may still have a claim for wrongful dismissal. Also, age discrimination becomes illegal in 2006.

Automatically unfair dismissal

There are certain cases where a dismissal is held to be automatically unfair. These are when the reason for dismissal relates to:

(a) membership or non-membership of a trade union;

(b) a transfer of undertakings when the employer's activities pass to someone else;

(c) unlawful discrimination (explained later);

(d) asserting a statutory right;

(e) performing the duties of a health and safety officer, or a pension fund trustee.

What is unfair dismissal

Since unfair dismissal was outlawed in 1971, employment tribunals and the courts have produced volumes of case law from thousands of hearings. It is impossible to repeat all this received wisdom in this book. However, we can provide some of the main principles and give at least a flavour of what has been decided in those areas most likely to be relevant to organists.

Any employee who is dismissed has a statutory right to a written statement of the reasons for dismissal. If no statement is given, it is assumed that the reason was redundancy which, if it cannot be substantiated, can be regarded as unfair dismissal.

A dismissal is fair if it relates to one of five statutory grounds given in Employment Rights Act 1996 s98:

> (a) capability;
>
> (b) conduct;
>
> (c) redundancy;
>
> (d) statutory restriction; or
>
> (e) some other substantial reason.

Capability means the employee's skill, aptitude, qualifications, health, and all other physical and mental qualities of a sufficient standard to do the job. An organist could be dismissed if he suffered an injury which seriously affected his ability to play.

Conduct includes anything improper which an employee does. In some cases, it can include conduct outside the workplace. This is the most problematic area of unfair dismissal, and is discussed further in a later section.

Statutory restriction means that a person is no longer legally able to do the job. The commonest example is a driver who loses his licence. It is unlikely to apply to an organist.

Some other substantial reason is a sweep-up clause for anything else. For any claim of dismissal, an employer must show that the facts of the particular case justified dismissal within the scope of one of the five broad reasons. If this reason is used, the employer must also first show that the reason could be a fair reason. Reasons which the tribunals and courts have accepted under this catch-all include:

> (a) refusal to accept a reasonable reorganisation;
>
> (b) working for a competitor or setting up in competition to employer;
>
> (c) an extreme case of pressure from a customer of the employer;
>
> (d) problems working with other employees;
>
> (e) expiry of a fixed-term contract (when not otherwise protected);
>
> (f) as allowed in a transfer of undertakings;
>
> (g) persistent absences for sickness;

(h) conduct in private life which is inconsistent with position held;

(i) imprisonment;

(j) making false statements to secure the employment; and

(k) refusing to move to a system of cashless pay.

As far as organists are concerned (d) and (h) are probably the most relevant and are discussed below. Regarding (b), churches do not have "competitors", so an organist who occasionally plays for another church does not justify dismissal unless it affects his ability to perform his employed duties.

Even if an employee's conduct falls within the scope of a reason for fair dismissal, that does not make the dismissal fair. The employer must show that dismissal is justified in the particular circumstances of the individual case.

Misconduct

While almost any improper execution of duties could be misconduct, dismissal is only justified if the conduct is sufficiently serious. This does not mean that the misconduct must be serious in itself. Tribunals have accepted minor acts of misconduct where the consequences are serious or where the misconduct is part of a deliberate course of conduct.

Misconduct need not be blameworthy, though it can be a factor. An organist who becomes disabled through illness may be fairly dismissed.

The most common forms of misconduct are lateness; absenteeism; abusive behaviour; disloyalty; disobedience; drink or drugs; smoking; attitude; appearance; sleeping on duty; dishonesty; violence; and inconsistent personal conduct.

A dismissal is fair if the employer can show "a genuine belief on reasonable grounds after reasonable investigation" *(British Home Stores Ltd v Burchell. EAT [1980]* and affirmed by Court of Appeal in *W Weddel & Co Ltd v Tepper [1980])*. Some forms of misconduct may also be criminal offences, such as theft and assault. It is not necessary for a criminal court to find a person guilty as this requires a higher level of proof, namely "beyond reasonable doubt". So a person may be fairly dismissed for a criminal act even though found not guilty in a criminal court.

Conduct outside work

An employee can be dismissed for improper conduct outside work in very limited circumstances.

Even for criminal convictions, dismissal is only justified "so long as in some respect or other it affects the employee, or could be thought to be likely to affect the employee, when he is doing his work" *(Singh v London Country Bus Services Ltd [1976] IRLR)*. The ACAS Disciplinary Code specifically states that criminal offences outside employment "should not be treated as automatic reasons for dismissal, regardless of whether the offence has any relevance to the duties of the individual as an employees. The main considerations should be whether the offence is one that makes the individual unsuitable for his or her type of work or unacceptable to other employees."

The tribunals have accepted that dismissal was justified when a shopworker shoplifted from another store, and when a cleaner in a bank pleaded guilty to three charges of obtaining property by deception. In each case, the conviction showed problems in the employee retaining the job. In the case *Gunn v British Waterways Board [1981]*, the Employment Appeal Tribunal held that an employer was entitled to sack an employee who broke into a surgery to steal drugs because this affected the employer's reputation and his relationship with colleagues.

As criminal convictions are often considered irrelevant, it becomes almost impossible to justify dismissal for out of work conduct which is not criminal. In the opinion of the authors, there is no reason to dismiss an organist solely on the grounds that he:

    (a) is divorced;

    (b) has had an affair;

    (c) is homosexual;

    (d) lives with a person outside marriage;

    (e) reads *Playboy*;

    (f) has been banned from driving;

    (g) has paid civil penalties for motoring or tax offences;

    (h) is a member of freemasons, Rotary, Round Table or a similar body;

    (i) smokes;

    (j) has been drunk at a private party;

    (k) has publicly expressed political or personal opinions unrelated to his work;

    (l) is bankrupt or has financial problems; or

    (m) is involved in civil litigation.

In saying this, the authors neither condone nor condemn such conduct; we simply state our opinion that the nature of these matters is not sufficiently legally relevant to justify dismissal of a church organist. Our observation is based purely on what we believe to be legal under UK law, not on what is morally correct.

The seriousness of any offence can be judged by the degree of trust an employer may reasonably have in the employee. In the case *Dairy Produce Packers Ltd v Beaverstock [1981]*, the Employment Appeal Tribunal held that an employer was justified in dismissing an employee found drinking at a pub during working time, even though three other employees were only warned for this offence. The dismissed employee worked away from the factory, so a greater degree of trust was needed.

In a church context, it may be argued that higher standards should be expected than in secular society, so dismissal of a church officer may be justified in circumstances which would not apply to a bank employee. Bible passages such as 1 Timothy 3:1-10 set high standards for bishops and less demanding standards for deacons. There is clear evidence that those who hold leadership positions in the church must abide by higher standards than other church members.

The first issue this raises is that these higher standards apply to those who "aspire to leadership" in the church. It is the authors' view that an organist may be a minister within the church, but is not a leader. Another issue is that many expressions are imprecise, such as being "temperate, courteous, hospitable" (verse 2).

The Church of England has had problems enough in defining acceptable standards for clergy. In general, it has taken action only when the conduct reflects on the person's work or brings the church into disrepute such as by attracting scandal.

Discrimination

Discrimination is only illegal if it comes within one of the statutory categories. These make it illegal to discriminate on grounds of a person's:

- race, colour or ethnic origin;
- sex or marital status;
- membership or non-membership of a trade union;
- (from 1 December 2003) religion; or
- (from 1 December 2003) sexual orientation;
- (from 1 October 2006) age.

In Northern Ireland it is illegal to discriminate against a person on the grounds of their religion or political view.

There is no law against discrimination on other grounds, so it remains legal to discriminate against someone for being left-handed, right-wing or ginger-haired, though such arbitrary discrimination is deplored.

The introduction of laws based on religion and sexual orientation are a significant development, as these are largely areas of personal choice, unlike sex, race, age and disability.

There are some exceptions for a genuine occupational qualification, such as allowing sex discrimination for models and actors, for example.

In general, the rules for each type of illegal discrimination are similar, though they derive from different Acts. Unless covered by a specific exemption, a refusal to employ someone or a dismissal would constitute unlawful discrimination for each of these reasons:

- an irrelevant job requirement which can be more easily addressed by one group than another. For example a minimum height discriminates against women;
- their partner is of a particular religion or orientation;
- an employee served a black person after being told not to do so because the person was black;
- believing that an employee is of a particular religion or orientation, even though he is not.

Exemption for religious bodies

There are limited exemptions for religious bodies who are allowed to discriminate, which is why it remains legal not to have women bishops.

The religious exemption is most explicitly spelled out in regulation 7(3) of the statutory instruments for religious and sexual orientation discrimination. These regulations are:

- *The Employment Equality (Religion or Belief) Regulations SI 2003 No 1660;*
- *The Employment Equality (Sexual Orientation) Regulations SI 2003 No 1661.*

These regulations permit discrimination if:

- the employment is for purposes of an organised religion; and
- the discrimination requirement is to comply with the doctrines of that religion; or to avoid conflicting with the strongly held religious convictions of a significant number of the religion's followers.

For these purposes, "organised religion" is defined more narrowly than Christianity generally. The Department of Trade and Industry notes say that each denomination is considered separately. Guidance notes from the Archbishops' Council go further and suggest that each church may be considered separately.

As regards religious discrimination, guidance from the Archbishops' Council of the Church of England says that:

- an Anglican church or body cannot have a blanket policy that all employees must be Anglican — a requirement to follow a religion must be relevant to the particular post;
- a requirement to belong to a particular denomination or religion is relevant when the work involves arranging worship.

While a church's religious identity is clear, the church's attitude to homosexuality is less clear with strong views held for and against.

The Archbishops' Council notes in relation to sexual orientation include the following:

20 The sexual orientation genuine occupation requirement

This is one of the most sensitive areas of the regulations. In arguing for something akin to regulation 7(3) [the religious exemption] the Archbishops' Council was not seeking freedom for the Church to discriminate on the grounds of sexual orientation. The Council made it clear to the government that it was opposed to such discrimination. The aim was simply to ensure that churches and other faith groups continued to have the freedom to set standards in relation to sexual conduct without these being held to be discriminatory simply because they were defined in relation to marriage.

21 The primary issue is that of consistency. A tribunal is likely, for example, to uphold a discrimination case from an actively gay, lesbian or bisexual person denied a job, if the parish wishing to invoke section 7(3) in order that its particular ethos is maintained, knowingly employs heterosexual people who are in a sexual relationship outside marriage.

It will be for each church, theological college, trustee body, church voluntary organisation etc to think through its own approach and be clear how it would justify it if challenged in a particular case. It is particularly important, for example, that people avoid assumptions about people's sexuality or lifestyles. It cannot be assumed that two people living together (regardless of gender) have a sexual relationship, or that someone is gay or that if someone is gay s/he is active sexually. Finding out about a candidate's private life without making assumptions will be particularly sensitive. Where employers conclude that they need to adopt a restrictive approach they may be vulnerable if they are selective in asking some of those being considered for appointment, promotion, training etc about their lifestyle, but not others.

In the House of Lords debate, government minister Baroness Blackstone said, "I return to the concern that the employment directive might require religious organisations that believe that homosexual activity is wrong to open all jobs to practising homosexuals. It would be unacceptable, for example, for a teacher in a Catholic school to challenge openly the teachings of the Church on homosexuality."

The government document *Towards Equality and Diversity* published in 2001 states that "a religious organisation may be able to demonstrate that all staff — not just senior staff or people with a proselyting function — should belong to the religion concerned, so as to ensure the preservation of the organisation's particular ethos. Alternatively, depending on the circumstances, the exemption might apply only to a number of key posts. However, this exemption does not allow religious or belief organisations to discriminate on other grounds".

Advisory Conciliation and Arbitration Service (ACAS) has also published guidelines. If an organisation believes that it has a genuine occupational requirement for a person to be (or not be) of a particular religion or sexual orientation, this must be explicitly stated in any advertisement for that post.

The requirement for sexual orientation is stricter than for religion. For orientation, the condition must be *necessary* whereas for religion it is sufficient if *preferable*.

Advertisements for organist posts since these regulations became law show only a minority requiring the organist to belong to a particular religion. We have not found any advertisement specifying a particular sexual orientation.

It may also be worth noting that most Christian bodies have welcomed the final form of regulations while pro-homosexual bodies have generally condemned them. The religious exemption is also being legally challenged by some trade unions, the result of which was not known when this book was written.

From all this, the authors conclude that a church may legally discriminate against an organist for his religious belief, as the organist is involved in worship.

For sexual orientation, a church may not discriminate, unless that is its clearly stated policy which has been consistently followed. This would seem to be reasonable. No advantage would be gained in a homosexual organist trying to exercise a ministry in a church whose members strongly condemned his lifestyle.

However, these are just the authors' views based on what has been published so far. These issues will not become clear until there have been some cases on the matter.

Sickness, maternity, family policies and similar

The law provides minimum requirements which employers must follow with regard to sickness, maternity and other family matters. An employer may agree to provide additional benefits to the employee, and most employers do.

For **maternity**, a woman has these rights:

- paid leave to attend ante-natal classes;
- maternity leave;
- statutory maternity pay;
- right to return to same or similar job at same pay and conditions; and
- protection against dismissal or other employment disadvantage.

The rules below reflect the changes for maternity, paternity and adoption introduced from 6 April 2003. Each right is subject to strict rules.

A woman is entitled to 26 weeks' maternity leave regardless of how long she has been in post. A woman is entitled to a further 26 weeks of additional maternity leave if she was employed for 26 weeks in the 15th week before the expected birth, which usually means that she became pregnant after starting that job. She must give notice, and may start up to 11 weeks before the expected birth.

Statutory maternity pay (SMP) is paid for up to 26 weeks. It is paid at 90% of average earnings for the first six weeks and (from 6 April 2005 to 5 April 2006) at £106 a week for the rest (unless this exceeds 90% of average earnings). It is subject to tax and national insurance. This and similar rates are revised each April as part of the Budget.

For **adoption**, a man or woman may claim 26 weeks or 52 weeks adoption leave and 26 weeks statutory adoption pay (SAP) on broadly identical terms to maternity. Where a couple adopts a child, only one may claim.

For **paternity**, the father is entitled to two weeks paternity leave and two weeks statutory paternity pay (SPP) of £68.20 (from 6 April 2005 to 5 April 2006), reduced to 90% of average earnings if less. Where a couple adopts, the one not claiming adoption leave and SAP may claim paternity leave and SPP, so it is possible for a woman to take paternity leave and receive SPP.

It is a condition for SMP, SAP and SPP that the employee earns at least the lower earnings limit, which is £82 a week for the tax year from 6 April 2005 to 5 April 2006, and is revised each year. A woman with insufficient earnings for SMP but who earns at least £30 a week may be eligible to claim maternity allowance of 90% of earnings. Many female organists may be eligible for this allowance but not claim it.

An employee does not receive any pay during a period of additional maternity leave or additional adoption leave, so basically a woman can take a year off work but only receives any pay for the first six months.

Time off work

In addition to maternity leave and similar, an employee is entitled to **paid time off work:**

- for certain duties as a trade union official;
- for acting as a safety representative;
- to look for work while under notice of redundancy;
- if disabled, to obtain certain forms of help;
- for acting as a trustee of an occupational pension scheme;
- to study, if under 18 and lacking in basic education.

An employee is entitled to **unpaid time off work:**

- for jury service;
- to sit in court as a magistrate;
- to perform certain other public duties;
- to look after dependants; and
- as parental leave.

Time off to look after dependants was introduced on 15 December 1999. It is strictly limited to such cases as a sick child or injured wife.

Parental leave was also introduced on 15 December 1999. It allows someone who has worked for at least one year to take a total of up to 13 weeks unpaid leave to look after a child aged four or under provided notice is given. Very little use has been made of this right.

In addition a parent has the right from 6 April 2003 to *request* **flexible working hours** to accommodate looking after a child. There is no right to be *given* flexible hours, though in the first year 75% of such requests were agreed by employers. The government plans to extend this right to those who look after adult dependants.

All the above are minimum statutory rights. An employer may agree additional rights.

Pay

An organist is entitled to such pay as the parties agreed *in advance*.

The issue sometimes arises of who is the other party who is legally obliged to pay the organist. In the Church of England, it is the minister, who is entitled to be reimbursed from church funds.

For a wedding or funeral, it is usually still the church which engages the organist, and not the couple or family. The Incorporated Society of Musicians has a form of contract for *visiting* organists who play for weddings. This is a contract between the couple and the organist.

Chapter 4 deals with rates of pay and fees.

There are strict rules about **deductions from pay**. In particular, an employer cannot deduct money from pay just because the employee owes money to the employer. Only the following may be deducted from pay:

- income tax and national insurance;
- occupational pension contributions;
- repayments of student loans;
- corrections of mistakes on previous payslips;
- attachment of earnings orders;
- amounts which the employee has authorised in writing;
- other deductions allowed by statute or the contract of employment.

Employment tribunals

Most employment disputes which cannot be resolved between employer and employee are settled by an employment tribunal. Most hearings are in public. Generally a complaint must be made within three months.

This is a less formal procedure than a court case. Costs are not usually awarded against a losing party unless the party has behaved unreasonably.

An application may be made by completing form IT 1 in writing or on-line from the website www.employmenttribunals.gov.uk. Forms are available from Jobcentres, Law Centres and Citizens Advice Bureaux, or you may print one from the website. A form is sent to the appropriate tribunal office according to your employer's address. This can be found on the website or by calling the enquiry line on 0845 795 9775. The website and enquiry line also provide guidance on procedure, but cannot comment on the merits of your claim. There is no fee for lodging a claim, but a frivolous claim can attract a penalty.

When a form is submitted, a copy is automatically sent to Advisory Conciliation and Arbitration Service (ACAS) who will try to help you and the employer reach an agreement. There is no charge for this service. The employer has 21 days to respond to a tribunal application. If a hearing is arranged, each side gets at least 14 days' notice.

The same procedure applies in Scotland, except there is just one office in Glasgow. The procedure does not apply in Northern Ireland.

An appeal against an employment tribunal may be made to the Employment Appeal Tribunal, and then to the Court of Appeal and House of Lords.

Canon Law

Canon law is the collection of laws which govern the Church of England. It therefore does not apply outside England, nor does it apply to other denominations which meet in England. These denominations do have their own rules, sometimes referred to as canon law, but these do not have the force of law in England.

There are two sets of laws which regulate the Church of England:

- canon law; and
- ecclesiastical law.

Canon law is a body of concisely (and often ambiguously) written rules. The entire body of canon law is contained in a single loose-leaf volume available from Church House.

The whole code of canon law was rewritten in 1964, amended in 1969, and has been continuously amended by General Synod since 1970. This repeals the previous canons of the church issued in 1603, apart from canon 113 (relating to confessions) which remains in force after 400 years.

The whole set of canons may be bought from Church House Publishing, or downloaded free from the website http://www.cofe.anglican.org/legal/canons.html

The canon most relevant to organists is canon B20 "of the musicians and music of the church".

Ecclesiastical law includes Measures passed by General Synod under its own quasi-parliamentary proceedings. A measure must then be approved by both houses of Parliament which can reject but not amend the measure. In practice, the measure passes to a parliamentary committee which decides whether it is "expedient" for the measure to become law. The measure becomes law when it receives the Royal Assent, as for an Act of Parliament. Such a Measure has the same legal status as an Act of Parliament.

Some ecclesiastical law is issued in the form of statutory instruments.

Further law

Canon law and ecclesiastical law does not just exist in the form of written rules. As with other branches of law, it also exists in the form of legal judgments where cases have been brought, and in opinions published by the law officers of General Synod.

For the latter, a book has been published on legal opinions in the church. There is a whole chapter relating to music.

It is also possible to obtain specific opinions from the law officers by submitting a written question from an authorised body (though the officers may answer a question from anyone), or by being formally tabled by a member of General Synod.

Canon B20 "of the musicians and music of the church"

Canon B20 is of such importance to Anglican musicians that it is given in full below. Organists should particularly note para 2.

1. In all churches and chapels, other than in cathedral or collegiate churches or chapels where the matter is governed by or dependent upon the statutes or customs of the same, the functions of appointing any organist or choirmaster (by whatever name called), and of terminating the appointment of any organist or choirmaster, shall be exercisable by the minister with the agreement of the parochial church council, except that if the archdeacon of the archdeaconry in which the parish is situated, in the case of termination of an appointment, considers that the circumstances are such that the requirement as to the agreement of the parochial church council should be dispensed with, the archdeacon may direct accordingly. Where the minister is also the archdeacon of the archdeaconry concerned, the function of the archdeacon under this paragraph shall be exercisable by the bishop of the diocese.

2. Where there is an organist or choirmaster the minister shall pay due heed to his advice and assistance in choosing of chants, hymns, anthems and other settings and in the ordering of the music of the Church; but at all times the final responsibility and decision in these matters rests with the minister.

3. It is the duty of the minister to ensure that only such chants, hymns, anthems, and other settings are chosen as are appropriate, both the words and the music, to the solemn act of worship and prayer in the House of God as well as to the congregation assembled for that purpose; and to banish all irreverence in the practice and in the performance of the same.

The second paragraph was inserted into what was then Canon 29 on 14 January 1949 by the Upper House of Convocation (bishops), and was subsequently accepted by the Lower House (clergy). The Archbishop of Canterbury said, "before this addition there was not a proper recognition of the duties of organists or choirmasters."

Appointment and dismissal

Appointment of an organist is made by the minister, not by the PCC or anyone else. A minister is not obliged to appoint any organist. If he does appoint any musicians, he may use any job title he likes. Canon law refers to organists, so that term is used here regardless of the job title used by the church, and regardless of whether the director of music (or whatever) actually plays the organ.

The appointment is made by the minister but must be agreed by the PCC. The General Synod office has confirmed that an organist cannot be appointed to a parish during an interregnum, with two limited exceptions:

- cathedrals and collegiate churches with their own rules on the matter; and
- team ministries where another team member is appropriately authorised.

The sequestrators of the parish may arrange for someone to play the organ and may pay that person, but when the minister is eventually appointed, the minister is not obliged to accept the organist who has no legal rights to remain. However, a new minister does not have this right with regards to an organist appointed by a previous minister. An appointment of organist made by the archdeacon, churchwarden or PCC is ultra vires. In effect, such an organist has not been appointed at all, and acquires no legal rights as organist.

An organist may only be dismissed by the minister with the agreement of the PCC, unless the archdeacon gives consent on the basis that the matter may not get a fair hearing at the PCC, such as when many PCC members are in the choir. An organist cannot be dismissed during an interregnum, except by the archdeacon under Canon B20.

Choice of music

The minister has the final say in the choice of music, though he must pay "due heed" to the organist. If a vicar wrote to the organist that he would ignore all advice from the organist, an action could therefore lie against the vicar, but the authors are unaware of any such attempt. Recommended practice on choice of music is given on page 18.

An organist who dissents from the minister's instructions must still follow the minister's instructions but has the right to appeal to the bishop if prevented from playing arbitrarily, according to the legal decision in the case *Wyndham v Cole [1875]*. The authors know of no recent example of an organist attempting this, and doubt if a bishop would ever rule in favour of an organist against the minister.

In practice, the minister can choose all the music if he wishes to do so. However, there is no obligation on the organist to accept any instructions from a curate, churchwarden, lay reader or anyone else. There is no provision for a vicar to delegate this power to anyone else in the church, including the PCC or a worship committee. A vicar who simply rubber-stamps choices made by someone else is probably complying with the letter of the law though not complying with its spirit.

Canon B20 itself does not define "minister", but *Halsbury's Laws of England* define a "minister" as the incumbent or priest-in-charge. Ordinarily this will be the vicar, rector or priest-in-charge. If there is not one, such as during an interregnum, it refers to the minister taking the service, provided that minister is ordained.

The obvious point should be made that matters should never get to the state where these provisions need to be considered. However, passions can become very heated over the choice of music. Some guidance on dealing with this matter is given on page 18. If choice of music becomes an issue, it is probably a sign of a deeper problem which should be addressed.

Right to play

An appointed organist has the right to play at all services, including weddings and funerals, and to receive the customary fee. If the organist declines to do so, the incumbent may arrange for another organist to play and pay him such fee as may be negotiated.

No-one has the right to tell an appointed organist that he may not play at a service. Sometimes **wedding couples** wrongly believe that they can choose their own organist. A wedding is a church service which comes under the authority of the minister who alone can direct what happens. In practice, ministers and organists usually go to some lengths to accommodate the wishes of wedding couples, but the minister does have the final say as for all services. No couple is obliged to use the services of a particular church. If they choose to do so, they cannot pick which of its officers to use, any more than you can choose which staff may deal with you in any business dealings.

The Church of England official guidance on weddings presupposes that the minister and organist will allow the couple a choice of music and hymns, which is clearly good practice. The minister has the final say as to whether any choice is suitable, and an organist may refuse to play anything beyond his ability or where he does not have the music or would have to spend a disproportionate time practising it. An organist is expected to be reasonably available to wedding couples and to suggest suitable music.

If a couple or funeral family wish another organist to play, such as a relation or close friend, the organist may agree. An organist is still entitled to receive the fee. The couple may make whatever arrangement it wishes with the visiting organist. In practice, we recommend that such requests are granted by the resident organist.

There is no requirement for any music at a wedding or funeral. If a service is arranged without any music, the organist is not entitled to any fee.

Canon law is silent on the position if other musicians are requested, such as a band, or if recorded music is used. In the opinion of the authors, this is the same as requesting another organist. It needs the permission of the resident organist who is entitled to the customary fee.

Organists are rarely asked to play for **baptisms** outside regular services. If an organist is asked to play for a separate baptism service, he is entitled to a fee unless his contract of employment has another provision. Because baptism is a sacrament, unlike weddings and funerals, the Baptismal Fees Abolition Act 1872 specifically bans the clergy from charging for baptisms. However, the services of an organist are not an essential element of the sacrament, and so an organist may be paid for playing.

Payment

The standard organ contract is signed by the minister and organist as contracting parties, and by the PCC as a third party.

Strictly, it is the duty of the minister to pay the organist and he must do so. If the PCC refuses to pay, the minister must pay the organist and recover the sum as a charge on the PCC.

A similar situation exists in the Roman Catholic church, but in the free churches, the church meeting has the legal duty to pay. In the Methodist church, this means the trustees.

Behaviour

Canon F15 prohibits "riotous, violent or indecent behaviour" in church. This includes interruptions to the service, such as heckling and demonstrations. Under Ecclesiastical Courts Jurisdiction Act 1860, the churchwardens must maintain order. They have the power of a police constable to arrest and remove trouble-makers. Page 231 notes what an organist should do in such circumstances.

In the case *Matthews v King [1934]*, which related to a dispute about Catholic furnishings in the church, it was held that the organist could not use the organ to drown out the minister in the dispute. Before 1860, this offence was covered by the Brawling Act 1551 which prescribed the punishment of having an ear removed.

Other disputes

Sometimes music can be dragged into other church disputes. Complaints about clergy or order in service can include complaints about musical style. Other complaints can involve organists.

One of the most bizarre relates to United Church of Canada, which has eight affiliated congregations in Bermuda. In 1992 Grace Methodist church allowed the ordination of homosexuals which led to 80% of church members leaving and claiming that they were the owners of the church. By 1996, the two groups were holding services in the same building at the same time, each trying to drown out the other. One had a pianist and one an organist. They also both tried to change the locks against the other. In the end, the Supreme Court of Bermuda ruled that the 80% who left had the right to the building.

Non-Anglican denominations

In the **Methodist Church**, the organist's contract is with the trustees. The rules of the Methodist Church specify that the person *taking the service* chooses the music.

In other **free churches**, the organist's contract is usually with the church meeting. Other provisions are as set out in the contract.

In the **Roman Catholic** church, the contract is with the parish priest who has ultimate responsibility for the liturgy and music used, though most priests delegate the choice to music leaders.

The **orthodox churches** do not use organs or other instruments, except in the United States. Choristers and the choirmaster are appointed by the church body.

Two case studies on how not to handle disputes

Case study 1: Westminster Abbey

In 1998, the Dean of Westminster Abbey sacked Martin Neary, their eminent organist, with the agreement of the chapter.

Martin Neary was a contracted employee of the Abbey from 1988. His wife Penny was concert secretary. Between April 1994 and December 1996 they organised 22 events for the choir, all of which were approved by the Abbey. In 1994, arrangements were made for funds payable to choir members to be paid into a limited company outside the Abbey accounts in the beliefs (both wrong) that this would avoid any PAYE and any personal liability by Neary should a promoter not pay. It is common for promoters to pay a fixing fee, typically equal to 10% of the musicians' fees. This account retained £11,958 in such fees.

Martin and Penny Neary were sacked because, as employees, they were agents of the Abbey and agents must not make a secret profit. This undermined the trust and confidence there should be between employer and employee.

There is a curious precedent, as in 1685 the Abbey organist was the composer Henry Purcell who neglected to pay over money charged to people in the organ loft for watching the coronation of William III. On that occasion the authorities took the money off him but did not sack him. He remained at the Abbey for another nine years till a year before his death. For Neary, 300 years later, the Abbey did the opposite — sacked him but let him keep the money.

Neary was summarily dismissed. The dismissal was suspended when Cherie Booth QC, the prime minister's wife, obtained a High Court order. Under the Abbey's constitution of 1560, Neary could not bring a claim for unfair dismissal but could appeal to the Queen as visitor. She asked the Lord Chancellor to deal with the matter, and he appointed a retired law lord, Lord Jauncey, to hear the matter. The parties agreed that the hearing should follow the rules of the High Court except that it was heard in private. The hearing lasted 12 days and cost an estimated £750,000.

Jauncey found in favour of the Abbey. He made clear that the charge against Neary was of impropriety and not dishonesty. His ruling also included the significant sentence "The fact that the Abbey authorities had all the information which would have enabled them to find out about the contracts, had they been so minded, does not alter the position." In other words, the organist has a greater duty of accountability than the accountants do! Employment law text books have quoted this decision as extending the legal principle of *Sinclair v Neighbour [1967]* so that any financial irregularity justifies dismissal.

Case study 2: St James' parish church, Wetherby

St James', Wetherby, is a parish in Yorkshire where a much-publicised dispute blew up in April 2000 between the evangelical vicar, the Revd Philip Evans, and the organist, Stephen Hartley.

Hartley was a 64-year old widower who became friendly with a widow called Joyce of a similar age. She moved in with him. There was no evidence of any sexual relationship (assuming that is anyone else's business anyway), but the vicar still condemned him for "living in sin" and required him to marry her or resign. Hartley said they may marry one day but did not wish to be rushed into it.

Hartley resigned and claimed constructive unfair dismissal and claimed £30,000 compensation on the grounds that it is sex discrimination to make it a condition of employment that someone is married or not married. Before the case got to the employment tribunal, the PCC reached a settlement of an "undisclosed sum" (£7,500), and we lost an opportunity to establish the employment status of church organists. The settlement also included a confidentiality clause and a reference for the organist.

The issue so incensed local feeling that a pensioner at the church stood up at the start of a church service to denounce the vicar. She became involved in a row with the vicar's wife, and police had to be called to restore order.

There were other background issues, such as the lack of a choir, the fact that the music had gone "happy-clappy", and the congregation had halved.

A special general meeting of the parish was called which passed "no confidence" motions in the churchwardens and PCC, who resigned en masse, and in the vicar. He had a breakdown. He remained the vicar, continued living in the vicarage (with the telephone disconnected) and drew his full stipend, but performed no real duties for three years.

By 2002, the churchwardens and PCC started legal proceedings to have the vicar removed on the grounds of pastoral breakdown. The Bishop of Ripon and Leeds attempted an unsuccessful reconciliation between PCC and vicar. The issue was resolved in July 2003, when Evans was appointed to be an assistant priest in a parish in Peterborough diocese. Meanwhile Hartley was appointed director of music at Frankfurt's American Episcopal/Anglican Church which serves the German city's English-speaking community.

4 Fees and Budgets

Introduction

An organist may deal with money in three ways:

- his own fees;
- choir budget; and
- handling income and expenditure.

An organist must show the highest ethical standards of handling money in terms of:

- honesty; and
- accountability.

ORGANIST'S FEE

Amount of fee

An organist may be paid:

- a salary;
- an honorarium;
- a stipend;
- fees; or
- expenses

or a combination of them.

A **salary** is reward for labour, typically quoted as so much per year but paid monthly in arrears. An **honorarium** is a sum paid in appreciation for the work, even though there is no legal obligation to do so. A **stipend** is a fee for a person not to work, so as to be available for pastoral duties. A **fee** is an amount for a specific task, such as playing for a single service. An **expense** payment is reimbursement for costs, such as travel.

The organist should be clear which he is being paid. In practice there is little difference; the tax position is generally the same for all of them.

The amount an organist is paid is a matter of contractual negotiation between the organist and church authorities. They may agree any amount they like, however large or small, and that is legally binding on both of them. This derives from the law of contract, as explained in chapter 3. The organist may agree to work for no fee at all.

A scale of fees is produced annually by the Incorporated Society of Musicians with the agreement of the Guild of Church Musicians, the Royal College of Organists and the Royal School of Church Music. These figures are widely used, even though they are advisory. Under contract law, an organist has no right to demand the ISM rate (or any other rate) unless this is agreed in advance. These fees are revised every year with effect from 1 September. Current rates can be found on the ISM website at http://www.ism.org/info.

It is ideal for the organist to be paid the rate set annually by ISM. The contract must specify exactly which rate applies to the organist. This is a good idea as it ensures that the rate will be increased annually without the organist having to negotiate pay rises.

Some Christian principles

There are several scriptural teachings about wages:

- the labourer is worthy of his hire (Luke 10:7);
- paying wages is settling a debt, not bestowing a favour (Romans 4:4);
- working for wages is righteous (John 4:36);
- wages should be paid promptly (Leviticus 19:13); and
- the wages of one employee are not the concern of another (Matthew 20:1-16).

It is as important to follow scripture in this area as in any other.

The Church also has a tradition of workers paying their own way. In biblical times, it was considered normal for a person to engage in remunerative work to support themselves in their ministry. In Acts 18:1-3, we learn that St Paul was a tent-maker. Some ministers and Christians practise this arrangement to this day.

By about 1000 AD, ministers were largely self-taught and itinerant. A minister would find a church which needed his services for which the lord of the manor would pay him. Much of this payment was "in kind", which means that most of it was in the form of food and shelter rather than cash. Even now, over half of a clergyman's remuneration may be paid in kind.

Organists are the last church workers for whom these "self-taught" arrangements still apply. Organists are self-selected, and pay for their own training and music. They are paid for the services they can provide.

The principle of a fair wage is well-established doctrine. For example, in the Roman Catholic church, the papal encyclical *Rerum Novarum 1891* required wages to be sufficient to support workers in an adequate lifestyle. This Church's catechism of 1994 includes section 2434 on wages. "A just wage is the legitimate fruit of work. To refuse or withhold it can be a grave injustice.... Agreement between the parties is not sufficient to justify the amount to be received in wages."

Should the organist be paid at all?

This a question which should properly be answered by the organist alone.

The scriptural principle of the labourer being worthy of his hire means that there can be no scriptural or moral reason against paying the organist. A minister who objects should be quietly reminded that he is paid for exercising his ministry. Many organists are professional musicians for whom organ fees are a significant element in their income.

Some organists may be prepared to work for no fee, such as when they already have adequate income from other work. There is a Christian principle of **stewardship** in which churchgoers should offer part of their wealth, time and talents to God as an acknowledgment of all that God has given us. The organist may offer his time and talents on the same basis as many other church workers, such as Sunday School teachers, cleaners, flower arrangers, sidesmen, magazine distributors and others.

A fundamental principle of all stewardship policy is that it must be *voluntary and willing*. This principle is clearly expressed in 2 Corinthians 9:7: "Each person should give as he has decided for himself; there should be no reluctance, no sense of compulsion; God loves a cheerful giver". A church can never justify not paying a fee on the basis that the recipient should be a willing giver. If he has no choice in the matter, he is neither willing nor a giver, and the arrangement is not stewardship at all.

Ministers who expect organists to work unpaid should reflect on Jeremiah 22:13, "woe betide him who builds his palace on unfairness and completes its roof-chambers with injustice, compelling his countrymen to work without payment, giving them no wage for their labour!"

Including unpaid fee in the accounts

When an organist waives his right to receive any fee, it is sometimes suggested that the accounts should still show the fee so that the principle of payment is established for the benefit of any future organist, and that parishioners know the value of the benefit they are receiving.

While acknowledging the admirable sentiments behind such a view, it is wrong.

A church produces accounts which must accurately reflect actual income and expenditure during the year. To include an item of expenditure which has not been incurred is false accounting.

An organist is just one job of many in the church which are sometimes paid positions and sometimes unpaid. Other such jobs include church cleaning, secretarial duties, grounds maintenance, youth worker, flower arranging and auditing. It is acknowledged that most churches could not survive financially without the generous stewardship of many volunteers. It is arbitrary to include some and not others, and would produce meaningless accounts, probably showing a massive deficit.

Giving the fees back

It is sometimes suggested that the organist should take the fee and then give it back to the church. This can be beneficial to the church if the giving back is done under Gift Aid, as the church can then also reclaim a sum equal to the tax on the amount, provided the organist has sufficient other income on which tax has been paid.

Such an arrangement is legal, but care must be taken in how it is set up.

If it is agreed that the organist will receive a fee *on condition* that he gives it back, Gift Aid must not be used. The gift is not voluntary and therefore is outside the scope of Gift Aid. To claim the tax back under such circumstances is an offence under tax law. The benefit of Gift Aid only works if the church agrees to pay the fee to the organist who is free to do what he likes with the money.

Sometimes an organist may be prepared to give the fee back provided it is applied only for musical purposes. Gift Aid may be used here, provided the giving back is genuinely voluntary. Church accounts must distinguish between **restricted funds** and unrestricted funds, where the former may only be used for a stated purpose, such as maintaining the organ or developing the music.

A restricted fund will often be held in a deposit account which earns interest. That interest may be applied to unrestricted funds. Suppose a music fund contains £5,000 and earns £200 a year in interest. Unless arrangements are made to the contrary, the fund will keep its £5,000 whose value slowly reduces through inflation, while the church's general funds benefit by £200 a year. If you believe this is inappropriate, you should raise the issue with the church treasurer or church council.

An organist should consider whether he really wants to donate back his fees to a restricted fund. If he provides £2,500 a year for ten years, the organ fund could contain £25,000 for work which is not needed when the church is obliged to go fund-raising to pay for a new boiler. Once the money is in a restricted fund, it may only be used for that purpose, even if the original donor is agreeable to changing its use. A church is legally obliged to maintain the organ anyway.

When clergy begrudge organist's fees

We have heard reports of clergy begrudging organists their fees on the grounds that an organist should not be paid more than a clergyman.

There are many possible responses to such an attitude, such as noting the considerable skill, practice and expense in becoming an organist. To become a competent organist can cost £3,500 in organ lessons alone (at 2005 rates).

It is perhaps worth noting that a clergyman's total remuneration package is much greater than the amount paid in cash.

In the Church of England, a clergyman receives a stipend of around £19,000 a year (2004 rate). To this should be added a non-contibutory pension scheme (worth about £5,000), council tax, water rates, travel expenses, and house insurance. These last four items must be paid by other workers out of net pay after tax, so to make a proper comparison with secular remuneration packages, they should be grossed up. This brings the total to over £30,000 before the value of the parsonage itself is considered. Few four-bedroom detached houses can be rented for less than £1,000 a month. This can easily create a remuneration package of £40,000 or even £50,000 a year. (This is not an entirely fair comparison as clergy must fund their retirement home, and if a minister already owns his own property, the parsonage can be seen as just additional expense rather than an asset.)

Nevertheless, a vicar who could be receiving up to £1,000 a week should not begrudge an organist £50 a week.

CHOIR BUDGET

Church funds

The **church funds** are owned by the PCC in the Church of England, and usually by similar bodies in other denominations. It is that body which decides how funds may be spent. The administration is handled by the treasurer.

There is a common exception for **legacies** where the deceased's will names who has authority to decide how the money is to be spent. It is common for the vicar and churchwardens to be named. In such cases only they have the authority to decide how to spend these funds. In most cases, the PCC will be invited to comment, but there is no compulsion to do so, and the vicar and churchwardens are not obliged to follow any suggestions made.

It is possible but undesirable for other sums of money to be held in small funds, such as by the organist, flower arrangers or catering team. As none of these bodies has any legal status allowing them to hold funds, such amounts are usually church funds which the officer holds on trust for the PCC and to whom the fund holder is accountable. It is not good practice for large amounts to be held other than by the treasurer.

If you do have a **choir fund** independent of the church accounts, there must be no doubt as to:

- who legally owns the funds;
- the purpose for which the funds are held; and
- who decides whether something is within the scope of that purpose.

There is no objection to choir members pooling their own money for whatever objective they wish, such as to pay for a dinner or outing. As such, the members have created a simple trust fund. This point is worth noting as any dissent over who owns the money or how it may be spent can cause considerable ill will, even when the amount is small.

Funding music

In the Church of England the Parochial Church Council (PCC) is responsible for funding the worship of the church, even though the PCC has very limited authority over the content of the worship. It has been suggested that this means the vicar can simply incur expenditure on worship, including music, and demand that the PCC pays the bills. In other churches, it depends on the church's constitution or trust deed.

There is no legal basis for a PCC to demand that the choir must raise funds to support itself, such as by concerts or fund-raising exercises. There is nothing to stop an organist or choir engaging in fund-raising activities if it wishes, but it cannot be compelled to do so. There are many imaginative ways a choir can raise funds, such as by asking congregation members to sponsor an anthem. Singing the entire hymnbook is not recommended as it puts great strain on the voice, and who really wants to listen to it?

The organ is as much part of the church property as the pulpit and the boiler. As such it is legally owned by the churchwardens (or equivalent authority outside the Church of England) who have a duty to maintain it. In practice, this function is usually delegated to the organist who liaises with the organ tuner. However an organist only does this as agent for the churchwardens, and should always inform the churchwardens of what is happening.

The PCC and churchwardens cannot demand that the organist must be responsible for finding the funds for organ maintenance, such as by giving recitals. The organist may do so if he wishes, but that does not discharge the parish from its legal duty to maintain the organ.

Fund raising for the organ

The responsibility for raising funds to replace, expand or maintain the organ is not a function of the organist. However, the organist should be willing to be involved, such as by being a member of the fund-raising committee. Fund-raising for the organ is likely to be hampered if the organist is seen not be interested.

Excellent advice on fund-raising is given in the booklet *Fund-raiding for your church building* (Church House Publishing) which includes specific provisions for organs. More general advice is in *The UK Church Fundraising Handbook* by Maggie Durran (Canterbury Press). For example, received wisdom is that fund-raising should only go public when about 60% of the funds have been raised.

Individuals give more readily to tangible projects such as organs, which can also be attractive to musicians and heritage bodies outside the church.

There are several funds which will consider grants towards organ fund-raising. A leaflet on sources of funds is produced by the British Institute of Organ Studies, and is available direct from them (address in appendix 1) or on their website www.bios.org.uk. The leaflet also explains how to prepare an organ appeal.

General guidance on finding grant-making trusts is contained in *Directory of Grant Making Trusts* available from Charities Aid Foundation, King's Hill, West Malling, Kent ME19 4TA. This is also available on CD-ROM.

Bodies that will consider grants towards organ fund-raising

Arts Council Arts Lottery Fund (see below)

Council for the Care of Churches, Church House, Great Smith Street, London SW1P 3NZ. 020 7898 1885

Foundation for Sport and the Arts, PO Box 20, Liverpool L1 1HB. 0151 259 5505

Manifold Trust, Society of Antiquaries, Burlington House, Piccadilly, London W1V 0HS. 020 7734 0193

O N Organ Fund, 36 Strode Road, Forest Gate, London E7 0DU. 020 8555 4931

Ouseley Trust, 127 Coleherne Court, Old Brompton Road, London SW5 0EB. 020 7373 1950

Pilling Trust, Waterworths, Central Buildings, Richmond Terrace, Blackburn, Lancashire BB1 7AP

The Arts Lottery Fund is administered by the Arts Council using funds collected from the National Lottery. Its address is Arts Council of England, Lottery Department, 14 Great Peter Street, London SW1P 3NQ. 020 7312 0123. Website: www.artscouncil.org.uk. It gives grants for improving cultural facilities, and accepts applications for major organ projects to be used for concerts.

Applications for the conservation of historic organs may be made to Heritage Lottery Fund, 7 Holbein Place, London SW1H 8NR, 020 7591 6042.

Some churches may object to using lottery funds on moral grounds. The Church of England's official position is in a House of Bishops' statement that lottery funds are appropriate to maintain heritage responsibilities, but not for worship, witness, evangelism and pastoral care.

Grants may also be available from Entrust (from landfill tax credit scheme), the diocese (or other church parent body) or the local council.

A listed building may benefit from the **Listed Places of Worship Grant Scheme**. This in effect reduces the rate of VAT from 17.5% to zero for work between 1 April 2004 and 31 March 2006, and to 5% for work between 1 April 2001 and 31 March 2004. Details are available from the scheme at PO Box 609, Newport NP10 8QD. Telephone:

0845 601 5945. Website: www.lpwscheme.org.uk. The church pays VAT at the full rate of 17.5% and claims it back as a grant. Usually, the building must be used for worship at least six times a year. However, the Historic Environment Designation Branch of the Department of Culture, Media and Sport has told the authors that "organs, no matter how built in to the fabric of a church, are excluded from the eligibility criteria for this scheme." (Letter dated 3 February 2003.)

Choir budget

In accounting terms, a **budget** is an allocation of funds whereas a **forecast** is an expectation of a financial position, though these terms tend to be used interchangeably. Strictly, a budget therefore is an order as to the amount which must be earned or may be spent. So a treasurer may say that the budget for the choir is £1,000 — that is how much of the funds were allocated for the choir — whereas the forecast is £900. In other words, he expects the choir to underspend by £100.

A choirmaster should run his budget by:

- deducting the expenses which he knows will be incurred anyway, such as choir pay and organ maintenance (if within the choir budget);
- divide the balance by 12 to give a monthly figure, or by three to give a termly figure on how much you can spend every month or every term;
- keep a running balance as you go during the year.

Always account for the money you handle. If you put on a concert, account for the ticket sales and expenses. If you prepare the children's choir pay, keep a record of how much you paid each child and how you calculated this figure. Keep a copy yourself and pass one to the treasurer with the cash or the bill as appropriate. Always be scrupulous and careful with money. If you find this particularly difficult, see if you can delegate the job, perhaps to an adult in the choir.

The issue of whether and when choir members are paid is a policy matter for the church council to decide. Outside cathedrals and colleges, it is unusual for adults to be paid unless the church has, exceptionally, decided to maintain a professional choir. It is more common for children to be paid for services, weddings and choir practices. The amount is usually fairly nominal, perhaps between 20p and 30p for each service and practice, with a few pounds for a wedding. However it means much to a child; as earned money it is worth more than pocket money. You should remember that children do not see such matters in the same way as adults.

Concert budgets

Sometimes an organist may organise a concert, publication or recording which requires its own budget.

The important principles are:

- always plan to make a surplus;
- know how any loss will be underwritten; and
- know to whom any surplus will be given.

A budget should identify all sources of income and expenditure. For a concert, these may include:

Income	Expenditure
Ticket sales	Hire of musicians
Programme sales	Hire of premises
Refreshment sales	Hire of music and equipment
Advertisements in programmes	Printing programmes
Sponsorship	Copyright fees
Grants	Printing tickets
	Commission for selling tickets
	Security
	Hire of rehearsal premises
	Refreshments for performers
	Advertising the concert
	Additional staff overtime

In preparing the budget, under-estimate income and over-estimate expenditure. When large sums are involved, it is also advisable to add to expenses a **contingency** of 10% of other expenditure to cover unforeseen expenses.

If booking a hall, read the agreement very carefully. You can find yourself liable for all sorts of "extras", such as use of chairs, use of piano, use of kitchen, display of promotional material, and commission on ticket sales. A particularly large expense can be the cost of the hall's own staff. It has been known for an organisation to be charged additional staff hours to have someone just to switch the lights on and off.

Even if your concert aims just to break-even rather than make a surplus, always budget for a surplus. Concerts have a habit of generating less income and more expenditure than expected.

Separate elements of concerts, such as programmes and refreshments, should be priced to ensure that they cover their own costs.

Even well run and properly budgeted concerts can make a loss, so know who will underwrite such a loss. This may be the church, the choir budget, a sponsoring body, a sympathetic individual or yourself.

Conversely, establish to whom any surplus belongs. You do not want competing claims for the surplus afterwards.

Many items of expenditure can be minimised. Advertisements and programmes may be inexpensively produced on modern computers and photocopiers. A4-size advertisements can be displayed free in shops, libraries, pubs and surgeries with permission. Local authorities often agree to allow local bodies to display notices on their noticeboards. Local newspapers are often happy to print details as a short story, but give them a month's notice.

Do not be tempted to indulge in **flyposting** on telegraph poles, lamp-posts and vacant premises. This is an offence under one or more of:

- Town and Country Planning Act 1990 ss224-225;
- Highways Act 1980 s132; and
- Town and Country Planning (Control of Advertisements)

Regulations 1992 (amended in 1994 and 1999).

This can lead to a fine of £1,000, plus £100 a day thereafter.

Recording budget

If making a recording, you must first check your obligations under copyright law (see page 140). The cost of recording a concert has two elements:

- the cost of recording; and
- the cost of copying each CD or cassette.

Companies offering this service instead tend to give you a single figure for so many CDs, because this looks cheaper. For example, in 2004 one company quoted £2.25

(plus VAT) for each CD provided you buy 200 copies, or £3.20 for 100 copies. These figures look excellent value for money when you can sell a CD for anything between £5 and £15. However it is very difficult to sell 200 local CDs even if you sell 500 tickets to the concert.

The two cost elements can be calculated as:

	200 CDs total cost	£450
less	100 CDs total cost	£320
	100 CDs unit cost	£130

So each CD costs £1.30 to produce once the recording is made. The cost of the recording is:

	100 CDs total cost	£320
less	100 CDs unit cost	£130
	Recording cost	£190

In other words, it costs £190 to record the concert and £1.30 for each CD produced. As 17½% VAT must be added, these costs are really £223.25 and £1.53 respectively.

Suppose you sell the CD for £10. The **marginal cost** of each CD is £1.53, so each CD sold makes a **contribution** of £8.47 towards the fixed cost of £223.25. This means that you must sell 27 CDs to break even.

£223.25 divided by £8.47 = 26.4.

This is provided that the company agrees to sell you only 27 CDs at these prices, and the contract does not commit you to buying 100 CDs.

You should also check whether the price for CDs includes travelling expenses for the engineer, and sleeves and labels for the CDs. Again, read any contract or agreement to look for "extras".

In practice, it is usually sufficient to pay just for the recording and make your own copies as required. This can easily be done on modern personal computers.

5 Copyright

The Law

What is copyright?

Copyright is the right to make copies of a legally protected work.

Organists must always respect copyright. Not only is this a legal requirement, but copyright income represents the income of writers and composers, many of whom are not wealthy. To deny someone their copyright royalty is not just against the law, in effect it is stealing from your fellow musicians.

An organist need not worry about copyright law if he does no more than buy music which he plays and the choir sings in the course of worship. When you buy the music, part of the price is passed by the publishers to the copyright owners. So you have discharged your duties under copyright law simply by paying for the music.

Copyright law becomes relevant for organists who wish to:

- compose music;
- photocopy music;
- transpose music;
- arrange music;
- perform music in a concert rather than in worship;
- set someone else's words to music; or
- record music.

Although the law on copyright can become complex, copyright need not be a huge problem in practice. Probably the commonest need for an organist to be involved in copyright is in taking copies of music. In practice, the use of Christian copyright licence (see page 151) or a phone call to the publishers may be all that is needed.

The current law is Copyright, Designs and Patents Act 1988, but this only applies to works created from 1 August 1989. Works created previously are still governed by Copyright Act 1956, though many provisions are the same.

Penalties for breaches of copyright have been strengthened by the Copyright, etc. and Trade Marks (Offences and Enforcement) Act 2002.

The Berne Convention provides a measure of international protection.

As this book is written for organists, it concentrates on copyright in music, and generally ignores specific provisions about art, drama, literature, typefaces and computer software. However you should note that copyright exists in all these areas, and be careful when using pictures, photographs or poems in programmes and posters. In practice, you avoid copyright problems in art, either by producing it yourself or by using copyright-free art, of which plenty is commercially available.

There is a separate but similar right of "performing right" which protects the performance of any work (regardless of whether the work is in copyright).

There are also "moral rights" to protect the reputation of composers, and "publication rights" for first publishers of copyright-expired material.

Many of the cases mentioned in this section relate to pop music. This is because that is where most of the big money is involved and where there has been most litigation. However, the principles behind these cases apply equally to any type of music.

What works are copyright?

Copyright exists in all original literary, artistic, dramatic or musical works. The work does not need any artistic value, so railway timetables and telephone directories are copyright.

The work must involve some labour, so a single note cannot be copyright. However a piece consisting of just four notes, a jingle for Channel 4, is copyright. An anthology, compilation or abridgment can be copyright in its own right.

In music there are certain standard patterns, such as scales, arpeggios, cadences, harmonic modulations, rhythms and riffs. These may be regarded as public property. There is no copyright in an arpeggio, but there can be copyright in how arpeggios are used in a piece of music.

There is no copyright in ideas, so copying someone's ideas in how they composed a work represents no breach of copyright if all the words and music are original. In 1989, Hughie Green failed to secure copyright for the format of his television programme *Opportunity Knocks*. There is no copyright in news or facts. The title of a work is not itself copyright *(Dick v Yates [1881])*. There are other forms of "intellectual property" such as scientific know-how and patents, but these are unlikely to be relevant to musicians.

There may be many copyrights in a single production of a musical work. For example, suppose you make a video of a group performing a French song translated into English. This may have these separate copyrights:

- the French words;
- the English translation;
- the music;
- the orchestration or arrangement of the music;
- the dance routine;
- the performance;
- the scenery; and
- the recording of the performance (both audio and video).

If you have a piece of sheet music, there can be separate copyrights in:

- the words;
- any translation of the words;
- the music;
- editing of the music;
- arranging the music; and
- the typesetting of the music.

Each of these copyrights may be held by more than a single person. Apparently it took seven people to write the words *I'll tell you what I want, what I really really want* for a song by the Spice Girls.

In some cases, some of these copyrights may have expired. For example a setting of a folksong may have no copyright in the words but still have copyright in the music.

Almost all copyright has a finite life. After that, the work is "out of copyright" or in the **public domain**, and anyone may do what they like with it without payment of any fee.

Copyright is a form of **intellectual property**. Other forms of intellectual property include patents, trade marks and know-how. Although copyright has no tangible form like a book, it has most of the attributes of tangible property. Copyright can be sold, given away or left in your will. You can give people rights to use it.

Moral rights cannot be disposed of and always remain with the creator of the work, except on death when it passes with the deceased's other property.

On death, copyright, performing rights and moral rights pass in accordance with your will, if you have one. If you do not, the rights pass in accordance with the laws of intestacy. This will be to any surviving husband or wife (but not any other type of partner), failing which to your children. Any dispute is settled by the courts. In October 2002, Italian courts ruled that copyright in Puccini's work rests with the Italian government until it expires in 2022.

Unintended copying

It is sometimes suggested that there is only a finite number of notes available to a musician, so there will come a time when every tune possible will already have been written. Mathematically that is not so. There are 12 semitones in an octave. If we confine ourselves to using notes from one octave, a tune of just eight notes gives us 35,831,808 possibilities. (That is 12^7.) And that is before we even consider harmony or rhythm. We are far from having written every possible musical work.

However, it is still possible for a composer to find that something he has written is similar to something else that has been composed, even allowing for natural harmonic and melodic progressions.

The law is that there is no breach of copyright for creating something which someone else has also created; however, the burden of proof can be difficult. The court would consider not only the similarities between the two works, but what opportunities you had to hear the first work. It can be advisable to play your work to other musicians to see if any of them recognise any of it as being similar to an existing work. When Paul McCartney wrote *Yesterday*, he played it to several musicians, convinced that someone else must have already written it.

There have been many cases where successful songs have led to copyright cases, hence the expression in the music business "where there's a hit, there's a writ." George Harrison, another Beatle, lost a copyright case when his 1971 hit *My Sweet Lord* was held to be based on *Sweet Talking Guy* recorded by the Chiffons in 1963.

Both songs had a similar use of alternating minor and diminished chords and there was a passing similarity of melody. Harrison even performed both songs in court to explain the difference. At the end of the case, the judge said that he "really liked *both* songs". Harrison's lawyer unsuccessfully pointed out that if he liked *both* songs, he was admitting that there were two songs.

One of the most bizarre copyright cases concerned Mike Batt (who wrote songs for The Wombles). He included a track called *Classical Graffiti* on an album by The Planets. The track comprised pure silence, and was credited to Batt and the avant-garde composer John Cage, whose work 4'33" also comprises pure silence. Cage sued for breach of copyright. In 2002, a six-figure sum was paid in an out-of-court settlement. As silence is hardly original music, Batt's mistake was probably in crediting Cage. Artists as diverse as The Goons and John Lennon have issued albums with tracks of silence and not been sued.

Use of copyright or even breach of copyright can be a consideration in contract law (as explained in chapter 2). This means that when copyright has been breached, the parties can make their own arrangements as to how to settle the matter. John Lennon, yet another Beatle, was accused of copying one of Chuck Berry's songs in *Come Together*. They settled the matter by John Lennon agreeing to record some of Berry's songs on a rock and roll album.

How long does copyright last?

The general rule is that copyright lasts from creation to the end of the 70th year after the creator's death. So if a composer dies on 8 July 2011, his work remains copyright until 31 December 2081 (assuming there is no change in the law before then).

This limit was increased from 50 years on 1 January 1996. This meant that some composers went out of copyright then came back in. This is known as **revived copyright**. Elgar died in 1934, so his music was copyright until 1984, and then from 1996 to 2004. It was out of copyright for 11 years between 1985 and 1995, and is again from 2005. Music acquired during the out-of-copyright period may continue to be used. For revived copyright, a user may simply send a notice to the copyright holder saying what use is to be made of the work. The notice constitutes a licence though the copyright holder is entitled to a fee, which the Copyright Tribunal will set if not agreed.

Where a copyright is sold, given away or passes on death, the copyright life is still determined by when the original creator died. Where the copyright is owned by a company or other body, the copyright lasts for 70 years from its creation. Where a work was created by two or more people, the copyright lasts until 70 years after the last death.

Copyright lasts for ever in the Authorised Version of the Bible and the Book of Common Prayer, in the UK only (see page 146).

Other liturgical material, such as *Common Worship* and other bible translations are bound by the normal copyright rules. *Common Worship* was published in 2000. Its copyright is owned by the Archbishops' Council of the Church of England. Its copyright therefore expires in 2070. The use of copyright liturgy is examined later.

Sound recordings are copyright for 50 years. This means that all Glenn Miller's recordings are now in the public domain. However, in the UK, copyright in the music and words will probably still exist when the recording copyright expires.

Government publications, such as Acts of Parliament, are copyright for 50 years from the end of the year in which it received Royal Assent. This provision applies equally to Measures passed by General Synod of the Church of England. Crown copyright in other works lasts for 125 years.

Typesetting lasts for 25 years from publication. Photographs are copyright for 70 years (50 years before 1 January 1986). Industrial designs are copyright for 15 years.

You must always be careful that all copyright has expired before treating anything as in the public domain. Bach died in 1750, so his work is well outside the protection of copyright, but that does not mean that you can photocopy any music by Bach. Almost all Bach's published work is edited, and there is a separate copyright in the editing. This means that such work does not become public domain until the editor has been dead for over 70 years.

Do not forget that there is a separate copyright in the typography of the page which lasts for 25 years from publication. If you want to photocopy an out-of-copyright hymn tune, photocopy it from *Hymns Ancient and Modern Revised* or *English Hymnal*. Do not photocopy it from *Common Praise* or *New English Hymnal*.

Note that public domain simply means that you may copy freely. It does not entitle you to access to the documents to copy them. If you do obtain access, the owner has no power to stop you copying it. Sometimes libraries or publishers suggest that you have a moral obligation not to copy. You should reply by asking what moral right they have to deny you what is already yours as a member of the public.

How do you copyright music?

There is no process for copyrighting anything. There are no forms to fill in and no fees to pay, as there are for patents. As you compose music, the copyright is automatically created and belongs to you. This right is given by section 9(1) of the 1988 Act.

Note that the copyright runs from when you "fix" the work, such as writing it down, recording or broadcasting it. There is no copyright for ideas in your head, even when you have performed them to others. If your work goes through several drafts, each draft has its own copyright. A later draft does not replace the copyright in a previous one.

There is an exception if you create a copyright work in the course of your employment, unless a prior agreement has been made between employer and employee that the employee owns copyright. In such cases, the copyright belongs to your employer and not to you. This is unlikely to affect organists. Although many organists do compose, it would be most unusual for this to be regarded as part of the job. However it may be advisable to include a clause in the contract of employment to make this clear.

Copyright law even states who owns the copyright in works created by a computer program written for that purpose (the programmer). And in 1978, paintings by the chimpanzee Yamasaki were the copyright of the circus which owned him.

It is normal for music to have at the bottom of the first page, the copyright symbol ©, followed by the year the work was created, and the name and address of the copyright holder. This is not strictly necessary under UK law, but it does give the work a measure of international protection.

Although you own the copyright in music, you may need to prove it in any enforcement action. Any evidence may be produced, such as witnesses, concert programmes or reviews in magazines.

The two commonest methods used by composers, in order, are:

- sending a copy to himself by registered post; or
- depositing a copy at a bank.

Other methods include:

- depositing a copy with a solicitor who certifies the date it was deposited; or
- depositing a copy with Stationer's Hall, for which a modest fee is payable.

None of these actions is essential. Evidence from reliable musicians about when they performed the work is just as good. Also, the evidence suggested above simply proves that the work existed by a certain date. It does not necessarily prove that you wrote it.

Editions

Copyright represents the human endeavour in creating works. The leading High Court case of *Sawkins v Hyperion Records [2004] EWHC 1530 (Ch)* established that this includes creating performing editions of old manuscripts of music *even though the editor creates no new music*.

Dr Lionel Sawkins spent a year preparing four editions of music by Michel-Richard de Lalande (1657-1726) by studying manuscripts round the world. Sawkins transcribed composer's "shorthands" and made informed guesses about missing notes, among other tasks. Lalande wrote sacred motets for Louis XIV and Louis XV. Hyperion Records used this music on the CD recording *Music for the Sun King* by singers called Ex Cathedra led by Jeff Skidmore. Sawkins was paid a hire fee of £1,278 for use of the actual performing materials (score and parts) but Hyperion refused to pay him copyright royalties, so Sawkins sued. Justice Patten said, "I am not persuaded that one can reject a claim to copyright in a new music work simply because the editorial composer has made no significant changes to the notes." Sawkins' claim was upheld for three of the four recorded works.

Hyperion was ordered to pay damages and costs. It immediately deleted the CD from its catalogue after sales of 3,332 copies had not recouped the recording costs. In May 2005, Hyperion Records lost their appeal against this decision.

This case means that copyright may exist in some editions of old manuscripts which were previously regarded as copyright-free.

Publication rights

There is a special copyright provision to protect the first publication of a work whose copyright has expired. All such works have copyright protection until 31 December 2039. Publication here includes exhibiting and lending copies; it is not necessary that the work is printed. This provision is contained in the 1988 Act Sch 1 para 12 and The Copyright and Related Rights Regulations SI 1996 No 2967 which implement EC directive 93/98/EEC.

This law refers to works "after the expiry of copyright". It is not clear what the position is for works which were never in copyright because they predate copyright law. Sheet music has been copyright in England since 1709, so this may be an issue for 17th-century and earlier manuscripts first published from 2040.

Rights of copyright holder

There are three sets of rights given to a copyright holder under the 1988 Act:

- the right to copy;
- secondary rights; and
- moral rights.

Anyone who wishes to exercise any of these rights for someone else's copyright work needs permission, which may require a payment. In some cases, permission may be refused. *Mission Praise* had to drop the song *We are one in the Spirit* for copyright reasons. You should therefore be careful before starting a major exercise such as orchestrating another composer's work. You could find that the composer refuses to allow you to perform it, or demands a very high fee to do so. Many composers will ask to see the finished work and demand the right to make changes.

A composer may ban all performance of his work during his lifetime. Saint-Saens did just that for *Carnival of Animals*. If a composer first destroys the work, it can never be heard, as happened to Sibelius' Symphony 8.

There are some exceptions where you do not need permission with regard to copyright works, as explained later. If you wish to use one of these exemptions, you must make sure that what you do is exactly within the scope of the exemption.

The first set of rights are called **acts restricted by the copyright** under s16 of the Act. There are five such rights:

- to copy the work;
- to issue copies to the public;
- to perform, show or play the work in public;
- to broadcast the work; and
- to adapt the work.

To **copy** a work means reproducing any or all of it in any form. It is not restricted to photocopying music. Copyright extends to copying out by hand. It includes photographing the music or storing it in a computer file. It includes forms of copying not even thought of when the music was created. In 2001, Walt Disney settled an eight-year court case with music publishers Boosey & Hawkes over the right to include Stravinsky's *Rite of Spring* in the video of *Fantasia* made in 1940 when videos were not invented.

Ten years previously, there was a similar resolution to a dispute about the inclusion of Peggy Lee's recording of *Fever* on a video.

With a few exceptions, it does not matter *why* you copy the work. You can still breach copyright by making a copy just to play for your private enjoyment.

To **issue** copies includes any form of publishing or public hire or loan by any means. This includes putting a work on the Internet or distributing it as a computer file.

To **perform** or **broadcast** the work includes any mode of visual or aural presentation, including broadcast on television or radio.

To **adapt** a musical work includes making an arrangement or transcription of it (section 21(3)(b)). An adaptation of a literary work includes a translation of it. Section 21(2) makes clear that an adaptation need not be written or otherwise recorded in any way, so an improvisation of a copyright work is an adaptation.

Transposing a work to a different key or register is not regarded as an adaptation, but this exception only applies when transposing on the spot, because writing a piece out (whether in the original key or not) is within the scope of copyright.

An improvisation on a copyright work as the final organ voluntary is clearly an adaptation. However this is a hollow right. As the improvisation would have been performed by the time the copyright holder knew about it, his only remedy would be damages which would probably be a nominal amount.

Secondary rights

Secondary rights are designed to help protect the main rights by imposing penalties in respect of **infringing copy**. This is material generated which contravenes copyright law.

There are five secondary rights:

- importing infringing copy;
- possessing or dealing with infringing copy;
- providing means for making infringing copy;
- permitting use of premises for infringement; and
- providing apparatus for infringement.

In each case, an offence is only committed if the person knew, or should have known, that it was to be used to infringe copyright. Without this provision, every photocopier supplier would be guilty.

Moral rights

Moral rights were introduced by the 1988 Act and therefore only apply to works created from 1 August 1989. It should be noted that these rights belong to the creator of the work, who may no longer be the copyright holder. If you sell your copyright, you still retain your moral rights, unless you have separately given them up.

European countries have been much readier to recognise moral rights. For example, France codified moral rights in 1957, having already given such rights through case law.

There are four moral rights:

- to be identified as author, director or composer;
- protection from derogatory treatment;
- protection from false attribution; and
- privacy in films and photographs.

The right to be **identified** is contained in s77 of the Act. This is sometimes called the **paternity right**. It gives the composer the right to be identified whenever music is published commercially, recorded for sale to the public, or included in a film for the public. The same rights are enjoyed by someone who has written words set to music. This right only applies if the copyright holder has "asserted" the right. This means that the holder has shown his name on the work, and stated it in any assignment of right. This right does not apply in respect of any of the permitted exceptions to copyright law.

The right to object to **derogatory treatment** is contained in s80 of the Act. There is a "treatment" of a musical work if someone does something other than transposing it to another key or register. A treatment is "derogatory" if "it amounts to distortion or mutilation of the work or is otherwise prejudicial to the honour or reputation of the author or director" (s80(2)(b)).

It should be noted that this involves much more than just not liking what someone has done to your work, such as parodying the words or producing a bad arrangement, though in such cases you may still have protection under other copyright provisions. For derogatory treatment, you must show that the treatment is likely to reflect badly on you, which is most likely when the person has not sufficiently identified himself as the arranger. One of the few cases on derogatory treatment of music was brought by the pop singer George Michael in 1993. Five songs he recorded as part of the duo Wham! were remixed and interspersed with music recorded by other musicians on the *Bad Boys Megamix album*. He demonstrated an arguable case and so was granted a temporary injunction.

The issue was raised again in the case *Confetti Records v Warner Music UK Ltd [2003]* where one of the issues was whether the inclusion of words from a song *Burnin'* on a rap record was derogatory treatment because of rap's association with violence and drugs. The answer is no, as derogatory treatment must reflect on the composer. The judge also questioned whether expressions such as "mish mash man" and "shizzle my nizzle" would be generally understood.

Other countries have applied moral rights more strictly. In Belgium, a band called Fortuna and Apotheosis made upbeat arrangements of Orff's *Carmina Burana* which reached numbers 1 and 3 in the Dutch pop charts. Orff died in 1982 and so is copyright until 2052. His estate successfully sued and the records were withdrawn from sale.

France allowed the director of the film *Asphalt Jungle*, deliberately shot in black and white, to stop a colourised version being broadcast, even though he did not own moral rights in the US where the film was made. Italy held that it was a breach of moral rights to insert advertising breaks during the broadcast of a film. In Canada a sculptor successfully defended his moral rights to stop ribbons being draped round his sculpture at Christmas.

A person is protected from **false attribution** by someone saying that you wrote a work which you did not. The right is contained in s84. It is easy to see how an eminent composer could have his reputation damaged by having some poor work attributed to him. This right lasts until 20 years after the alleged composer's death. A false attribution could also lead to a claim for libel or malicious falsehood. This right does not allow a composer to disown works which he has written but may now wish he had not. Alan Clark MP used this law to sue Associated Newspapers for publishing a diary which was falsely attributed to him.

There is a similar offence known as "passing off" which is widely used when a product is manufactured to look like another. This is a difficult case to prove, and many blatant examples seem to avoid action, as a stroll round the shelves of any supermarket will demonstrate. Passing off could apply in music, such as falsely describing your choir as Kings College, Cambridge to help sell recordings.

The right to **privacy** only applies to films and photographs taken for private and domestic purposes. The photographer owns the copyright and may prevent it from being used in any work issued to the public. The right is in s85 of the Act. It should be noted that a separate law of privacy is being developed under Human Rights Act 1998.

Except for false attribution, moral rights last for as long as the work is in copyright.

Permitted acts for copyright works (exemptions)

The 1988 Act allows you to do certain things which would otherwise be a breach of copyright law. However, you must be careful to ensure that you come exactly within the scope of the exemption. These exemptions were modified from 31 October 2003 by a statutory instrument SI 2003 No 2498. Much of this statutory instrument relates to broadcasts and computer files.

These rights are those which the law allows you to do, *regardless of whether the copyright holder agrees*. This law does not stop the copyright holder agreeing to let you do anything else you wish.

The main permitted acts are:

- research and private study;
- criticism, review and news reporting;
- incidental inclusion;
- education;
- librarianship; and
- public administration.

There are additional exceptions for non-musical copyright, such as for computer programs, statues, buildings, industrial designs and typefaces.

The exemption for **research and private study** is given in s29 of the 1988 Act. It allows a person to take one copy for research and study. This need not be as part of any formal education, but may be to help write a book or even for personal curiosity. Although the Act does not expressly say so, in practice this right is limited to a single copy which should be destroyed when the research or study has been completed.

An unsuccessful attempt was made in the case *Ashdown v Telegraph Group Ltd [2001]* to argue that freedom of expression under Human Rights Act 1998 provided an extension to this exemption. The case concerned *The Sunday Telegraph* publishing a leaked memo of a meeting between Paddy Ashdown MP and the prime minister.

The exemption for **criticism** (s30) allows fair dealing with a work, such as quoting it. If you wish to review a piece of music, you may print a short quotation without bothering to get permission, but you must acknowledge the source. In practice this means identifying the work, composer and publisher. From 31 October 2003, the requirement to acknowledge the source may be dispensed with, if this is impractical.

It would appear that this section may permit short quotations of musical works in other works. However even short quotations have often got composers into trouble. In 1997 the group Verve had a hit with *Bitter Sweet Symphony* written by Richard Ashcroft. It included a sample from a 1965 recording by Andrew Oldham Orchestra of the Rolling Stones' song *The Last Time*. Verve's record company paid a fee to Decca Records for this sample, but this does not cover all the copyright owned in this brief extract. Ashcroft was sued twice and in effect lost all the copyright in the music.

If quoting someone else's work, it is always advisable to get permission. Some record companies have adopted a **three-second rule**, that they will not take action if no more than three seconds of music is copied, such as when an extract is taken as a "sample" for a dance or rap record. However this is their own rule; it is not the law.

A more generous approach seems to be adopted for the printed word than for music. In the case *Chappell v D C Thompson & Co Ltd [1928-35]*, a paper called *Red Star Weekly* got away with printing four lines of words from the song Her Name is Mary. In contrast, any performance of *Happy Birthday to You* attracts a demand for payment, which is why you never hear this song in a film.

In the United States, the case *Campbell v Acuff-Rose [1994]* held that there was fair use when the group 2 Live Crew copied the bass line from Roy Orbison's song *Oh Pretty Woman.*

The exemption for **incidental inclusion** in s31 exempts such situations as where a few bars of a tune may be heard in the background during an item in a news bulletin. It does not apply in any instance where the inclusion of the work is deliberate. This could be relevant when a wedding video includes some of your organ music, as explained on page141.

There are many exemptions in relation to **education** set out in sections 32 to 36 of the 1988 Act. These generally exempt performance and copying of short passages for the purposes of teaching or examining students. It does not extend to copying whole works or substantial passages, nor to performances in school concerts.

The exemptions for **libraries** are set out in sections 37 to 44. This allows a librarian to provide a copy for a permitted purpose, such as for private research and study. From 31 October 2003, the law is tightened up so that libraries need permission to provide copies for commercial purposes.

The exemptions for **public administration** are set out in sections 45 to 50. They allow copies to be made for court cases, statutory enquiries and in similar circumstances.

From 31 October 2003, a new section 28A exempts making a temporary copy as part of a permissible use of copyright. An example is preparing a master tape for a broadcast, provided the broadcast complies with copyright law.

There are also some minor exceptions which are mostly irrelevant for musical works. Section 61 allows folksongs to be recorded for an archive, if the performers agree. Section 63 allows extracts to be issued for promotion, such as including an extract of a work on a sampler recording. Section 64 allows a creator of a work to use his own material in a later work, even if he is no longer the copyright holder.

There are also some rules about implied permission for copyright such as when music is used in a video which is offered for hire. Section 71 allows someone to video-record a television programme to watch later.

Unknown copyright holder

Sometimes it is not possible to know who the copyright holder is. In church music this often happens with worship songs which may be composed in one fellowship and copied by others. It is almost a form of modern folk music in that no-one knows who actually composed the work. Common examples include *A new commandment, Be still and know that I am God, Great is the Lord and greatly to be praised, Holy holy holy is the Lord,* and *Peace is Flowing Like a River.*

Section 57 provides one measure of protection when it is not possible to identify the copyright holder by reasonable effort, and it is reasonable to assume that the copyright holder died more than 70 years ago.

Otherwise a work remains in copyright even though no-one knows who is the holder. In such cases, the work is indicated as "composer unknown". It is often shown as ©

Copyright control. This means that the copyright is acknowledged and any fees are collected and payable should the copyright holder ever be identified.

Performing rights

Performing rights are separate from copyright, though similar in nature. Performing rights basically protect performers while copyright protects composers. Performing rights are now governed by Copyright, Designs and Patents Act 1988 sections 180 to 212.

This point should be clearly understood as the two rights are separate. There is some possible confusion in that the Performing Rights Society deals with copyright enforcement as well as performing rights.

A performance of copyright music attracts a copyright payment for the performance in addition to that paid when you bought the music. However, there is an exception for acts of worship. But you must remember to make a payment for any performance which is not an act of worship, such as a concert.

Illicit recordings

Otherwise, the main protection of performing rights is against illicit recordings. This may be directly, such as recording a concert, or indirectly such as copying a radio broadcast or another recording of a concert.

Illicit recording or copying is commonly known as **bootlegging**. This has been widely practised since the tape recorder became available, but has become much more common since the 1980s as recording equipment has become better technically and more affordable. Until the 1980s, fines for bootlegging were usually too small to be a deterrent, so bootleg albums were openly advertised in music magazines. In 1988 this changed when the estate of the late actor Peter Sellers sued a film company for £1 million for using out-takes from previous films to make a new Pink Panther film which neither the actor nor his estate had authorised *(Rickless v United Artists Corporation [1988])*.

The Internet provided new opportunities for good quality performances to be passed freely between millions of subscribers at no cost. The website operators derived their fees from advertisements. The main website Napster was shut down in 2000. Napster has now reopened with other websites operating a low-cost download service which complies with copyright law.

Own recordings

There is no law which stops you recording your own performance of any music, even of music in copyright. Restrictions only start to apply under s182(1) when you:

- wish to use the recording other than for "private and domestic use"; or
- do not get the consent of the performer.

Issues can arise if you record a concert or service and wish to make copies, such as for members of the choir to enjoy, or to raise funds for the church. Even though this is not a commercial activity, it is not for your private and domestic use, and so you need the permission of the performers, even if the performance is in an act of public worship. (There are other issues you must consider if recording an act of worship.)

Another issue is in defining the "performer", such as when a choir, orchestra or ensemble is involved. Does permission need to come from the choirmaster, the vicar, or every member of the choir? The answer is probably all three.

In practice, the best course of action is to state in advance any intention to record the performance and what you intend to do with the recording.

There is a separate offence under s184 of importing, possessing or dealing with illicit recordings. Section 185 deals with issues concerning exclusive rights in recording contracts.

Performing rights last for 50 years from the date of performance.

Fees for wedding videos

Performers who take part in films, television programmes and even television advertisements acquire a right to **repeat fees**. This is because each showing of a film, programme or advertisement is a separate performance.

To avoid the administrative burden for broadcasters and uncertainty for performers, it has become common practice to buy out these rights, which is known as a **pre-performance payment**. The performer receives a lump sum for giving up his right to receive repeat fees.

There is an element of this payment when an organist is paid an additional fee when a wedding is video-recorded. The recommended rate is that an organist should be paid double the normal rate for a video recording, and 50% extra for an audio recording. One fee is for playing at the wedding; the other is the pre-performance payment when the video is subsequently shown. As a wedding video is only likely to be watched in private domestic circumstances, it is questionable whether the organist has any performing right for which to claim a fee. However the fee for an organist is a matter for contractual negotiation, so if the parties are content with the fee, that is the end of the matter.

The organist and any music group leader or soloist has a right to refuse to allow their performance to be recorded, or to ask for an additional fee for recording. This right is independent of whether the minister allows the service to be recorded. In practice, an organist or other musician should not refuse permission. An organist who is concerned about having his performance recorded should probably not be an organist at all. If the choir is paid for singing at a wedding, they may also be entitled to additional fees.

Once permission has been granted it cannot be retrospectively withdrawn, however bad your performance. But remember the recording is only for domestic use.

An issue can arise when a couple say that they will not record the wedding and so do not pay the additional fee to the organist, and then Uncle Fred turns up with his video camera anyway. Neither the couple nor the bride's father can be made vicariously liable for what an independently minded guest chooses to do. However, church authorities have the right to restrict all forms of photography and recording during a church service, which includes weddings. The minister is within his right to ban all photography and video-recording during the service, or (as is normal) to limit it to certain parts of the service such as processions and signing the register. A minister who does permit recording has full authority over where lights, cameras, microphones and personnel may be placed.

The best course of action is for the churchwarden, minister or verger (or someone acting in such capacity) to tell the guest to stop recording or pay the additional fee. Such a request can be enforced. Another alternative is simply to increase the organist's fee and give everyone the right to take whatever amateur video recordings they want.

The issue is different if the video is shown on television. This may happen if something funny happens at the wedding and is shown in a programme of short video clips. It could also happen if the wedding or a party to it became newsworthy for some reason. If your music is merely background to the bridesmaid fainting during the second hymn, or whatever else is deemed hilarious enough for public consumption, there is probably no copyright issue as this would be covered by the exception for incidental use, explained above.

For a professional recording, ie where the video recordist is paid or by a television company, there should always be a separate agreement between the company and the organist. The Incorporated Society of Musicians has a draft written contract for visiting organists.

These provisions apply to all audio and video recordings of church services; however, weddings are most recorded.

Copyright Tribunal

Disputes about performing rights are administered by a Copyright Tribunal. These tribunals were established under the 1956 Act under the name Performing Rights Tribunal. The 1988 Act renamed the tribunals and extended their jurisdiction. These tribunals hear disputes about licensing schemes, such as whether the terms offered are reasonable and fair to all users.

The tribunal also sets terms when a person has the right to use copyright material but the terms cannot be agreed. A common example is playing a recording. The 1956 Act allowed anyone to broadcast a recording once it had been issued to the public. The 1988 Act abolished this right, but it was reintroduced under Broadcasting Act 1990. This allows radio and television stations to broadcast publicly issued recordings, provided the broadcaster is willing to agree the terms subsequently set by the Copyright Tribunal.

Brief history

The first copyright law was an Act of 1709 which took effect from 10 April 1710, giving copyright in books. Before this, there was a measure of protection under common law, and by various licences granted by the king.

The next major step was the Berne Convention to provide a measure of international acceptance of copyrights. The UK ratified this convention on 5 December 1887. This has been periodically amended, most recently in Paris in 1971. The UK Act extended copyright to English translations of foreign works. There is also a United Nations Universal Copyright Convention.

The first major piece of copyright law was Copyright Act 1911. On 1 June 1957, Copyright Act 1956 became law. This consolidated previous Acts and allowed for copyright in new media, such as films and television.

On 1 August 1989, the current Copyright, Designs and Patents Act 1988 became law. This consolidated the 1956 Act and, again, reflected technological changes, such as computer programs and video recorders.

There have been several amendments since then, mostly prompted by European Union directives. There is a European Copyright Treaty designed to harmonise copyright laws between EU member states. This has largely been adopted in the UK, but its adoption has yet to be tested by the courts.

New regulations were introduced from 31 October 2003 under the Copyright and Related Rights Regulations SI 2003 No 2498.

United States law

Because so much church music comes from the United States where the law is different, some brief notes about US copyright law are included.

For music published from 1 January 1978, copyright lasts for the lifetime of the copyright holder plus 70 years, as for the UK and most of the rest of the world. For music published previously, copyright lasts for 95 years from publication.

Copyright is automatically created with the work, as in the UK. A work is said to become copyright when it is "fixed" in a copy or recording.

However there is a registration process with the United States Copyright Office. The filing fee is $30. The address is:

> Library of Congress Copyright Office
>
> 101 Independence Avenue, SE
>
> Washington DC 20559-6000.

Generally, it is necessary for a work to be registered to bring infringement proceedings.

The rights of the copyright holder are broadly similar though sometimes expressly differently. For example there is a specific right "to synchronise music to visual images".

The rights to do anything with a copyright work may be given by the copyright holder, as in the UK, but there is a greater reliance on having it in writing, known as a licence (except the Americans spell it "license").

To make recordings, a "mechanical license" must be obtained. The rate is set by statute as so much per song per recording:

Calendar years	Statutory rate
2004 and 2005	8.5 cents
2006 and 2007	9.1 cents

There is a body called Church Music Publishers Association (CMPA) which combines copyright and similar concerns for church musicians.

CCLI operates a licensing system in the USA on a similar basis to that offered in the UK. Its American address is:

> 6130 NE 78th Court
>
> Suite C-11
>
> Portland, OR 97218.

Penalties have high statutory limits. A copyright holder may recover damages from $500 to $100,000 per copyright infringed. For wilful commercial infringement criminal fines of up to $250,000 and five years imprisonment may be imposed.

Isle of Man

The Isle of Man's copyright law is governed by the Tynwald's Copyright Act 1991. The main differences from UK law is that copyright lasts for the composer's lifetime plus 50 years, not 70 years.

Other countries

Works created in other countries enjoy copyright protection in the UK for 70 years after the composer's death unless the copyright expires earlier under the laws of the country of origin. All European Union countries have the same 70-year time limit.

European directive

In 2001, the European Union passed EC Directive 2001/29/EC on the Harmonisation of Certain Aspects of Copyright.

The directive will give new powers to copyright holders, such as controlling the right to quote works, to restrict electronic provision, and to allow copyright holders to track on-line use of their works.

The Profits

Using someone else's copyright

As copyright is a form of property, using someone else's copyright is just like using someone else's tangible property. If you want to use a piano belonging to someone else, you ask them. If they want to charge you for borrowing the piano, you must agree a price. So it is with copyright. If you want to use someone else's copyright work, you must ask them and agree any price.

Not all copyright holders want payment to use their work. Many composers are only too delighted that you wish to perform their work and will happily let you do so freely. There are many Internet sites which offer free material for church use. Some of these sites allow free downloading for worship purposes only.

A person may agree subject to a condition. While Gilbert and Sullivan was copyright, D'Oyly Carte opera company had an effective monopoly on their operettas which they used to enforce their standards of production. Now that has expired, people are free to do what they like with their works — and have done.

Another example concerns the rap singer Coolio who wanted to "sample" part of a song by Stevie Wonder in *Gangsters' Paradise*. (Sampling is taking a short extract from an old recording to be used in a new recording.) Wonder only agreed if the new words were cleaned up, as he did not want to be associated with the original violent lyrics. The words were cleaned up, and the result was the best selling record of 1995.

Whatever agreement you reach with the copyright holder, he can enforce under the normal law of contract (see chapter 3). For example, if he allows you to make 100 copies and perform it twice, he could sue you for making 101 copies or performing it three times. You must follow the agreed conditions in the same way as you must comply with agreed conditions when hiring a hall or a piano.

The commonest such arrangement is **publishing right** where the copyright holder allows someone the right to publish the work without owning the copyright. The publishers of this book have publishing rights but not copyright in the cartoon on the cover.

Liturgy and Scripture

Suppose you write your own **Communion setting** for a *Common Worship* service. You own the copyright in your music, but the copyright in the words rests with the Archbishops' Council of the Church of England. If all you have done is to reproduce the words of the parts usually sung, there is unlikely to be any problem about getting agreement. No fee is likely to be requested.

Church House Publishing's third edition of *A Brief Guide to Liturgical Copyright* says that no prior permission is needed for a local music setting, provided:

- the words faithfully and accurately follow the text of *Common Worship*;
- the copies bear the name of the parish, cathedral or other church body;
- settings are not offered for sale; and
- there is an acknowledgment which reads "*Common Worship*, extracts from which are reproduced in this setting, is copyright © The Archbishops' Council 2000."

The same arrangement may be used for other copyright material owned by the Archbishops' Council

The Book of Common Prayer is still in copyright owned by the Crown. No permission is needed to reproduce up to 500 words. Otherwise, permission is needed from The Permissions Controller at Cambridge University Press.

The reference to "faithfully and accurately" means that a composer cannot drop text to fit the music (as Schubert did). However, there appears to be no objection to repeating words, such as changing "Glory to God in the highest", to "Glory, glory to God in the highest, in the highest". In practice, the reference to setting words includes reproducing "cue lines" as plain text, such as "Great is the mystery of faith" before the acclamation in the Communion service.

This concession does not apply when a setting is commercially published or otherwise offered for sale. In such cases, an agreement must be reached with the Copyright and Contracts Administrator at Church House.

The Church of England gives parishes a similar right to make their own **service books** using copyright material owned by the Archbishops' Council. The copies must give the name of the parish, and must include a statement of the copyright in the form as above. No charge is made for this, as parishes have already paid through the diocesan quota (also known as parish share). It is a requirement that the church must own at least one copy of *Common Worship*. These home-made service books must not be offered for sale, but may be given away. Similar provisions apply to liturgy available in electronic format, such as on CD or downloaded from a website.

The exemption from prior agreement also applies to:

- service sheets to be used for a single occasion, such as orders of service for weddings and funerals;
- overhead transparencies;
- reproductions in pew notices, service leaflets and prayer cards;
- large print versions for people with poor sight.

Where a service book contains material from several sources, an acknowledgment must be included for each source, and you must comply with the rules for each source. Ensuring compliance with copyright law does not mean that such a book is canonically acceptable as worship.

It should not be forgotten that translations of **The Bible** are copyright, and so permission may be needed when passages of scripture are set to music or included in service books. In practice, copyright owners allow a certain amount to be used without prior agreement or payment of a fee, but their copyright must still be acknowledged.

Table of Bible translations, copyright maximum and copyright holder

Translation	Copyright-free maximum	Copyright holder
Authorised Version	500 verses	Cambridge University Press
Contemporary English Version	50 verses	Bible Society
Good News Bible	1000 verses	Bible Society
Grail Psalter	5 psalms	A P Watt Ltd
Jerusalem Bible	500 words	Darton, Longman & Todd Ltd
Liturgical Psalter	5 psalms	HarperCollins Religious
New English Bible	500 verses	Cambridge University Press
New International Version	500 verses	Hodder & Stoughton
New Revised Standard Version	500 verses	RSV/NRSV Permissions, USA
Revised English Bible	500 verses	Cambridge University Press
Revised Psalter	5 psalms	Archbishops' Council
Revised Standard Version	500 verses	RSV/NRSV Permissions, USA

Photocopying music

There is no law against photocopying music, only against photocopying it without permission. Permission to photocopy copyright music can often be obtained easily, sometimes by just a single telephone call to the publishers and asking for their copyright department.

Many modern Christian songs are covered by a music reproduction **licence** (MRL) issued by CCLI, as explained later. This allows you to pay a single annual fee and then freely photocopy music from a list provided by them.

Commercial publishers are not trying to stop you performing their music. They are trying to stop you avoiding payment for doing so. Publishers are usually co-operative when you seek permission and are willing to pay an agreed fee.

Several, but not all, leading music publishers have agreed that you may photocopy their music without getting their express permission or making a payment in these circumstances:

- to avoid a difficult page turn;
- to keep a record of bowing marks in parts for stringed instruments;
- as temporary copies when you have ordered copies and while you are waiting for them to arrive;
- to generate additional copies of orchestral parts, provided that the total number of parts generated does not exceed one quarter of the number of parts you have bought.

If music is out of print, most publishers will arrange either to produce authorised copies from an archive for you, or will allow you to make your own copies, possibly on payment of a fee.

You may wish to perform an anthem from a book containing 50 anthems without buying 30 copies of the whole book. In such cases, you should contact the publishers and ask permission to copy the one anthem or other extract. Permission is likely to be refused if the anthem or extract is published separately as the publishers will expect you to buy that copy. In other cases, the publisher is likely to agree to let you photocopy the music on payment of a fee. This is rarely a large amount, typically around 30p a copy, but the exact amount must be agreed with the publisher. The publisher will ensure that the composer receives the appropriate royalty. The publisher will usually give you a licence number to be written on each photocopy and will send you a bill for the amount. Sometimes the publisher will send you self-adhesive labels printed in red ink to stick on each copy. Once you have legally photocopied this music, it is your property to use in exactly the same way as any other printed anthem. You may sing the anthem as many times as you wish without payment of any further copyright sum.

Sometimes you may wish to photocopy music for convenience. For example, a carol service may involve several books with only short readings between carols to find the next place. You may wish to photocopy all the music in order to make life easier for the choir. Another example is in large **anthologies**. Many publishers produce collections of up to 100 anthems in a single book. These represent very good value for money. However such books can be heavy for some choristers who are happier with a photocopy. Yet another example is a chorister with poor sight who may wish to have an enlarged photocopy.

In all these cases, contact the publisher and ask if they are in agreement to what you wish. Publishers are more concerned about losing income than in being awkward to law-abiding musicians. In practice, most publishers agree, though they will often insist that you destroy the copy after first use. In other words, if you have 30 copies of an anthem book, the publisher may be willing to let you leave them in the cupboard and produce 30 photocopies of an anthem. They are not losing any profit or royalty by so agreeing.

When you have been given permission to take photocopies, always note the date and name of person who gave you permission. Always write on the copies the basis for your permission to photocopy. Sometimes music stands are inspected by representatives of publishers looking for illicit photocopies.

Some publishers now offer books on terms which permit the purchaser to make their own copies.

Remember that illegally photocopied music remains illegal. If you discover what appears to be illicit photocopies in a choir cupboard, you must throw them away or agree any payment with the copyright holder.

Licensing schemes

In reality, making a private agreement with a copyright holder may only be practical if you want to perform a work written by an organist you know. It is unlikely to be practical for a major composer or for any published work.

In such cases, there are various licensing schemes, which are legislated for in sections 116 to 125 of the 1988 Act. A licence may be granted to permit the holder to do anything protected by copyright law. Perhaps the most relevant for organists is the Christian Copyright Licence explained below.

CCLI licence

Christian Copyright Licensing International (CCLI) offers a simple solution to copying church music. By acquiring one of several licences, you can legally reproduce music in certain ways. You pay an annual fee for this licence.

The Church Copyright Licence, the most well-known, is for the reproduction and projection of words of Christian hymns and worship songs. This licence includes a Mechanical Copyright Protection Society (MCPS) licence allowing recording of music for non-commercial use, such as maintaining an archive or providing copies to housebound members of the congregation.

There is also a Music Reproduction Licence for the photocopying of music from authorised music publications. This licence also allows for small arrangements where no arrangement already exists, such as for brass ensemble.

When you buy the Licence, you are given a list of which works and composers are included. You should check that any music you wish to copy is on this list. This list contains 150,000 sets of words from 2,500 catalogues. If a work is not on the list, you must make separate arrangements with the copyright holder.

The different types of licence offered to churches are:

- church copyright and music reproduction licence;
- Performing Rights Society (PRS) performing licence;
- Copyright Licensing Agency (CLA) church licence (for photocopying material from magazines and books);
- church event copyright licence; and
- church video licence, showing films and film clips.

A similar set of licences is offered to schools.

The church copyright licence (CCL) allows the church to:

- include words of hymns and songs on notice sheets or similar;
- produce your own hymn book or supplement;
- project words from an overhead acetate;

- store and retrieve words of hymns from computer files;
- make an audio or video recording for those who cannot attend.

The last of these is administered by CCLI as agent for the Mechanical Copyright Protection Society.

The **music reproduction licence (MRL)** is an addition to the CCL. It also allows the church to:

- photocopy music.

In all cases, the words or music must be on the list provided by CCLI Europe.

A requirement of a licence is that you complete an annual return of which songs you have actually reproduced, recorded or projected. This allows CCLI to apportion the copyright royalties to copyright holders in proportion to the use of their material.

The annual fee is based on the average size of your church's congregation. Current rates (in 2004) are:

Category	Church Size	Annual Fee
AH	0 - 14	£48
A	15 - 49	£72
B	50 - 99	£132
C	100 - 249	£216
D	250 - 499	£300
E	500 - 999	£393
F	1,000 - 1,499	£489
G	1,500 - 2,999	£603

These amounts include VAT.

A **church event copyright licence** is issued by CCLI for occasions of short duration, such as missions, rallies, conferences, weddings and funerals. The licence lasts for 14 days and costs about one third of the annual licence. This licence cannot be used for any event where admission is charged.

The address of CCLI is given in Appendix 1.

CCLI also operates in other parts of Europe, USA, South Africa, Australia and New Zealand.

CCLI provides other services, such as news updates, copies of articles and annual lists of the top 25 Christian songs.

Music outside CCLI licence

The CCLI licence covers a huge amount of Christian music, but does not cover it all. However some other leading publishers have made their own arrangements.

For **Taizé chants**, you can obtain a Calamus licence from Decani Music. For this they provide you with a copy of the chant, if not otherwise published, for which you acquire the licence. Its address is given in Appendix 1.

Calamus also covers other sources of music such as New Dawn Music, OCP Publications, GIA Publicatons Inc, World Library and McCrimmons Publishing Co Ltd, as well as its own Decani Music. They also license Bernadette Farrell *(Christ be our light)*, Daniel Schutte *(Here I am Lord)*, Sebastian Temple *(Make me a channel of your peace)* and Marty Haugen *(All are welcome)*.

Iona songs are now covered by a CCLI copyright licence. Previous copyright permissions granted directly by Wild Goose Resource Group remain valid. One consequence of the change is that you need a licence to reproduce the words of an Iona song, such as in a service sheet. Previously, Wild Goose allowed free copying of words.

Enforcing copyright

Copyright is a civil law, not a criminal law. So if you breach a copyright you are more likely to receive an invoice than a summons.

A copyright holder may issue court proceedings for an action to recover damages. Under s 97(2) of the 1988 Act, these damages may be increased according to the flagrancy of the breach and the benefit accruing to the infringer.

Where there would have been no infringement of copyright had the infringer obtained a licence from the Copyright Tribunal and the infringer subsequently agrees to obtain such a licence, the maximum damage is twice the amount of the licence.

Damages

In all but the most serious cases, breach of copyright attracts compensatory damages under the 1988 Act s96(2). This is a sum of money designed to compensate the copyright holder for lost profits or the fee that could have been charged.

A court may award additional damages when:

- the infringement has been particularly flagrant; or
- the defendant's profit is so large that compensatory damages are an inadequate remedy.

Breach of moral rights is also actionable for damages, assessed as a sum to put the right-holder in the same position as if the moral right had not been infringed.

A court can order an infringer to provide an account of profits, and to deliver up copies of the offending works.

Before the 1988 Act, it was also possible to claim conversion damages equal to the value of the infringing article, which could be huge. This right is now abolished.

In practice, breaches of musical copyright usually attract only damages as a remedy, as a musician does not normally suffer other than financially when his copyright has been breached. However, other remedies are given below for the sake of completeness.

Injunctions and searches

An injunction may be granted by a court to prevent or remedy a breach of copyright. An injunction may not be granted if:

- the infringement is slight;
- there is unlikely to be any repetition; or
- there has been unreasonable delay in seeking the injunction.

Since 1976 the courts have been able to grant Anton Piller orders (from the name of the case where such an order was first granted). The order is usually made by a judge at a secret hearing to which the premises owner is not a part. These draconian orders allow a copyright holder to enter premises to look for, seize or copy material. Such orders are only allowed in extreme cases.

Destruction of infringing material

Musicians are sometimes fond of saying that if their copyright is infringed, they have the right to tear up the offending music or seize the illicit recording. This is rarely so. Any musician that does this is liable to prosecution for criminal damage under Criminal Damage Act 1971. This is an "arrestable offence" which means that you can make a citizen's arrest, in other words detain them while you wait for the police. Threats and attempts at damage are also offences.

If you find material that infringes your copyright, a strict seizure procedure is set out in section 100 of the 1998 Act. You, or someone acting for you, may seize material which breaches your copyright only if:

- you first give notice of the time and place of the proposed seizure to a local police station;
- you stay in areas open to the public (such as a shop's sales floor but not its stock room);
- the offending material is not in the possession of a person at work;
- you do not use force; and
- you leave a notice which states what has been seized, by whom, on whose authority, and for what reason.

An alternative and much safer procedure is to use the courts. Section 99 allows a copyright holder to get a court order requiring infringing material to be delivered to the copyright holder or someone else named by the court. Section 114 allows the court to order that infringing material be destroyed or delivered to the copyright holder.

The Copyright, etc. and Trade Marks (Offences and Enforcement) Act 2002 allows the police to apply to the court for an order to seize copyright material.

Someone to whom a licence has been given in respect of a copyright work has similar rights to enforce the copyright to the extent that it breaches his licence.

An action may be brought for breach of moral rights. The court may grant an injunction on such terms as it thinks fit.

Criminal offences

It is not a criminal offence just to breach someone's copyright, but it becomes a criminal offence under s103 of the 1988 Act if you breach the copyright:

- on a commercial basis; or
- to an extent that prejudicially affects the copyright holder.

The enforcement of this criminal law is the responsibility of the local weights and measures authority.

The maximum penalty for a criminal conviction is an unlimited fine and ten years in prison when the Copyright, etc. and Trade Marks (Offences and Enforcement) Act 2002 becomes law. Until then, the maximum penalty is a fine of £5,000 and two years in prison. If the offence is committed by a company or other corporate body, any officer of that body who acted or connived in the breach of copyright is also liable.

Goods which infringe copyright can be "prohibited goods". This means that HM Revenue and Customs can stop them being imported into the UK. This provision is widely used to stop importation of pirated CDs.

Electronic enforcement

Technology now means that some equipment is fitted with electronic devices to make copying difficult or impossible. Section 296 of the 1988 Act gives these devices legal protection in that it is an offence to find ways of defeating the security feature or of making known how to do so.

From November 2002, some CDs have copyright control technology on them. A consequence of this is that the CD cannot play in some players, such as in computers. A CD must indicate that such a device has been put on.

There are similar protections for computer software.

6 Protecting our children

Introduction

Children's choirs have been an important part of church life for centuries in which both the children and adults benefit. In the vast majority of cases, there is no problem in ensuring that children and adults can happily and properly enjoy working together. But just as we must take precautions to protect ourselves against the minority of citizens who are burglars, so we must take precautions against the minority who are child abusers.

> *Provided simple precautions are taken, good child protection practice should not get in the way of running a choir.*

It is important to take a balanced view. You should neither be so concerned about child protection that you are discouraged from working with children, nor should you regard all this as just a fad of a politically correct society.

First, understand that there is a problem. The National Society for the Prevention of Cruelty to Children (NSPCC) launched its Full Stop campaign against child cruelty on 22 March 1999 with these horrifying statistics:

- around 35,000 children are on child protection registers in the UK. These are considered to be suffering from or likely to suffer significant harm - at the hands of their parents or carers; and

- there are at least 110,000 adults living in this country who have been convicted of sex offences against children;

- for rape, 26% of all victims are children;

- in the UK one child a week is killed each week through abuse;

- the homicide rate for infants is five times higher than for adults.

This reality must take precedence over the popular mythology of a choirmaster clouting naughty choirboys round the ear with a full music edition of *Hymns Ancient and Modern* "which did them no harm". Like most tales of the good old days, it never really happened. We now know that such fondly imagined fiction hid much child abuse which ruined lives.

For the sake of thoroughness, much information is given in this chapter. This is for the sake of completeness, and should not be seen as indicating a formidable problem.

The church, being a body based on trust, has proved a fertile ground for serious abuse. It is estimated that about a quarter of all serious child abuse is in a religious context. Research has found that a higher proportion of convicted offenders against children is found in church congregations than in the population generally. Many abusers are male.

An organist with responsibilities for a children's choir must comply with child protection procedures, including being checked. An organist who refuses must not be allowed access to children, however talented he may otherwise be. It must be appreciated that no system of child protection can guarantee to prevent all child abuse. However, that is no reason to avoid doing what can be done.

A system of child protection is also a system of organist protection against false claims.

The Churches Child Protection Advisory Service (CCPAS) commissioned Christian Research in 2003 to undertake a study of child protection policies. The report found that 9% of churches had no child protection policy (Source: *Churches, children and child protection (2004) ISBN 1 85321 157 5)*.

Compliance with child protection policy is usually an essential element to comply with the terms of the church's insurance policy. Ecclesiastical Insurance Group (EIG) insures many Anglican churches (though churches are free to insure with any company). EIG issued its statement on child abuse in September 2003. Where EIG provides public liability (third party) insurance for death and bodily injury to third parties, they will pay if the church is legally liable. The policy does not indemnify the abuser himself. As with all insurance, the insured must take all reasonable steps to prevent loss. "A duty therefore exists upon the insured to research and adopt best practice based upon current and ongoing guidelines." It is also a condition that any incident or allegation is reported to the insurance company immediately.

In the context of this book, child protection only applies when a child is not with a parent or legal guardian. If a child is with a parent or guardian, such as when mother and daughter are together at choir practice, the child is in the protection of the parent and not the organist. However an organist or any other adult who witnesses any child abuse on any occasion still has at least a moral duty to report the matter.

No-one should ever exclude someone from child protection policy on the basis of "I know him". You cannot identify a child abuser by looking at him, nor by whether he is married or has children of his own. Every time a child abuser is exposed, dozens of people are stunned by the "I would never have guessed" emotion.

In March 2004, Stephen King was convicted of sexual abuse against dozens of children. He was a child protection expert who trained police and the Crown Prosecution Service, and appeared as an expert witness in court.

In July 2004, Judge David Selwood of Portsmouth Crown Court was sentenced for child pornography. He had presided over many similar cases in his 12 years, and denounced child pornography in strong terms when passing a seven-year sentence on Paul Hobbs in July 2002.

Official guidance

Guidance on protecting children was published by the Home Office in 1993 in a document entitled *Safe From Harm* (which relates to children up to the age of 16 in voluntary organisations). *Safe from Harm* is concerned with the welfare of children and is therefore wider in scope than just protection from abuse.

This book went to press as the Queen's speech of May 2005 announced that the government was to introduce the Safeguarding Vulnerable Groups Bill designed to provide a central register by 2007 of all who work with children and vulnerable adults.

Development of policy in the churches

In the Church of England, the bishops first introduced child protection policies in 1995. This was followed by *Policy on Child Protection* in 1999, which was replaced by *Protecting All God's Children* in February 2004.

In the Roman Catholic Church, the Nolan Report was published in September 2001, following a first report in April 2001. This was an investigation commissioned by the Archbishop of Westminster and conducted by Lord Nolan into child abuse in the Roman Catholic Church. (Between 1995 and 1999, 21 Roman Catholic priests of the 5,600 in Britain were convicted of child offences.) Nolan endorses *Safe from Harm*, and gives 83 recommendations to prevent abuse. Previous policies introduced in the Roman Catholic Church in 1994 were found wanting. The Nolan report does not specifically deal with organists; its Annex F of sample job descriptions did not include organists.

The Anglican and Roman Catholic policies are identical in their main provisions. Other denominations have produced their own similar guidance. The denomination, diocese or church may have its own guidance. The Roman Catholic church's point of reference is the Catholic Office for the Protection of Children and Vulnerable Adults (COPCA), address in Appendix 1.

Several denominations use the Churches Child Protection Advisory Service (CCPAS) "Guidance to Churches" model policies. CCPAS works across the denominations throughout the UK and provides child protection resources, training, and a telephone helpline. Details are given in Appendix 1.

Secular agencies such as NSPCC have produced useful guidance and co-operated with church bodies in developing appropriate policies.

We recommend that exactly the same standard of child protection should be followed regardless of the denomination or territory, and therefore believe that the guidance contained in these documents should be followed by all organists.

Some legal background

The law on child protection is mainly contained in Children Act 1989 and Protection of Children Act 1999, in addition to provisions of the criminal law generally. The 1989 Act establishes that "the best interests of the child" are the guiding principle in all decisions regarding children. The 1999 Act establishes a stricter regime to prevent unsuitable people working with children. It became law on 2 October 2000.

Legally, a **child** is someone up to the age of 13. Someone between the ages of 14 and 17 is legally a **young person** (Children and Young Persons Act 1933 s107). Child protection applies to both children and young persons, although some provisions become less relevant for young persons. For example, someone aged 16 may legally consent to sexual intercourse. For convenience, we refer to all people under 18 as children.

The two Acts mentioned above are complemented by the Criminal Justice and Court Services Act 2000, of which sections 26 to 42 introduce a **child disqualification** order which prevents a person from working with children. Further details are given in a statutory instrument SI 2000 No 2419.

Sexual Offences Act 2003 ss114-122, effective from 1 May 2004, introduces a **foreign travel order**, which can prevent an offender going overseas. Sections 123 to 129 introduce a **risk of sexual harm** order to stop an adult repeating offences such as sending pornography to a child. The Act also creates notification orders and sexual offences protection orders, which are designed to protect the public of any age.

On 15 September 2000, the Care Standards Act 2000 was introduced which makes provisions regarding looking after children. This is relevant for such places as boarding schools.

Responsibility for children generally rests with the parents or other adults who have parental responsibility, such as guardians. This responsibility can be delegated by the parents to any other adult on a temporary basis, as happens when a child is at school, at a choir practice or with a babysitter. Such a person is said to be in *loco parentis* (in the place of the parent) and has similar rights to a parent in dealing with the child in such areas as discipline and dealing with emergencies.

The criminal law on sexual offences was updated by Sexual Offences Act 2003 from 1 May 2004. The Act tightens up many definitions (such as consent), extends the scope of sexual offences and introduces some new offences, such as a new offence when a person aged 18 or over engages in any sexual activity with a child in his care. Many sentences are increased. Inappropriate touching of a child under 13 can attract life imprisonment.

Recruitment checking

All applicants for the post of organist must be vetted for child protection if the church has a children's choir. This applies even if the church has a separate choirmaster.

Recruitment checking comprises:

- providing references;
- signing a confidential declaration; and
- being cleared by the Criminal Records Bureau (CRB).

Protecting All God's Children says that all those who work with children must also complete an application form, be property interviewed and first be appointed for a probationary period, typically six months. Volunteers must be checked as thoroughly as paid workers, which accords with CCPAS advice.

With regards to **references**, *Protecting All God's Children* says that two references should be obtained, one of which must be from a current employer or previous church. It is possible for an organist to be someone still at school with no employer or previous church. In such cases, we recommend that the equivalent reference is sought from the head teacher.

The **confidential declaration** asks organists to tick yes or no to each of these questions:

1a Have you ever been convicted of a criminal offence (including any spent convictions under the Rehabilitation of Offenders Act 1974)?

1b Have you ever been cautioned by the police, given a reprimand or warning or bound over to keep the peace?

1c Are you at present under investigation?

1d Have you ever been found by a court exercising civil jurisdiction (including matrimonial or family jurisdiction) to have caused significant harm to a child or young person under the age of 18 years, or has any such court made an order against you on the basis of any finding or allegation that any child or young person was at risk of significant harm from you?

2a Has your conduct ever caused or been likely to cause significant harm to a child or young person under the age of 18, or put a child or young person at serious risk of harm?

2b To your knowledge, has it ever been alleged that your conduct has resulted in any of these things?

3 Has a child in your care or for whom you have or had parental responsibility ever been removed from your care, been placed on the Child Protection Register or been the subject of a care order, a supervision order, a child assessment order or an emergency protection order under the Children Act 1989, or a similar order under any other legislation?

4 Have you any health problems which might affect your work with children or young people under the age of 18?

5 Have you, since the age of 18, ever been known by any name other than that given below?

6 Have you, during the past five years, had any home address other than that given below?

The form must be signed and dated, and give the applicant's name, address and date of birth. Any "yes" answer must be accompanied by relevant details.

A determined abuser is unlikely to volunteer details, which is why there is a system of checking.

The **Criminal Records Bureau** was established in 2002 to provide certificates to individuals summarising their criminal record, or stating that they have no criminal record. It is established under Police Act 1997 s112-127.

The Bureau will issue three types of certificate:

- criminal conviction certificate;
- detailed certificate; and
- enhanced certificate.

These are respectively known as:

- basic disclosure;
- standard disclosure; and
- enhanced disclosure.

The first certificate is not yet available. When it is, any individual may obtain a certificate which lists all unspent convictions, including police cautions. If a person has no unspent convictions, the certificate will state that.

Protecting All God's Children says that all who have access to church premises (ie key holders) and who do not require a higher certificate, must produce a criminal conviction certificate when available. This will include all adult members of a choir that includes children. This requirement has proved controversial as being unnecessary and intrusive, and is being challenged by bellringers. We have been informed of adult members of choirs found guilty of abusing children where contact was made in the choir.

A **conviction** is where a court has found you guilty of a criminal offence, such as theft or criminal damage. It does not include most fines for motoring or tax offences which are regarded as civil penalties. Police cautions are included as you can only be cautioned if you admit the offence.

A conviction is **spent** when sufficient time has passed for it to be considered irrelevant for most purposes. This law prevents a youthful indiscretion blighting one's whole life. A period of imprisonment of more than 2½ years is never spent. Shorter periods of imprisonment and other penalties, such as fines and community service orders, are spent after periods of between six months and ten years depending on the severity of the penalty. In general, a spent conviction does not have to be disclosed. The concept of spent convictions was introduced by Rehabilitation of Offenders Act 1974. However those who work with children must always disclose details even of spent convictions under Rehabilitation of Offenders Act 1974 (Exceptions) Order 1975.

About one fifth of the UK adult population has a criminal record. The majority put the matter behind them and go on to lead lawful and responsible lives.

A **standard disclosure** is available on joint application with the applicant and a registered person, usually an employer, both of whom must sign the application. This certificate also includes details of spent convictions. The 1974 Act provides a list of circumstances when spent convictions must be disclosed.

An **enhanced certificate** is the most comprehensive of all, and is the certificate needed for an organist. It checks the applicant against four files:

- criminal records (for all convictions, including spent ones);
- information held under Education Act 2002 s142 (sometimes known as "LIST 99" held by Department for Education and Skills;
- the Protection of Children Act 1999 list held by the Department of Health (and known as the Po Ca list); and
- information held by the local police.

Local police may disclose acquittals and arrests which did not lead to charges. It will give (subject to some exclusions) local intelligence such as known associates.

For such a certificate, the employer must be registered with the Bureau (or with an umbrella body which has registered with the Bureau) and the job must involve working with children. The applicant must agree to comply with a strict code of conduct. Organists complete exactly the same form as Sunday School teachers, youth workers, clergy, bellringers, scout masters, school teachers and anyone else who may have unsupervised access to children.

In practice, the church is usually registered through a central body such as the diocese. This requires the church to follow the policy of that central body. Each parish or church appoints a child protection officer. The organist must see that officer in person with documents proving the organist's identity. At least one document must contain a photograph, such as a passport or new driving licence. Details of what documents are suitable are provided in notes with the form. The form must be completed by both the applicant and child protection officer. This form is sent to the registered umbrella body (usually the diocese or similar central church body). This body countersigns the application and sends it to the Bureau. They take about two months to check, but hope to reduce this period.

The certificate is sent to both the applicant and the employer. It records details under each of the four boxes. If there is nothing to report, it says "nothing reported". A certificate does not mean that anyone can absolutely guarantee that the person is safe — every offender has to commit a first offence. Also some offences may not be disclosed, particularly those committed overseas. There is also no disclosure of prosecutions originated from Customs and Excise (now HM Revenue and Customs) or British Transport Police, though it is hoped this will be resolved soon. Despite these shortcomings, the certificate does indicate that there is no recorded reason to exclude the applicant. It is believed that in the first year of operation, about a dozen church volunteers were found to be unsuitable.

A certificate relates to a particular post. Originally, this was taken to mean that an organist must be checked for a new position even though he has already been checked for another position, such as when the organist is a school teacher.

However, portability of CRB disclosures is now accepted. Each organisation should decide what portability to accept. For the Church of England, the conditions laid down in *Protecting All God's Children* are:

- The disclosure must be less than two years old.
- The person must still be in the same job or post for which the disclosure was sought.
- The disclosure must be clear (ie nothing disclosed).
- The disclosure must be of the same level as that required, ie an enhanced certificate where appropriate.
- A disclosure for working with vulnerable adults is not adequate for working with children, and vice versa.
- A reference must be obtained from the employer or appointer that the person was appointed following the disclosure, and that the person is still in post.
- The date and reference number of the disclosure must be recorded, with the name and date of birth of the applicant.
- The applicant's identity must be verified as if making a new application.

If any of these conditions cannot be met, a new certificate must be sought.

A certificate has no time limit. Once an organist has been checked for a position, there is no legal requirement to check again. Organists who were appointed before the Criminal Records Bureau started are not required to be checked under this system, though a church may decide to do so voluntarily. The Church of England now recommends that a new confidential disclosure and CRB certificate is obtained every three years. The CRB's view is that each denomination should make its own decision. It is good practice that all who work with children are checked.

Disclosure of any matter does not automatically prevent a person being appointed. A judgment must be made on the relevance of the disclosed matter. Any disclosure in the second or third boxes (offences in an educational or health post) and any disclosure of a child-related offence will almost certainly exclude the applicant. The view is that a child offender rarely changes his nature. This may seem tough and unforgiving to the offender, but protecting children is a higher priority.

Protecting All God's Children states that any **positive disclosure** must first be checked with the applicant. If he disputes the disclosure, this must be taken up with the CRB. Where there is a positive disclosure, a **risk assessment** must be conducted by a professionally qualified person or a panel. This assessment comprises advice to the employer or appointer, who makes the final decision. A panel from an adjacent diocese is recommended if an appeal is made against the risk assessment.

For other offences, consideration is based on:

- the seriousness of the offence;
- the nature of the offence; and
- how long ago it happened.

A single offence of shoplifting 30 years ago is unlikely to exclude, but a recent offence for violence may well do so, even if the violence was against an adult. A recent ban for drink-driving may be relevant if the position includes driving children. At the least, it is expected that the child protection officer will question the applicant about any conviction disclosed.

Enhanced certificates are only required for those who have *supervision* of children. Those who only have regular contact will need just the basic certificate. This means that **adults in the choir** and members of the congregation do not have to be checked as thoroughly as organists. It is recommended that adults in the choir at least be asked to complete the self-declaration form. If they refuse, or disclose a child-related offence, it is necessary to exclude them from a choir with children present. *Protecting All God's Children* introduces a new requirement that adults in a choir who do not need an enhanced certificate should obtain a standard criminal conviction certificate if they have regular contact with children. Some choir adults may need an enhanced certificate, such as if they drive children or do any individual teaching or testing. This may all seem draconian, but we have learned of choir adults using their position to groom children and then abusing them.

In February 2004, the Criminal Records Bureau was severely criticised by the National Audit Office for overspending and not being able to process applications promptly enough.

There was also criticism of police vetting when it was discovered that Ian Huntley had been investigated in 1996 for under-age sex, and had been reported by a deputy head teacher, among at least seven allegations made about him. Huntley secured a job as a school caretaker in Soham which enabled him to murder the 10-year-old schoolgirls Holly Wells and Jessica Chapman in 2002. No references had been taken up for Huntley.

Child abuse

There are four types of child abuse:

- physical abuse;
- neglect;
- emotional abuse; and
- sexual abuse.

Physical abuse includes inflicting any action leading to actual or likely injury to a child. This includes such actions as hitting, poisoning and suffocation. It also includes a failure to prevent injury.

There is a condition known as Munchausen's Syndrome. The Oxford Textbook of Psychiatry defines Munchausen's Syndrome by Proxy as "a form of child abuse in which the parents, or carers, give false accounts of symptoms in their children and may fake signs of illness (to draw attention to themselves). They seek repeated medical investigations and needless treatment for their children." The government issued guidance for professionals working in situations where Munchausen's is suspected in *Safeguarding Children in whom Illness is Fabricated or Induced (2002)*.

Evidence by its pioneer, Prof. Sir Roy Meadow, has been successfully challenged in UK courts, though the existence of the Syndrome remains generally accepted.

Neglect is a persistent or severe neglect of a child, such as failing to protect a child from starvation, cold or danger.

Emotional abuse is significant or potential adverse effects on the emotional and behavioural development of a child caused by persistent or severe emotional ill-treatment or neglect.

It should be appreciated that abuse involves much more than a temporary upset or hurt. The authors know of an organist suspended merely for calling a choirboy a "twerp".

Sexual abuse is actual or potential involvement of a dependent, developmentally immature child or adolescent in sexual activity they do not truly comprehend and to which they are unable to give informed consent. Much public concern about child protection relates to sexual abuse, though this is the reason for only 11% of children being on the child protection registers (with a further 16% for more than one type of abuse).

Code of Practice

Safe from Harm lists 13 recommendations:

1   Adopt a policy statement on safeguarding the welfare of children.

2   Plan the work of the organisation so as to minimise situations where the abuse of children may occur.

3   Introduce a system whereby children may talk with an independent person.

4   Apply agreed procedures for protecting children to all paid staff and volunteers.

5   Give all paid staff and volunteers clear roles.

6   Use supervision as a means of protecting children.

7* Treat all would-be paid staff and volunteers as job applicants for any position involving contact with children.

8* Gain at least one reference from a person who has experience of the applicant's paid work or volunteering with children.

9* Explore all applicants' experience of working or contact with children in an interview before appointment.

10* Find out whether an applicant has any conviction for criminal offences against children.

11 Make paid and voluntary appointments conditional on the successful completion of a probationary period.

12 Issue guidelines on how to deal with the disclosure or discovery of abuse.

13 Train paid staff and volunteers, their line managers or supervisors, and policy makers in the prevention of child abuse.

* These guidelines were issued before Protection of Children Act 1999 and the start of the Criminal Records Bureau. These subsequent developments can impose stricter requirements as previously explained.

In practice

In general, the law says what you should not do, rather than what you should do.

Some basic practical principles are given in Annex C of the Nolan Report 2001. Although written for the Roman Catholic Church, it is good guidance for all churches.

You must

- treat all children and young people with respect;
- provide an example of good conduct you wish others to follow;
- ensure that whenever possible there is more than one adult present during activities with children and young people, or at least that you are within sight or hearing of others;
- respect a young person's right to personal privacy;
- encourage young people and adults to feel comfortable and caring enough to point out attitudes or behaviour they do not like;
- remember that someone else might misinterpret your actions, no matter how well intentioned;
- be aware that even physical contact with a child or young person may be misinterpreted;
- recognise that special caution is required in moments when you are discussing sensitive issues with children or young people;
- operate within the Church's principles and guidance and any particular procedures of the diocese, parish, order or club;
- challenge unacceptable behaviour and report all allegations/suspicions of abuse;
- provide access for young people to talk to others about any concerns they may have.

You must not

- have inappropriate physical or verbal contact with children or young people;
- allow yourself to be drawn into inappropriate attention-seeking behaviour;
- make suggestive or derogatory remarks or gestures in front of children or young people;

- jump to conclusions about others without checking facts;
- either exaggerate or trivialise child abuse issues;
- show favouritism to any individual;
- rely on your good name or that of the Church to protect you;
- believe 'it could never happen to me';
- take a chance when common sense, policy or practice suggests another more prudent approach.

You should give guidance and support to inexperienced helpers.

Recommended practice

To provide some guidance, the authors set out their interpretation of what the requirements mean in practice.

1 Have adequate supervision

There should always be at least two adults present at a choir practice attended by children, and both must have been satisfactorily checked by the Criminal Records Bureau. It is good practice that at least one adult is a woman. Assuming that one adult is the choirmaster, it is often possible to organise a rota of adults (usually women) to be the **second adult**. Most churches love rotas and will enjoy producing one more.

There should be arrangements for an emergency standby if the second adult cannot attend or forgets. The second adult should pay attention to what is going on at the choir practice, which usually means sitting at the front facing the children and not becoming engrossed in a novel or crossword puzzle. One of the functions of a second adult is to be a witness if any incident happens or is alleged.

The second adult should be present at least 10 minutes before the choir practice as children arrive, and should stay until the last child has left.

If the choir is particularly large, it may be desirable to have more than two adults. Child-minding groups must be registered with a local authority and comply with various regulations. One requirement is to have one adult for the first eight children aged at least 9, and another adult for each further 12 children. This means three adults for 21 or more children aged between 3 and 8. The ratio is one adult per eight children under the age of 8. A church choir is not a registered child group and so does not have to comply, but it is good practice that it does follow this guideline.

The requirement for a second adult is not restricted to choir practices. It applies whenever you have custody of a child, and so will include private tuition (such as rehearsing a solo) or when testing a child alone for an RSCM award.

2 Have clear delivery and collection arrangements

A child is not in your custody until delivered to your care. Parents should be told not to leave young children until both adults are present, and should escort young children to the place where the practice is being held and not simply to the church entrance.

Parents may decide that the child may come on their own when sufficiently old. Most child welfare bodies agree that this is usually around the age of 10, but the decision must be made by the parents for their own children. Entrances to premises must be well-lit. Children must not be expected to walk down dark passages alone.

If a parent fails to collect a child, an adult must stay with the child. After waiting perhaps 5 or 10 minutes, you should try phoning the parent. If there is no reply, you should keep the child at church in case the parents turn up late. If they still do not arrive, take the child to their home yourself. You should not leave the child at the home until you see the child go indoors. If there is no-one at home, the child must stay with you, even if it means the child going to your home. You should first return to the church, in case the parent turned up late. If you have other contact details, such as for a grandparent or neighbour, you may try contacting that person to see if the child may be delivered there. You may also ask the child for such a contact. Otherwise, if you cannot contact the parents after an hour, you must call the police.

3 Have contact details

For each child, you must record:

- name;
- date of birth (so you know the age);
- address;
- at least one telephone number.

You should give parents details of your own name, address and telephone number, and those of the minister and church's child protection officer.

If a child has any medical condition which could affect them during choir practice, the choirmaster should be informed of this and told what to do. Examples of such conditions include asthma, epilepsy and certain personality disorders.

A register should be kept, recording attendance at all choir practices, services and other choir-attended occasions. If a child is late, the time of arrival should be recorded. You must not allow a child to leave the choir practice early except by prior arrangement, even if the child is collected.

4 Have First Aid available

The church authorities should have First Aid and an accident book readily available to you. It is advisable to have a First Aid kit in a choir vestry or where you are practising. In the Church of England, it is the churchwardens' function to provide it.

If a child has an accident, you should deal with it to the best of your ability, possibly using the skills of your second adult. The accident must be recorded in the accident book and be notified to the parents as soon as possible. This applies even to minor accidents — a cut finger can turn septic.

If it is necessary to call an ambulance, you do this first. Then notify the parents. Then obtain further assistance such as from a standby second adult or the minister.

You must not prescribe any medicine to a child unless, exceptionally, you have appropriate medical qualifications to do so. If a child needs to take medicine during a practice, you should hold the medicine and administer it in accordance with the instructions. In practice, the second adult is well placed to perform such tasks.

5 Know the limits of discipline

An organist or other choir trainer will routinely administer discipline in the form of telling children to stop talking and pay attention. We recommend that the standard a choirmaster follows should be the same as for state schools.

Naughtiness from children is normal. Merely telling off a child is not a matter which need concern anyone. However any rebuke should be the mildest necessary to have the desired effect. You should be careful not to be intimidating or bullying. You must never threaten a child, except with reporting them to their parents. A child should never be ridiculed or humiliated. A child who has difficulty finding hymn numbers or remembering what you said five minutes ago needs help, not discipline.

Discipline should be immediate and should rarely involve more than a rebuke. If it is necessary to raise your voice, this should be to the whole choir rather than just one child. A child should never fear that you may be about to hit him or her. Never lose your temper. If a rebuke is insufficient, a possible further sanction is to make a child sit nearer to you or stand near you. Where children are encouraging each other in naughtiness or are annoying each other, you should separate them.

Making deductions from choir pay is ineffective. If normal discipline does not contain the problem, you must discuss the matter first with the minister and then, possibly, with the parents. Expelling a child should always be the last resort, but should not be avoided if that is necessary. In the Church of England, an organist may not expel any member of the choir without the agreement of the vicar.

If a child is playing with something, confiscate it until the end of the practice or service. The item should then be returned to the child, except if you think it is something the child should not have (like cigarettes) which you should return to the parents. Children and choirmasters often forget about returning items, and choir cupboards can accumulate a treasure chest of confiscated items.

Discipline should be administered by the choirmaster. Other adults, such as sidesmen and choir adults, should only deal with a naughty choir child if absolutely necessary, to prevent damage for example. Other adults should not otherwise give a child a telling-off but should report the matter to the choirmaster. Discipline is compromised if adults in the church each seek to enforce their own standards and methods. They could put themselves at risk if they discipline a child inappropriately.

What appears to be misbehaviour may just be confusion. Church services, with various books and times to stand and sit, can be difficult to follow for young children. It is a good idea to have a **buddy system** whereby every new child is assigned to a responsible older child to help them in these areas. If a child gets something wrong, assume it is confusion unless it is clearly misbehaviour.

6 Never ask a child to keep a secret

A child must never be told to keep something a complete secret. A child must always be allowed to tell at least one parent what you have told them.

Keeping secrets is part of the grooming process used by child abusers. Any evidence that you are asking a child to keep a secret can raise suspicions.

If the secret is innocent, such as a surprise for a parent's birthday:

- refer to the secret as a "surprise";
- make clear that the child will eventually be able to tell; and
- ensure that there is at least one other adult with whom the child can share the surprise.

Similarly, you should not promise a child that you will keep a secret.

At a purely practical level, children often have great difficulty keeping secrets. So it is probably better to avoid surprises.

7 Your own conduct

Your own conduct can help prevent incidents and accusations. You should always remember that children are people in their own right, with their own rights to dignity and respect, however young.

You must:

- not appear before children while under the influence of alcohol or drugs;
- be careful about your speech, tone of voice and body language;
- only supervise a child washing or using the toilet if necessary (which is most unlikely for a child capable of singing in a choir), and otherwise respect the child's privacy;
- never mock, humiliate, harass or embarrass a child;
- never scapegoat, ridicule or reject a child;
- avoid any remark which could be regarded as sexually suggestive or threatening;
- avoid favouritism;
- discourage "crushes" or any inappropriate attention the child shows to you;
- prevent other children engaging in bullying and mockery.

You should avoid giving children **lifts in your car** unless the parent has given specific consent. You should not give a lift to any child who has displayed a crush or similar inappropriate behaviour to you. If giving a lift is unavoidable, the child must sit in the back.

An element of fun in a children's choir practice can help prevent misbehaviour and false allegations. Many singing methods can be taught as a game. Part of the practice can be spent asking children what news they have. Young children love telling you what has happened to them.

8 Get permission for photographs

You should be careful about taking photographs or videos of children, and even more careful what you do with them. If you wish to publish a photograph of a child, such as in a choir newsletter or church magazine, it is advisable to get the parent's permission first, unless it is a crowd scene where it is difficult to identify any particular face.

Physical contact

It is sometimes said that an adult must not touch a child under any circumstances. This is not true.

Useful guidance is provided under section 550A of Education Act 1996, introduced on 1 September 1998 (by Education Act 1997 s4) and explained by Department for Education and Employment guidance issued at the time. (This department is now known as Department for Education and Skills, or DfES.) This applies to state schools, but as we recommend that churches maintain the same discipline procedures as state schools, this guidance should be followed by church choirs.

Corporal punishment must never be used. This includes smacking, cuffing round the ear, tweaking the ear, and hitting choirboys on the head with a hymn book. You must not use corporal punishment even if the parents say you may.

Everyone has the right to use reasonable force to protect themselves from attack, however young the assailant. Reasonable force should be sufficient to overpower the assailant and not extend to retribution. Most adults do not realise their own strength, particularly with regard to children. You should be very careful about using force in such circumstances. It is essential that the second adult notes what happened.

You may use reasonable force to prevent a child from:

- committing a criminal offence;
- injuring themselves or others;
- damaging property, including the child's own property;
- engaging in any behaviour prejudicial to good order.

There is no legal definition of **reasonable force**, but DfES guidelines say there are two relevant considerations:

- circumstances must be sufficient to justify force, failing which even the mildest force can be construed as assault. Trivial offences, such as dropping litter, do not justify force;

- the degree of force must be proportionate to the circumstances of the incident and the seriousness of the behaviour or its consequences. Any force must be the minimum necessary to achieve the desired result. The degree of force will also depend on the sex and age of the child.

Examples where reasonable force is usually justified are listed as including:

- fighting;
- vandalism, including being about to commit vandalism;
- risk of accident, dangerous play, or handling dangerous materials;
- running in a way likely to cause an accident;
- trying to abscond;
- serious disruption.

Where force is used, it should be in a way likely to cause no injury to the child, nor should it cause the least injury or pain.

Children who are fighting will often stop (and freeze) on hearing a sufficiently authoritative command from an adult. If that fails, you should try placing yourself between the children.

Sometimes reasonable force can be administered by blocking a child's path, or putting your hand on a child's back to steer them in a particular direction.

Only in "the most exceptional circumstances" should you use force which will cause pain or injury to a child. It is most unlikely that you will ever be able to justify:

- holding a child by the neck or collar so that breathing may be restricted;
- slapping, punching or kicking a child;
- twisting or forcing limbs against a joint;
- tripping up a child;
- holding or pulling a child's hair.

You should always try a non-physical method of dealing with a matter if possible. In some circumstances, such as a child about to run into a road, that may not be possible.

If force is used, a contemporaneous written report must be made. This must record:

- the name of the child;
- date, time and place;

- who witnessed the incident;

- reason for using force;

- how the incident began and progressed, including details of the child's behaviour and what steps (if any) were taken to calm the situation before using force;

- what force was used, how it was applied, and for how long;

- the child's response and the outcome;

- details of any injury suffered by the child, by the adult, and to any property.

Any other adult present should make a similar record. These records should be kept factual and avoid expressing opinions.

You must report any such incident promptly to your church's child protection officer. You may also wish to report it to the minister and the child's parents or guardians.

While much of the guidance is concerned with force to maintain discipline, the guidance does deal with other forms of physical contact. It is recognised that some physical contact is necessary to administer first aid, for example.

Physical contact can be justified in the course of physical activities, such as sports coaching. This could apply in instructing children in singing posture, though normally telling a child should be sufficient.

Sometimes it may seem appropriate to provide a cuddle, arm round the shoulder, or similar action to a child who is upset or hurt. This is not ruled out, but great care should be exercised, particularly for older children, those of the opposite sex, and those from certain minority backgrounds where such contact may be considered less acceptable. Even well-intentioned contact can be misconstrued.

In practice, if you follow reasonable conduct with restraint and common sense, you are unlikely to go wrong.

Guidance on physical contact is also contained in Annex D of the Nolan Report 2001:

> *Any physical contact should only take place in public.*
>
> *Physical contact should reflect the child's needs, not the adult's.*
>
> *Physical contact should be age appropriate, and initiated by the child, not the adult.*
>
> *Avoid any physical activity that is, or may be thought to be, sexually stimulating to the adult, or the child.*

Children have the right to decide how much physical contact they have with others (except in exceptional circumstances when they need medical attention).

Team members should monitor one another in the area of physical contact.

They should feel able to help each other by pointing out anything that could be misunderstood.

If an adult persists in inappropriate touch with a young person this must be challenged.

If there are concerns about an adult's contact with a young person, advice must be sought.

These notes are drawn from guidance originally given by CCPAS to Mothers Union. In their latest guidance CCPAS, says:

Keep everything public. A hug in the context of a group is very different from a hug behind closed doors.

Employment of children

A child is not regarded as employed when taking part in a religious service or a choir practice for a religious service. This specific provision is contained in Children and Young Persons Act 1933 s30(1). It applies whether or not the child is paid for being in the choir.

If a child is engaged in other work, including performing in a show or secular concert, you must consider the requirements of employment law for children. The current regulations are The Children (Protection at Work) Regulations SI 1998 No 276, which became effective from 4 August 1998. There are separate regulations for child performers.

In Scotland, the main law is Children and Young Persons (Scotland) Act 1937. Although both the Scottish Parliament and the Welsh Assembly have indicated possible changes to their own laws, no such changes appear yet to have been made. In Northern Ireland, the law is governed by Children (Northern Ireland) Order 1995. Therefore the law seems to be about the same throughout the United Kingdom, though some of the authority derives from different Acts.

This is an area where European law is beginning to have an influence. It is advisable to check details with your local authority in plenty of time.

For these purposes, a "child" is someone under the age of 16. From the age of 16, there are almost no work restrictions.

The main provisions of the law are:

- a child under 13 may do no paid work, except light work for a parent (such as helping in a shop or on a farm);
- at 13, a child may do light work as permitted by the local authority's bye-laws.

When a child does work, the maximum hours must not exceed any one of these limits:

- eight hours a day at 15; five hours under 15 (except for Sundays and school days);
- 25 hours a week, except that a 15-year old may work 35 hours in a non-school week;
- four hours in a single shift, with at least one hour's break before the next shift;
- (from 11 October 2000) 12 hours in any week the child is required to attend school.

A child must have at least two weeks without work during a summer holiday. In the last year of compulsory schooling, a child may engage in work experience as approved by the local authority.

Under Education (Pupil Registration) Regulations 1995, a pupil is not generally allowed to take time off school for paid employment except for performances with a local authority licence. A head teacher is not allowed to give permission for a child to be absent from school for an audition or rehearsal, other than rehearsals that fall within the period of a licence.

A licence for a long absence, such as cathedral choir tour, must include provisions for maintaining a child's education unless in a holiday period. This usually means private tuition. The private tutor need not be a fully qualified teacher, but must be approved by the licensing authority, and is limited to teaching a maximum of 12 children at a time if they are of a similar age and standard, failing which the maximum is six children.

In England, a child may leave school on the last Friday in June in the school year in which the child reaches the age of 16. The law is slightly different in Scotland and Northern Ireland.

An employer who engages a child must conduct a risk assessment under Health and Safety (Young Persons) Regulations SI 1997 No 135. This is in addition to any risk assessment conducted in respect of adult workers.

For performances, which includes singing and playing instruments, there are further laws under Children and Young Persons Act 1963 ss37-43, plus regulations under the Children (Performance) Regulations SI 1968 No 1728. This imposes no further restriction if:

- the performance is organised by the school; or
- no admission charge is made; or
- the work involves fewer than three days in six months.

The term "performance" is not defined, so there is scope for local authorities to make their own decisions in marginal cases. In practice, a performance is usually regarded as something which is directed.

For other performances, a local authority licence is required by the person producing the performance. Such a licence commonly includes provisions about maximum hours and the child needing to be chaperoned. Some of these restrictions were reduced from 1 February 2000 under SI 2000 No 10. To grant a licence, the local authority must be satisfied that:

- the child's education will not suffer;
- the child's health will not suffer;
- the places of performance and rehearsal conform to standards laid down in the regulations; and
- the conditions of the licence will be observed.

An application form must be signed by the child's parent or guardian, or the person with whom the child lives. The licence must be sought at least 21 days before the performance, though a local authority has a discretion to waive this time limit.

The licence will show:

- the child's name (with any stage name);
- a photograph of the child;
- the nature of the performance;
- the place of performance;

- the actual dates of performance, or the number of days of performance within a six-month period.

Rehearsals do not count towards the total number of performances, but must be included in the hours of work. A child may work at night if it is "absolutely essential" and a further set of restrictions are followed.

There are separate provisions regarding children taking part in sport, working as models, or engaging in dangerous acts (such as in a circus).

A child may make a valid contract of employment at any age, but the contract may only be enforced against a child if the contract, as a whole, is beneficial to the child *(Clements v LNWR [1894])*.

A child is liable to pay income tax from any age, but every child is entitled to a full personal allowance, so it is unlikely that a child is likely to pay income tax.

A child is liable to pay national insurance (of any class) only from the age of 16. The liability arises from the first pay day after the 16th birthday and applies to the whole of the pay, even if some of it was earned before the 16th birthday.

If you learn of abuse

A good choirmaster will win a proper place in children's affection. A child will tell you many details about his or her private life. Much of it will be childish trivia. However it is possible that a child will tell you something which indicates abuse. In such cases, you must be very careful what you do.

The advice is:

- listen carefully and take the matter seriously;
- avoid leading questions;
- do not make any judgmental comments;
- assure the child that he or she is doing the right thing in telling you;
- carefully make a written note of what was said as soon as possible;
- report the facts to the child protection officer, regardless of your views about the matter;
- tell the child what you intend to do.

You must not:

- attempt to investigate the matter yourself;

- promise confidentiality to the child;

- speak about the matter to the accused;

- discuss the matter with anyone other than those officially involved.

Once you have passed on the information to your child protection officer, you should generally take no further action until asked to do so. Exceptionally, if you believe the child protection officer has not taken the matter sufficiently seriously, you have the right as a member of the public to report your concern to the police.

If a child is being systematically abused, particularly sexually abused, the child may be groomed not to tell anyone. The child may be told that something is "our secret" and they will be not believed or may be put into care if the secret is revealed. Even in such cases a child may let something slip which alerts you.

If an adult tells you of suspicions about a child, you should pass on the comments to your child protection officer. If an adult tells you of abuse he or she suffered as a child, the adult should be told to speak to the child protection officer. The child protection officer has a procedure for dealing with allegations.

Equally, children live in a fantasy world, fed by fanciful programmes, books, films and computer games. Children can say the most outrageous things which have no truth in them. That is why it is important that anything revealed is dealt with by someone with training and experience.

If you are accused

Every organist's nightmare is to be accused of child abuse himself. This section assumes that you are innocent. CCPAS reports that such false accusations are very rare in practice.

Children become "street-wise" and may make an allegation to get attention or to get back at you for being disciplined or not allowed to sing a solo. If you have followed the guidance in this chapter, such as having a second adult present, you will be in a strong position to demonstrate your innocence.

In this area, *Protecting All God's Children (2004)* is a welcome improvement on the previous guidance from bishops, which seemed to call for suspension in all circumstances, however baseless the accusation and however serious the consequences.

Under the 2004 guidelines, the investigation is co-ordinated by the diocesan child protection officer who must alert the statutory authorities. Confidentiality must be maintained so that only those who need to know anything are informed. The diocesan media communications officer manages media queries.

Under the 2004 guidelines, **suspension** is only automatic if you have been charged with a criminal offence against a child. Otherwise, *suspension is not automatic.* A decision to suspend may only be made after seeking legal advice and consulting with the diocesan child protection officer. Children's charities recommend that a person be suspended only if the police so advise. In some cases, suspension may be necessary because of excessive press interest.

Children's charities have policies which state that a worker would be suspended in consultation with social services and the police. There are two points to note about suspension:

- suspension should be seen as a neutral act — it does not assume a person's guilt (nor innocence);
- the reason a suspension is in consultation with the statutory authorities is that the act of suspension could "tip off" the alleged abuser giving them opportunity of silencing children and removing incriminating evidence before an investigation can commence.

An organist must always challenge any attempt to suspend him when these procedures have not been followed, such as when the minister has decided not to refer the matter to the diocesan child protection officer. To accept suspension when the procedure has not been followed leaves you open to accusations of a cover-up.

In some cases, you may agree to stand aside to assist an investigation. This is a matter solely for you to decide, though it may properly be suggested. Such standing aside is not a suspension. In other cases, it may be sufficient that your duties are curtailed to limit contact with children. You should only agree to any of these options after taking legal advice.

In no case, should you attempt to contact the child or the child's family until the investigation has been satisfactorily concluded.

Both you and the child are entitled to pastoral support. This must be from someone who is not involved in the investigation and is not providing support to the other party.

An investigation may lead the Crown Prosecution Service (CPS) to decide to bring proceedings. At that point, you must be suspended.

However, a lack of prosecution does not mean that the matter is over. If the CPS decides not prosecute, the agencies involved will be asked to provide reports which may be used in disciplinary proceedings. A professional risk assessment is undertaken by a person qualified to make it. This will determine whether you are considered safe to continue working with children. It may conclude that you may do so with additional supervision or after training.

Anyone who is cautioned or convicted for a sexual offence with children is barred from working with children. This also excludes them from singing in a choir with children. For a non-sexual offence against children, the person is barred except in exceptional circumstances.

However an investigation ends, all parties must be told of the outcome, including what arrangements have been made as a consequence and what lessons can be learned.

Little thought appears to have been given as to what to tell the choir and congregation while an investigation is pending. In the absence of suspension, it should be possible to say nothing. Any information passed between bodies must be strictly on a need-to-know basis.

With all scandals and rumours, imagination quickly fills in gaps in statements, usually with details more lurid than real. If there is a scandal, the choice is "all or nothing". It is ideal if the information can be kept completely confidential until the facts are established. This means that those who know say *nothing* to anyone else; it is not sufficient that information is passed with some details omitted as those details may be found out elsewhere. If the news does leak, as often happens in churches, it may be advisable to publish the facts. The effect of a scandal is minimised if you break the news yourself. However you should not act in a way which could compromise any criminal case. It is essential to get legal help.

Someone accused of child abuse is quickly demonised. There is a prevailing view of "no smoke without fire" (which is as untrue literally as it is untrue metaphorically). There have been instances of hostile reaction to innocent people.

If accused, it is essential to get a lawyer. Do not delay as the longer you leave it, the worse the problem will be.

The church may tell you what you must and must not do, but the church is only protecting its own interests. It is essential that you are advised on what is in your own interests. You still have rights. Properly designed child protection policies properly enforced are designed to protect all parties.

There are offences of libel and malicious falsehood which prevent people from spreading or publishing defamatory material. It may be in your interests for your lawyer to remind people of these facts. It may be in your interest to make a full statement to the press, choir parents and congregation if the church is refusing to do so. The church has no power to stop you exercising your rights, but you must act on proper legal advice, remembering the huge repercussions any disclosure may have. It is unlikely that any disclosure by you is appropriate if proper procedures have been followed on a need-to-know basis.

You should refrain from taking any action if the investigation is being conducted properly by the appropriate bodies and nothing is being disclosed improperly. However, if there is any breach in the investigation, you should not hesitate to act.

You are entitled to full pay during any period of suspension. You may bring proceedings to receive this pay without waiting for the investigation to finish.

If you are cleared, you may find it difficult to come back. Child abuse has become the one offence when, not only are you guilty until proven innocent, but where some will see you as guilty even after you have been proven innocent. Don't think that you can simply come back as if nothing has happened. At the least, you must allow choir members and choir parents to discuss what happened with you.

False accusations are not new. A hundred years ago, the eminent opera composer Giacomo Puccini was accused by his wife Elvira of having an affair with a servant girl who committed suicide. A court case in 1909 established that there had been no affair, and his wife was jailed for five months.

A summary of advice to an accused organist is:

- ensure that the matter is referred to the diocesan child protection officer (or equivalent) and to the statutory authorities and not left with the vicar or parish child protection officer;
- co-operate with proper authorities;
- consult a lawyer;

- do not accept suspension unless the matter has been dealt with properly, or you otherwise believe that suspension or standing aside is appropriate;

- insist on your pay during any period of suspension;

- consider with your lawyer what statements to make to the choir and congregation, and whether to take any action if the investigation is not conducted properly or if sensitive information is leaked.

Some cases

The majority of organists and others in the church cannot understand why anyone would want to abuse children. It is difficult for a normal person to imagine what pleasure can be gained from sexually abusing a child. However, our revulsion and bewilderment must never act as a cloak preventing our acknowledging that it does happen. This section gives a selection of actual reported cases.

Published examples include:

- a cathedral organist sentenced to five years in 2004 for sexual offences;

- a Roman Catholic priest sentenced to five years in 1997 for nine sex attacks, including one on a boy with learning difficulties;

- a choir tenor sentenced to four years in 1991 for sexual assault on boys aged between 12 and 14;

- a church organist jailed in 1991 for repeated sexual abuse on a 9-year old boy over six years;

- two vicars and a choirmaster imprisoned in 1988 on 21 specimen charges.

At the beginning of 2004, it was estimated that over 10,000 children had been abused by Roman Catholic clergy in the USA alone. Even bishops have appeared in court. Since 1990, the Church of England has had one bishop obliged to resign because of child abuse, another bishop appointed despite a criminal record for cottaging, and an archdeacon arrested for possessing child pornography, though no charges were brought.

One final observation

Most organists have to suffer supposed jokes about touching up choirboys and "playing with your organ".

These supposed jokes are not funny. They are distasteful, unfunny, tired, sad and pathetic. So are the people who repeat them.

7 Tax

Income Tax

Scope

All income for playing the organ is taxable. It does not matter whether the money is called fees, salary, wages, stipend, honorarium, allowance, expenses or anything else. Under UK law, income is taxed according to its nature, not what it is called.

However, the fact that fees are taxable does not always mean that any tax needs to be paid. Income tax is charged on net income, after deducting expenses, allowances and reliefs. Such deductions can reduce net income to zero or less.

Income tax is collected for **tax years**, which run from 6 April in one calendar year to 5 April in the next year. The tax year from 6 April 2005 to 5 April 2006 is shown as 2005/06.

At its simplest, income tax is calculated by:

- adding up all your income;
- subtracting tax-deductible items such as personal allowances and allowable expenses; and
- multiplying the balance by various percentages on slices of income.

Suppose you are a single person who is a music teacher earning £26,000 a year with no other income, reliefs or expenses. In 2005/06 your income tax will be calculated as:

income	£26,000
less personal allowance	£4,895
taxable income	£21,105
£2,090 taxed at 10%	£209.00
£19,015 taxed at 22%	£4183.30
£21,105 taxable at	£4392.30

And so, you will pay £4,392.30 a year in income tax.

The rates of personal allowance, tax bands and (sometimes) tax rates change each year in the Budget, but the method given above has remained unchanged for decades.

How tax is paid

An organist pays tax in one of two ways:

- by Pay As You Earn (PAYE); or

- a self-employed person by self assessment.

Which one applies depends on whether you are employed or self-employed. In this context, employment includes holding an office.

If you are employed, your income tax is normally deducted at source under PAYE by your employer. Every time you are paid, you receive a payslip showing how much tax has been deducted. Your employer pays this to HMRC (Inland Revenue before 18 April 2005) for you. Soon after the end of the tax year, you receive a form P60 from your employer which tells you how much you earned during the tax year and how much tax you paid. In the normal course of events, you do not have to do anything else about your tax as your employer does it all.

If you are self-employed, you receive payment without tax being deducted and must pay your own tax. You must complete a self assessment tax return which may be obtained from your local tax office. The address can be found in the local telephone directory under HM Revenue and Customs (or Inland Revenue, if printed before April 2005). Further details are given later.

So is the organist employed?

In most cases, yes. The answer for tax is not necessarily the same as for employment law (chapter 3), though in most cases the answer is the same.

Although the amount of tax for employed organists and self-employed organists uses the same figures and rates, there are still advantages of being taxed as self-employed:

(a) you pay the tax later;

(b) you may deduct a wider range of expenses; and

(c) you pay less national insurance.

Against this, you must remember that a self-employed organist does not have any employment rights, such as the National Minimum Wage, protection against unfair dismissal and the right to holidays with holiday pay, and paid sick leave.

However whether someone is employed or self-employed is a matter of fact to be determined in each case. It is not a matter of choice for the employer or for the employee. Guidance is given in a free HMRC leaflet IR 56.

For musicians, the distinction between employment and self-employment has often been marginal, and there have been several test cases. The tax authorities are obliged to follow the decision in a case where the facts are the same, and treat the case as guidance when facts are similar. Here are some tax cases:

Found to be employment

- a daytime teacher also teaching at an evening class *(Fuge v McClelland [1956])*

- a professional singer working four days a week as a lecturer of music at a college *(Walls v Sinnett [1986])*

Found to be self-employment

- an actor working part-time as a drama teacher *(Argent v Minister of Social Security [1968])*

- a freelance television vision mixer who worked for television companies on contracts for one or two days *(Hall v Lorimer [1993])*

The case *Hall v Lorimer* is a leading case which led to clarification of the position in HMRC's Employment Status Manual at ESM1094.

Benefits and expenses

Benefits in general

Income tax is not only paid on money you receive in cash. Income tax is also payable on benefits you receive for working, though there is a long list of exceptions.

Benefits in kind most commonly arise in employment, though they can arise in self-employment. For example if you give someone a music lesson in return for a pile of music, you are liable to pay tax on the value of the music as it is **payment in kind**.

Tax-free benefits

There are many benefits which are specifically exempt from income tax. Those which may be of relevance to organists include:

- pension contributions by the employer to an approved scheme;
- car parking near the place of work;
- canteen facilities, including tea and coffee;
- workplace nurseries and some other childcare facilities;
- mobile telephone;
- cheap or interest-free loans up to £5,000 a year;

- up to £8,000 in relocation expenses;
- accommodation and meals whilst working away from home;
- up to £5 personal expenses per day while away (£10 if overseas);
- up to £2 a week if you do some work from home;
- sports and recreational facilities;
- work-related training;
- long-service awards;
- Christmas and other annual parties up to £150 a year;
- medical check-ups.

Expenses in general

Income tax is only charged on the profit element of employment or self-employment, so some expenses incurred may be deducted from taxable income. However the rules are strict, and many items which seem to be expenses are not allowed. The rules are stricter for employees than for the self-employed.

Expenses in employment

An employee may deduct from his taxable income an expense if the employee "is obliged to incur and pay it as holder of the employment", and the expense is incurred "wholly, exclusively and necessarily in the performance of the duties of the employment" *(Income Tax (Earnings and Pensions) Act 2003 s336(1))*.

In practice, the only expenses an employee may claim are:

- subscriptions to professional bodies;
- special clothing;
- travelling in the course of employment;
- some books, music, shoes and similar;
- payments into an approved pension fund.

Some of these are discussed further below.

Expenses in self-employment

The main difference for the self-employed is that the expense does not have to be necessarily incurred, but it must be incurred wholly and exclusively for the purposes of the business.

In practice, magazines, recordings, and visits to concerts are more readily deductible from self-employed income as it is difficult for an employee to prove that such items are necessary for the employment.

Cathedral organists' accommodation

Because of its particular importance, special consideration is given to the taxation of accommodation usually provided for a cathedral organist. The issue is whether the organist is liable to pay tax at all on this benefit.

If taxable, the level of benefit on which the employee pays tax depends on the cost of providing the benefit. If the cost is less than £75,000 then the notional benefit is the annual rateable value of the property, or, if it is leased, the rent paid. If the cost of provision is over £75,000 the notional benefit is:

- its annual rateable value; plus
- an official rate of interest (currently 5%) on its value above £75,000.

These figures can easily give a taxable benefit of more than £5,000 a year.

There are three exceptions when accommodation for an employee is not a taxable benefit, namely when the accommodation is:

(a) necessary for proper performance of duties (such as caretaker);

(b) for the better performance of the duties and is customary; or

(c) needed to protect against a security risk.

A cathedral organist may be able to claim under one of the first two reasons, though (b) is the more likely. Note that the rules for organists are different from those for cathedral clergy who may claim exemption under separate rules.

For (a), the house must be within cathedral grounds and be a specific dwelling provided by the cathedral. This is unlikely to arise in practice.

For (b), HMRC accepts that it is customary for a cathedral organist to be accommodated, but the "better performance" may need to be demonstrated. An example is where the organist teaches at a boarding school and must be accessible during the day and night.

It is not necessary for the words "for the better performance of the duties" to appear in the contract of employment. What is relevant is the employment duties mean that the employee is regularly required to work outside normal hours at *short notice*.

Choral scholars who are employees are only entitled to the exemption if on a full-time course of study at a recognised institute of further or higher education.

Capital gains tax is payable when you sell a house or other item at a profit, though this is subject to many reliefs and allowances. There is an exemption for your main residence, but an individual or married couple may only have one main residence.

Sometimes an organist may be provided with accommodation but own another property. If so, the capital gains tax liability will arise when the other property is sold *unless* the organist intends to live in that property when he ceases to be cathedral organist. It is the *intention* that matters, so you can claim main residence relief even though you sold the house while still at the cathedral, or while employed at another cathedral.

Other benefits and expenses

Accommodation owned by organist

If you are employed and do some work from home, your employer may (from 6 April 2004) pay up to £2 a week tax-free for your home expenses.

You may claim for any direct household expenses incurred working at home and not reimbursed by your employer. HMRC's Employment Income Manual gives a music room used for business purposes as an example at EIM32836.

You may calculate a portion of household expenses equivalent to that room, such as one seventh of household expenses. These include council tax, water, gas, electricity and insurance. You can claim for business use of telephone and Internet, which may be calculated as an apportionment of total cost on any basis which appears fair.

Claiming some of your household bills for part of your house means that you lose the main residence relief for capital gains tax on the same proportion. In practice, this is subject to so many reliefs and allowances that the capital gains tax payable is unlikely to exceed the income tax saved.

Capital items

Any item you buy which is allowable but which is expected to last for more than one year is generally regarded as a capital item. Examples include pianos, organs, hi-fi, furniture and computers.

Instead of claiming the item as an expense, you may claim the capital allowance for plant and machinery used in a business. This is usually 25% on a reducing balance basis. So if you spend £1,000 on musical equipment, you claim capital allowances of £250 against your taxable income in year 1, and capital allowances of 25% of the balance of £750 (which is £187.50) in year 2, and so on, until you get rid of the item.

If the capital allowances claimed to the date of disposal plus disposal proceeds are less than the cost of the item, there is a balancing allowance which may be deducted from your income in the year of disposal. If capital allowances and disposal proceeds exceed the cost, there is a balancing charge which is added to your taxable income. There are some exceptions to this general rule.

Childcare

You cannot generally claim the cost of childcare as it is not incurred in your work but is incurred to allow you to work. (Tax law is full of such semantics.)

But there is a range of ways in which an employer can provide tax free childcare.

Workplace nurseries are exempt from tax and national insurance contributions if the nursery meets certain conditions. If your employer provides childcare, for example by buying places direct from a local childminder or nursery, the first £50 a week of the cost of providing the benefit is exempt from tax. The £50 exemption limit also applies to the national insurance contribution due on such a benefit. Similarly a £50 per week tax and national insurance exemption limit applies if the employee is provided with childcare vouchers. More information about the types of qualifying childcare can be found in the HMRC Internet site.

Clothing

As you must wear clothes anyway, clothing is only deductible if it is of a type not suitable for normal wear. Organ shoes therefore qualify. Robes and hoods only qualify if, exceptionally, it is a condition of your engagement that you *must* wear them; not that you are simply expected to or choose to. Even then, it is only the *replacement* of the robes which is deductible, not the original cost.

Evening dress and ball gowns for performing are not deductible as they can be worn outside your musical work (even if they never are). Specialist stage clothing is deductible. An organist may no longer claim for additional trousers worn out because of exceptional wear on the organ bench.

If clothing is tax-deductible, any repairs and laundry of it are also tax-deductible.

Gifts

Gifts which you receive from your employer are a taxable benefit, though the employer is able to pay your tax for you. Tips are taxable as income.

If you receive a gift from a third party, such as a bottle of wine for playing at a funeral, that gift legally belongs to your employer under the law of agency. If the employer agrees that you may keep it, it is only taxable if the value exceeds £250.

Loans

A loan from an employer of up to £5,000 creates no tax liability. A larger loan creates a tax liability if it is interest free or at a low rate of interest.

Medical expenses

There is no taxable benefit when your employer pays for you to have a health check-up. There is no taxable benefit if the employer pays medical expenses while you are overseas on work, or pays for insurance to cover such benefit (though you should note that you receive free medical treatment in all 25 European Union countries if in advance you have completed form E111, available from post offices).

Otherwise you are liable to tax on the amount your employer spends paying for medical treatment or for medical insurance (such as BUPA).

In the case *Prince v Mapp [1969]*, the High Court disallowed a claim from a professional guitarist for private surgery to a finger which hampered his playing. He admitted playing the guitar for pleasure as well as for money, so it was held that there was a dual purpose of business and personal use.

Music, books, magazines, records and concerts

An employed organist may claim for organ music which he needs to buy. The organist must be able to prove the "need" rather than want. He is unlikely to be able to claim for books, magazines, records or concerts, as it is difficult to see how these may be regarded as "necessary". The self-employed organist does not need to prove that expenses are necessary, so most of such expenditure is tax-deductible.

Parties and social activities

Annual parties at any time of the year are tax-free, provided the cost to the employer does not exceed £150 per person in the tax year. Incidental entertainment in the course of work, such as a bun fight after a special service, is also exempt.

Professional subscriptions

You may claim for subscriptions to a professional body if the body is:

- relevant to your work; and
- is on a list kept by HMRC.

It is not necessary for membership to be a condition of employment.

The list of bodies is very long, and may be accessed on HMRC's website. The Royal College of Organists and the Incorporated Society of Musicians are both on the list, so any fees to them are tax-deductible. The Guild of Church Musicians and Royal School of Church Music are charities. This means that you cannot claim tax relief on subscriptions, but you can make your payment under Gift Aid.

Telephones

There is no tax charge when the employer provides you with a telephone exclusively for your work. If your employer reimburses you for business calls from your private telephone, and such reimbursement includes a proportion of the rental charge, that proportion is chargeable to tax.

Provision of a mobile telephone is specifically exempt from tax. However the provision of other gadgets, such as personal organisers, is taxable. If the equipment provided by your employer is a computer, there is an exemption up to a certain limit linked to the cost of providing the computer. As long as the market value of the computer equipment is below £2500 when first provided, the benefit is considered exempt.

Training

Training provided by your employer which is related to your job is not a taxable benefit. So there is no tax liability if your employer sends you on a course on music, liturgy, child protection or first aid, for example. There is a separate tax exemption for longer courses, such as supporting a university student.

If you are an employee and incur your own training costs without reimbursement from your employer, no expense deduction is available because such an expense is not seen as being incurred "in the performance" of your employment duties.

If you are self-employed, training which you pay for yourself is tax deductible to the extent that it is wholly and exclusively for your self-employment.

Travelling

Commuting from home to work is not a tax-deductible expense. If the employer reimburses any commuting charge, it is taxable. There are a few exceptions for:

- disabled employees;
- occasionally working late when public transport is unreliable;
- a car-sharing scheme which has broken down;
- times when public transport is disrupted for any reason.

Sometimes it can be an issue of where the place of work is, as most organists will have a music room or study in their home from which they do some work. In practice, it is difficult to establish a home as a place of work. Even where a deduction is granted for using the home as a workplace it doesn't mean that travel from home to the place where the main work is performed will qualify for a deduction. It was held that travel was not allowable in the case of *Newsom v Robertson [1952]* which related to a self-employed barrister. This decision was upheld recently by *Powell v Jackman [2004]* in which a self employed milkman was claiming the cost of travel from his home to depot. This position was also reflected in the employment case of *Kirkwood v Evans [2002]*, when again travel between home and the workplace was not allowed even though some work was carried out at home.

Travel in the course of work is tax-deductible (or tax free if refunded by the employer). If an employee uses his own vehicle in the course of work, the employee may be reimbursed tax-free at a rate of up to 40p a mile for the first 10,000 miles, and 25p for any further miles in the tax year. An additional 5p a mile may be claimed for each passenger carried. The rate is 24p a mile for motorcycles and 20p for a push bike.

These rates do not establish a legal right to be paid that amount. That is always a matter of negotiation between you and your employer. If paid less, you may claim the shortfall as a tax-deductible expense. If paid more, you are taxed on the excess.

If you have two jobs with different employers, travel between them is generally not tax deductible.

Travel overseas is more generous as you can even claim for a husband or wife to accompany you, subject to limits. And if you are employed to play the organ on an oilrig, you are specifically exempted from tax on the value of the helicopter ride there.

Whilst away on a qualifying business journey, you can claim the reasonable costs of accommodation and meals. You are also not taxed on personal incidental expenses borne by the employer on occasions when you have to stay away from home overnight. Payments up to £5 a night in the UK or £10 a night overseas are exempt. This payment is meant to cover such items as newspapers, laundry, confectionery, bar bills, and sightseeing trips.

National Insurance

National insurance is a separate charge on income. An employee and the employer pay class 1. The self-employed pay classes 2 and 4.

The self-employed pay less national insurance but are entitled to less social security cover. In particular, they cannot claim jobseeker's allowance. The employed and self-employed are both entitled to state retirement pension, provided they have paid sufficient national insurance.

If you are employed in one job, and self-employed, you pay class 1 on your income from employment, and class 2 and class 4 from self-employment. However the total national insurance of all classes cannot exceed the maximum class 1 payable by an employee.

National insurance is only payable on earnings, not on other sources of income such as pensions or investments. National insurance is only paid between the ages of 16 and normal retirement age. Normal retirement age is 65 for men. It is 60 for women born before 6 April 1950; 65 for women born after 5 April 1955; and between 60 and 65 for women born between 6 April 1950 and 5 April 1955.

Value Added Tax

Value added tax (VAT) is charged on goods and services. The standard rate has been 17½% since 1992.

VAT is only likely to be of concern to organists who are self-employed. If your earnings from self-employment exceed an annual limit, you must register for VAT. From 1 April 2005, the limit is £60,000. This figure is reviewed each year. If your turnover is below this limit, you *may* register, though there is no obvious reason to do so.

You should also be careful if you work in conjunction with other people, such as passing tuition or performance work to others. It is possible that HM Revenue and Customs may decide that you are all running one business and aggregate your earnings so that, collectively, you exceed the registration threshold. There have been scores of cases on this, particularly involving pubs, hairdressers and mini-cabs.

For musicians, a relevant case is the VAT tribunal decision in *18816 Selwyn Dorfman [2004]*. Dorfman ran a band known as the Gershwin Gang of variable size and line-up. Engagers of the band dealt solely with Dorfman who set the fee. He then engaged the necessary musicians, usually including himself, and paid them from the fee. He argued that his income was solely that left over for himself and not the total amount. The tribunal held that the fee was the total amount for the booking, which was sufficient to require him to be VAT-registered.

If you are registered for VAT for another business activity, you must be careful that your musical activities are not also caught. This is because *you* are registered for VAT, not your business. If you are VAT-registered as a musician (or as anything else), you must charge VAT on all your fees (unless it is for something specifically exempt or zero-rated). If obliged to add VAT to organ fees, you are simply increasing your price which the church cannot reclaim. There are two ways to avoid this.

Robert Leach, one of the authors of this book is VAT-registered because of his earnings writing books. Customs directed him to charge VAT on fees for playing the organ. This was successfully challenged on the grounds that his organ playing was a hobby and not a business. The distinction is that the organist routinely spent more on music than he earned, and therefore it could not be run commercially. This depends on the facts of each individual case. HMRC would need to be convinced that the organ playing was a hobby. If there was consideration, the starting point would be that this was an economic activity, and therefore part of the VAT-registered business.

A supply of **education** is exempt under Value Added Tax Act 1994 Sch 9 Group 6 item 2. This item exempts "the supply of private tuition in a subject ordinarily taught in a school or university, by an individual teacher acting independently of an employer." Choir training delivered by self-employed individuals or partnerships is currently treated as exempt. When this book went to press HMRC was reviewing its policy over what subjects are allowed under this exemption.

Note that VAT is not charged on pipe organs which are installed as part of a new church building. Repairs to organs are not eligible for the Listed Places of Worship Grant Scheme, as explained on page 120.

8 Health and safety

Introduction

This chapter is not intended as an exhaustive guide to all aspects of health and safety in the church. It is simply a guide to those aspects which are of particular relevance to the organist.

Health and safety is the obligation to take reasonable steps to prevent injury. Its obligation is both legal and moral, with the former attempting to enforce the latter. Compliance demonstrates a Christian commitment to look after each other. At a mundane level, it helps the church avoid claims and ensures compliance with insurance policies.

Many of our churches were built long before there was such awareness of safety, and so there can be particular problems applying modern standards to old churches. Also many churches are listed buildings. However, local authorities are sympathetic and can usually find satisfactory ways of making adaptations without undue damage.

Almost anything can be dangerous if improperly used. A pencil can blind someone, for example. There is a balance of duty between the individual to exercise personal responsibility and the occupiers of premises to avoid potential dangers. For this reason, health and safety legislation is full of provisions using the word "reasonable". Procedures are laid down by parliament and other authoritative bodies not to prevent all accidents, but to indicate a standard where the balance is between collective and personal responsibility. Following such procedures not only helps avoid accidents but helps avoid claims should an accident happen.

While most health and safety issues at church are the responsibility of the churchwardens and church council (or equivalents in non-Anglican churches), safety is a matter for everyone. In particular, an organist must consider:

- candles;
- fire;
- cassocks;
- stairs;
- galleries;
- electricity;
- shelves;

- pianos;

- light;

- heating.

Each of these is further discussed later.

Proper precautions not only avoid accidents, but prevent the **pendulum attitude**. This is where no-one takes an issue seriously until something happens, and then everything is banned. It is much better to have a balanced approach from day one.

Legal basis

The legal basis for health and safety derives from four main sources of law:

- Health and Safety at Work Act 1974;

- occupier's liability;

- negligence; and

- Disability Discrimination Act 1995.

There are, however, many other aspects of law which can be relevant.

An organist is a representative of the church, and therefore can be liable under the law as a manager.

Health and safety at work

The main law is Health and Safety at Work Act 1974. This is designed to ensure that workplaces are safe for employees. If the church employs five or more people, it must have a written health and safety policy. The Health and Safety Executive recommends that volunteers are treated the same as paid employees.

Previously there were various regulations concerning factories and offices, which imposed a ragbag of conditions on the employer. The 1974 Act approaches the subject differently and puts a duty on employers and employees *together* to create a safe environment.

The general duty is summarised in section 2 of the Act, which imposes a general duty on the employer to safeguard the health, safety and welfare of employees with regard to:

- safe plant and safe systems of work;

- safe handling, storage, maintenance and transport of articles and substances;

- necessary information, instruction and supervision;
- a safe place of work with safe access and egress; and
- a safe working environment with adequate welfare facilities.
- having a written safety policy.

The Act has been complemented by many regulations covering many aspects of health and safety.

The Health and Safety Executive (HSE) is responsible for enforcing the Act and its regulations. Health and safety inspectors have the right to enter and inspect premises, see records, examine equipment, interview anyone, and take other reasonable steps. From 1 April 1990, local authorities are responsible for checking churches.

An inspector may serve an **improvement notice** which gives the employer at least 21 days notice to remedy a shortcoming. A **prohibition notice** takes effect immediately, unless it is a deferred prohibition notice. Inspectors may institute prosecution if there is no compliance with notices.

An inspector will first check what employees the church has. The legal adviser to General Synod has stated that volunteers playing the organ are not covered by this Act, however there is no reason why an unpaid organist should be put at greater risk than a paid organist.

In the Church of England, building work must also comply with the faculty jurisdiction, see page 225.

Occupier's liability

A separate body of law relates to the liability someone has from occupying premises, whether as owner, tenant or licensee.

This imposes a general liability on the occupier to ensure that premises are safe, and creates a possible liability to anyone on the premises. This liability is not limited to those who are legally on the premises. In extreme circumstances, this can create a liability towards trespassers and even burglars.

The two main Acts are the Occupiers Liability Act 1957 which created the liability for employees and visitors. The Occupiers Liability Act 1984 extends that liability to others who are on the premises. This Act also requires notices for any temporary hazard, such as a slippery floor just after washing.

Employers' Liability (Compulsory Insurance) Act 1969 requires employers to have at least £5 million insurance for injury or illness sustained by an employee. The certificate of insurance must be conspicuously displayed.

Negligence

Negligence is a tort (a civil wrong) for which it is necessary to prove two things:

- that you owed a duty of care to someone; and
- that you failed to discharge that duty.

The failure to discharge the duty can involve little more than thoughtlessness or carelessness, that is not realising that there could be a danger or not taking sufficient steps to prevent it.

Where the negligence arose from not complying with the terms of a contract, it is usually easier to sue for breach of contract.

Disability Discrimination Act 1995

This Act became law on 2 December 1996. It imposes a general duty on service providers not to treat disabled people less favourably than able people. It was introduced in three stages.

From 1 October 1999, service providers must make reasonable adjustments to how they provide services.

From 1 October 2004, all service providers, including churches, must make reasonable adjustments to the physical premises. This includes provisions such as handrails, hearing loops and ramps.

Organists must similarly be prepared to adapt any choir procedures to accommodate disabled choristers. Examples may include:

- excusing a person with walking difficulties from processing;
- providing enlarged music for those with sight problems;
- allowing a wheelchair-bound chorister to sit at the front.

A church should also make available large print sizes of hymn books and produce large print versions of service books.

Specific concerns

Candles

As a minimum, candles should:

- not be carried while lit, unless designed for that purpose;
- be in a secure holder of the right size;
- placed so they cannot fall over;
- not left lit and unattended without a glass chimney;
- not available to unsupervised children; and
- kept distant from hair, robes, foliage and paper.

A candle flame burns at 1000°C. It will ignite flammable material within 1½ times the height of the flame, and scorch material further away.

It is unlikely to be a good idea to have lit candles in the choir stalls where the risk of igniting hair and paper is great. Girls' long hair often has wispy strands which can easily ignite and set hair on fire. If quick enough, a hair fire can safely be smothered with bare hands, but don't take the risk of fire in the first place. Similarly, a surplice can easily catch in an open flame.

Care should be taken to acquire the right type of candle. Slow-burning candles are the safest, and are usually more economical than cheaper but faster-burning candles. Candles and holders of various types are readily available from suppliers such as the Church Purchasing Scheme.

If the congregation must handle lit candles, they must be of a suitable type with adequate protection. Some candles are specifically made for this purpose. If children hold candles, they must be properly supervised.

In the Church of England there is unrepealed 19th century case law that the ceremonial use of candles is illegal. For example, the case *Sumner v Wix [1870]* held that holding lighted candles each side of the minister while the gospel is read was an illegal addition to ceremonial. However, several modern liturgies from the Alternative Service Book 1980 onwards include candles in the rubric. Candles purely for illumination have always been legal.

Fire

Guidance on fire precautions for the church are contained in a free Council for the Care of Churches leaflet, available from Church House Bookshop.

A main concern about fire is not to block exits. This is particularly relevant for concerts; the audience must be able to go straight to the exit without having to negotiate kettledrums or loudspeaker cabinets first.

Churches are generally exempt from fire regulations while having services but not for concerts. However good practice is that the same standards of compliance apply at all times. The local chief fire officer is able to give free advice, which should be followed.

You should know where the fire extinguishers are. There should be between one and four depending on the size of the church. There should be a carbon dioxide extinguisher by the organ console. This and dry powder extinguishers are the only type safe to use on electrical appliances, but powder and pipe organs do not mix – it can cost £8,000 or more to clean out the powder if an extinguisher is discharged by the organ.

Ensure that you have adequate exits even while rehearsing. One side door down some stone steps is not enough for a rehearsal with 50 singers.

For regular practices, you should include a fire drill at least once a year.

If the fire alarm goes off, never assume that it is an accident or a drill. Evacuate the building immediately, tell people where to assemble, do not take belongings with you and call the fire brigade.

Flammable material, such as paper and old robes, should not be stored in the organ chamber. If a fire starts, flue pipes, not surprisingly, act as flues.

Cassocks

A cassock should be at least three inches above the floor. This should reach no lower than the ankle so the chorister cannot trip while processing.

If you have children in the choir, cassocks should be checked every year against the child's growth, and changed or adjusted as necessary. Do not be tempted to give a child a long cassock to "grow into". If it reaches below the ankles, take up the bottom hem, which is a simple job for someone adept at such things. The hem can always be lowered again.

Stairs

Sometimes a choir may need to negotiate a user-unfriendly staircase, such as a stone spiral staircase to a tower or gallery. You must:

- allow adequate time for ascending and descending, so there is no rush;
- if possible, put on robes after climbing stairs;
- if choristers must climb stairs in robes, tell them to lift up their cassocks a few inches to avoid tripping;
- carry as few books as possible; and
- have at least two adults, preferably able-bodied men, bringing up the rear, in case anyone does slip.

Organ chambers are not designed for public access. It is advisable for the organist to see the pipes and workings of the organ at least once. While it is good practice to encourage interest in organs and how they work, be very cautious about allowing people into the organ chamber. Any person let in must be supervised by the organist, organ tuner or other experienced people. If using a ladder, take extra care with one person remaining on the ground. There are specific safety guidelines on the use of ladders.

Section K1 of the building regulations gives these requirements for the building of staircases in institutional buildings. Building regulations apply only to what may be built, not to existing staircases, but give an indication of what is considered safe. There are further regulations for spiral staircases.

Galleries

Provision K2 of the Building Regulations 2000 requires that a gallery should have a protecting wall up to 1.1 metres (3 feet 7½ inches) high. This only applies to new buildings, but indicates what may be regarded as safe. (Similar sentiments are found in Deuteronomy 22:8.) A rail should be fitted to an existing gallery of less than 1.1 metres. The wall should either be solid, or at least designed so that a child cannot slip through it.

Choristers, particularly children, should be told not to stand near the edge, not to lean over, and not to lark around.

Electricity

Electrical work is subject to many specific regulations, particularly Electricity at Work Regulations. In general, fixed electrical work must be inspected every five years. There are regulations produced by The Institution of Electrical Engineers, British Standard BS

7671 and Part P of the Building Regulations. General guidance is available in the book *Wiring in Churches* published by Church House Publishing in 1997.

From 1 January 2005, electrical work in a home or garden must generally be undertaken by an approved electrician and not by yourself or an unapproved friend. This restriction does not apply to:

- adding power points to an existing circuit (unless in a kitchen or bathroom);
- maintenance work; or
- fixing appliances, such as changing a plug.

Strictly, these regulations do not apply to churches, but it is considered good practice that the same standard is followed there as for homes. If the church engages an approved electrician (as it should), that electrician is obliged to follow BS 7671 and other regulations. A church which permits electrical work by someone not approved to do it could find itself in difficulties with its insurance company and its own church authorities.

The main concerns for electricity are that:

- trailing wires are fixed;
- the system is not overloaded;
- connections are secure; and
- power points near the floor are covered.

Perhaps the most important consideration for an organist is that all trailing wires are securely fixed to the floor across the whole length where anyone may walk. There are special **cable protectors** made for this. In 2005, the cost approximated to £10 per metre, though with regular re-use this can become cheaper than tape. It is also much cheaper than an accident. Masking tape or gaffer tape (also known as elephant tape, duck tape and by other names) is widely used, and is better than nothing, but it will not properly protect cables from stiletto and similar heels or other forms of mechanical damage. Without any protection, people will easily trip over a loose wire. Unused lengths of extension leads should be coiled and kept away from any passage.

The organist may know where the church's **fuse box** is, but should only change a fuse if he can do so properly. Modern fuse boxes are circuit breakers which you simply switch back on. If a fuse keeps blowing, there is a problem with the electrical circuit somewhere. The organist must always report a blown fuse to the appropriate church officer, as this could indicate a problem with the electrical supply. The organ and fixed electrical heaters usually have their own power supply.

For normal 240-volt mains electricity, one kilowatt uses about four **amps**. Mains plugs are fitted with 13-amp fuses, though lower fuses are available. Thirteen amps is sufficient for just over three kilowatts. Power points are usually on circuits which typically have a total output of 30 amps. It is possible for ten amps in a 13-amp power point to overload the system if you already have 25 amps on other points. Unless running many free-standing heaters, it is most unlikely that you will ever get near that limit to overload a system. If you do have a power cut-out, there is probably a problem elsewhere, for which the church should get an electrician.

Electrical heaters are the heaviest users of electricity; a one-bar fire, fan heater or electric kettle uses one kilowatt. Amplifiers use little electricity. A deafening 100-watt amplifier uses about one fifth of one kilowatt. A standard 100-watt light bulb uses one tenth of a kilowatt. Electric keyboards, hi-fi systems, computers and clocks use tiny amounts of electricity.

Provided the total kilowattage does not exceed the total for the power point or circuit, there is no limit to the number of plugs that may be connected to a single power point using adaptors and gangboards. Gangboards are preferable to adaptors.

Note that some modern organs are vulnerable to **power surges** in the mains supply in the same way that computers are. This is because they use similar circuitry. A power supply to a modern organ will need a surge protector, which is simply a special type of plug or adaptor, readily available from electrical stores.

All electrical **connections** should be properly made and protective covers securely fixed. It is worth learning to wire up a plug properly; it is not difficult. A badly-wired plug is more likely simply to stop working than be dangerous, but that is also a situation to avoid. Plugs must be securely closed with no wires other than the outer cable showing. Poorly wired plugs in amplification systems can cause sound problems.

Portable electrical appliances, including heaters, kettles, amplifiers, keyboards etc. should be **"PAT tested"** on a regular basis, dependant on usage. The regulations do not state any specific interval, but give criteria to allow the user to decide.

For organs, Ecclesiastical Insurance Group offers this guidance:

- do not tolerate any amateur wiring;
- console lights must be permanently wired;
- console lights must be as low a wattage as possible;

- it must not be possible to put music, hymn lists or other paper on top of a console light;

- maintenance lights should be fitted above each section of pipework;

- maintenance lights should preferably be fluorescent (less heat);

- maintenance light switches should be at the entrance of the organ chamber;

- a wandering lead from a 13-amp socket should be fitted in the lower section of the organ, and be fitted with a proper inspection lamp (see below);

- any portable heater should be a convector or fan-assisted type, fitted with a thermostatic cut-out;

- a portable heater should be unplugged when not in use;

- inspection, maintenance and repair of an organ should be entrusted to an experienced builder who has appropriate knowledge of its electrical system;

- organ maintenance should not overlook the blower and humidifier which need to be examined periodically;

- a humidifier should be inspected every six months;

- the organ console should have a "power on" indicator light.

In addition, the Institute of British Organbuilding recommends the use of low voltage (50 volts) inspection lamps and circuit breakers on all power sockets.

Sometimes an **anglepoise lamp** is used instead of a permanently wired console light. This is not ideal, but if it must be used, it should either be bolted to the organ console or otherwise have a weighted base and be situated where it cannot readily fall over.

You should know who checks the organ's electrical wiring. It is not unknown for the organ builder to assume the electrician checks it, and for the electrician to assume that the organ builder does.

A general safety guide for electrical appliances is:

- plug in appliances before switching on the power;

- do not touch electrical equipment with wet hands (as the chances of an electric shock are vastly increased);

- keep water and liquids away from electrical appliances, and disconnect power immediately if any liquid is spilled inside;

- check electrical equipment periodically;

- switch off mains before removing plug.

Power points near the floor in buildings used by young children should have safety covers fitted, which should be used. As these covers are easily lost, the church should keep a plentiful supply.

In addition to these electrical hazards, many organ blower housings contain asbestos. This can mean that any work on the housing must comply with the Control of Asbestos at Work Regulations.

Organ humidifiers which are not properly maintained can spread Legionnaires disease. There is a code of practice which must be followed to minimise this risk.

Shelves

Choir vestries soon accumulate vast amounts of music and junk. Items can be precariously piled on top of cabinets and can easily fall on top of you.

Avoid unstable piles of music. Find proper homes for all sets of books, even if it means putting some music in storage. Alternatively use some of the choir budget for a new bookcase, if you have room.

Some modern furniture, particularly flat-pack furniture, is not strong enough to carry the full weight of music. Full size sheet music weighs 36 pounds per foot (53 Kg per metre). This means that a four-foot shelf can be required to support more than a hundredweight of paper. Flat-pack furniture shelves need to be braced along their whole length.

Music must be accessible without having to balance on one foot while standing on the piano. Even standing on a chair can be dangerous. A short set of aluminium steps is inexpensive, takes little space and is readily available.

Pianos

Pianos can be dangerous in three ways:

- weight;
- string tension; and
- stability.

A piano weighs from 650 pounds (300 Kg, or a third of a ton) for a small upright, up to 1400 pounds (635 Kg, or two-thirds of a ton) for a model D Steinway Grand. Lifting them requires great care and knowing how to lift properly. There are companies which specialise in moving pianos. Normally you need four men to lift a piano safely, fewer if particularly strong and trained. Even digital pianos can be surprisingly heavy. Don't even think of moving a piano if you have back trouble.

The tension on a piano string is about 165 pounds (75 Kg). As there are over 200 strings, the total tension across a piano frame ranges from 18 tons for a normal upright to 30 tons for a concert grand. If a string snaps it can be like a cheesewire with sufficient force to cut off a man's arm. So do not tempt fate by plucking strings or smashing up an old piano. A broken string should be replaced promptly by a piano technician.

Most of a piano's weight is in the iron frame which holds the strings. In an upright piano, this is at the back making a piano unstable while being moved. Most pianos have special castors for moving. There is a special school piano castor, which must be fitted properly.

On carpets, it is advisable for the piano castors to sit in castor trays. Although a carpet provides enough stability for a castor, it will leave a permanent mark in the carpet.

Light

Rehearse in plenty of light. Churches are full of hazards, made much worse if visibility is poor. Also poor light for singing causes eye strain.

It is a fool's economy to keep lights off to economise. Twenty lights provides plenty of illumination. Even at 10p per unit, this costs less than 20p an hour. Your choir is worth it.

Heating

The organist, and the choir, should be warm when practising. This may require portable heating appliances. The recommended portable heater is convector or fan assisted and fitted with a thermostatic cut-out. If the existing appliance is 'of some age', ie "resting and rusting" in the back of some kind person's garage for 20 years until resurrected and donated to the church, it may be cheaper to replace it with a modern brand than to PAT test it.

The use of LPG (bottled gas) heaters is not recommended. Changing bottles is hazardous to feet when the full bottle is dropped on them, and to backs when changing bottles in the heater. Cassocks can catch fire if the flowing robe is too close to the flame.

It is reasonable to expect the church to be warm for services and choir practices. It is not reasonable to expect the church to be heated for private organ practice, unless this is part of the organist's employment. A traditional stone church has a high thermal capacity where it can take weeks for its mass to warm up in summer and cool down in winter.

An organist may need to practise in a freezing building. The following advice is offered in *A Practical Guide to Playing the Organ* by Anne Marsden Thomas (published by Middle Eight Music Ltd):

- place a fan heater by the organ (but keep it focused on you, not the pipes or the organ bench);

- find or bring a kettle to provide hot water and/or drinks;

- immerse your hands in hot water for at least five minutes before playing;

- strap one or two hot water bottles to your body with a long scarf;

- play in fingerless gloves;

- bring a second pair of gloves warming underneath the hot water bottles. Periodically pause in your work and put your hands in the hot gloves;

- organise your tasks, so that you avoid wasting time. Thus you can achieve what you need before the cold forces you to stop.

Cold weather affects an organ tuning by making flue pipes go flat by up to a painful quarter-tone. This is to do with the speed that cold air travels through pipes. It does not affect reed pipes in the same way. Cold weather makes pianos go sharp as the metal strings contract. An organist should always leave swell boxes open, and be careful of tuning in cold weather.

Working conditions

Ideal working conditions are:

- lighting at 1500 lux to see music clearly;

- temperature between 15°C and 20°C;

- background noise around 35 decibels (explained more on page 228); and

- air movement of about ten metres per second, which can just be felt on the face.

For temperature, the Workplace (Health, Safety and Welfare) Regulations SI 1992 require a minimum temperature of 16°C for sedentary work.

A person's physical output halves for every additional 5°C above 20°, so someone is working at one eighth capacity at 35°C.

The 1992 regulations also require:

- buildings kept clean;

- adequate working space;

- suitable and adequate ventilation and lighting;

- adequate toilets and washing facilities;

- availability of drinking water;

- provision to hang outdoor clothing;

- a seat for each employee in sedentary work;

- eating facilities for employees who eat on the premises;

- protection for non-smokers from smoking (but no requirement to provide facilities for smokers);

- floors, stairs, steps, passageways and gangways to be soundly constructed and properly maintained;

- staircases to have a handrail on any open side;

- openings in floors to be securely fenced;

- dangerous parts of machinery to be securely fenced; and

- vehicles and pedestrians separated as necessary.

Other hazards

An organist shares responsibility with other church officers for ensuring that the church is safe, and should therefore ensure that he does nothing to compromise that safety. This requires an appreciation of general safety checks.

A health and safety inspection of a church should check:

- the floors are sound, level and not slippery;

- carpets and mats are securely fixed;

- availability of fire extinguishers;

- extinguishers have been checked;

- safe electrical and heating systems;

- protection from bells and clock weights;

- secure marking of open graves;

- restrictions on access to dangerous towers and galleries;

- safe access to all public areas;

- provision of first aid;

- toilets are clean;

- no accumulations of junk and debris;

- chairs not stacked too high;
- loose chairs in rows clipped together in four or more;
- cupboards not overfilled;
- no damp kitchen equipment;
- windows properly fastened.

Churches can be required to carry out risk assessments on particular aspects of their work. There are separate health and hygiene regulations for kitchens. The Central Council of Church Bell Ringers has produced its own safety guidance.

All Anglican churches must be inspected by an architect once every five years under Inspection of Churches Measure 1955. Any defects he identifies must be corrected within the timescale stipulated.

The local authority is always pleased to advise in these matters.

Personal security

In addition to the risks from tangible items, there are other safety factors which need to be considered.

Personal safety

Organists are frequently **in the church alone**, practising or sorting music. Organists are usually church keyholders. It is good practice to organise activities such as cleaning and flower arranging to ensure a presence in the church most of the time it is open. Sometimes churches organise a rota of church sitters. Any presence is a deterrent. It is also good practice for there to be visits by church officers at random times. Organ practice contributes to church security.

Churches are not immune to theft and vandalism, but **attacks** on people are much rarer. An organist is not at greater risk in a church than elsewhere. The following good practice can help:

- keep the doors locked at night;
- during the day, only leave doors unlocked if there are other people in the church;
- have a mobile telephone with you;
- switch on sufficient lights to see the whole building, rather than just the part by the organ console;

- make sure someone knows where you are and when you expect to return;

- keep valuable items locked away;

- always comply with the churchwardens' (or equivalent) instructions about locks and alarms.

Do not see people who come into a church as being a threat. Most **casual visitors** simply want to admire the architecture or enjoy quiet. This need not stop your organ practice. Most visitors quite enjoy hearing organ practice even when you are tediously repeating a difficult pedal passage.

If someone starts talking to you about their problems, you may wish to listen, but explain that you are the organist. You should not attempt **counselling** unless trained. Direct them to the vicarage, or call someone who may be able to help. People rightly seek help from the church, and are entitled to see those able to provide it.

Sometimes **church entrances** are used by tramps or addicts. It is recommended that such areas are fitted with locked gates and kept illuminated. Such people may seem intimidating but are rarely any physical threat. Avoid dark passageways to get to a side-door. Either insist on using a well-lit main entrance or for side entrances to be adequately lit.

Many organists in empty churches at some point believe they are joined by **ghosts** through hearing footsteps, voices and similar. Perhaps we are. However it is more likely to be the effect of a church's cavernous acoustics on wind, pigeons and heating pipes. If you are still spooked by this, remember there is no known incident of an organist being attacked by a ghost.

Stress

A different sort of personal issue arises from stress.

Most organists have frantic periods. Stress becomes an issue when the organist cannot cope. Stress is a state of mind rather than a state of play, in that some people can happily cope with a situation which stresses someone else.

Stress derives from the concept of **fight or flight**. If faced with a physical threat, such as from a dangerous person or a wild animal, the human instinctively prepares either to fight or run away. This instinct involves arching the back, clenching fists and draining blood from the skin and releasing glucose and fat into the bloodstream to produce energy. The same phenomena happen even when the threat is not a physical one.

About two-thirds of employees suffer from some form of workplace stress. About half of all stress is caused by colleagues rather than the job itself.

The body can take short periods of stress quite easily. However, prolonged stress can lead to personality changes in attitude and behaviour. More serious cases can lead to weight loss, headaches, skin disorder and other symptoms. Eventually stress can lead to a breakdown, for which time off and treatment is necessary.

An employer is obliged to take reasonable precautions to avoid stress. An organist should not be put under unreasonable pressure, nor should an organist expose choir members or others to unreasonable pressure.

An employer can be liable for stress to an employee on the same basis as for any other accident or illness suffered in the workplace. This legal principle was established by the case *Walker v Northumberland County Council [1995]*. The position was clarified by the case *Rorrison v West Lothian College and Lothian Regional Council [2000]* which held that an employer is liable for psychiatric injury only to the extent that such injury was foreseeable.

This law was further explained by the House of Lords in the leading stress case of *Barber v Somerset County Council [2004]*. The Lords made the following points:

- an employer becomes liable from when the employer first becomes aware of a problem, such as being told by the employee or receiving a sick note indicating stress as a problem;
- an employer is obliged to investigate complaints of work pressure;
- an employer must provide assistance, at least in the short term, to an employee in difficulties;
- where official guidance is published on the subject, an employer is expected to follow it;
- budgetary constraints and similar pressures on colleagues are no reasons to do nothing;
- an employer must investigate cases of stress and depression, particularly when an employee has taken sick leave for that reason;
- even a small reduction in duties and being sympathetic can make a difference.

Fatigue

Fatigue is a reduction in energy which prevents completion of a task. Fatigue is a purely physical condition; there is no such thing as mental fatigue. The sensation is caused by a change in the chemical composition of certain body fluids.

Research done more than 100 years ago has established that:

- fatigue is avoided by performing more tasks. It is better to make 10 trips easily carrying 20 pounds, than 5 trips struggling to carry 40 pounds;
- rest leads to a complete recovery from fatigue;
- a rest period is most effective at the first signs of fatigue;
- there are no long-term consequences of fatigue.

As with stress, the abilities to pace yourself, stay calm and prioritise helps greatly.

9 Everything else

Licensing Act 2003

New provisions about the performance of live music are contained in Licensing Act 2003. This Act takes full effect from 1 November 2005. The law applies to England and Wales, not to Scotland. Most of the provisions about music and entertainment are contained in Schedule 1 of an Act primarily concerned about selling alcohol.

There has been a considerable amount of misinformation, particularly in the press and from certain musicians' groups, that this Act outlaws live music. It does not. Most of the music in which an organist is involved needs no licence. Where a licence is required, the process is simplified.

Under the Act, three types of activity need a licence:

- provision of music and other licensed entertainment;
- sale of alcohol; and
- sale of hot food or hot drink between 11pm and 5am.

The first two replace a raft of over 50 previous licensing laws (particularly Licensing Act 1964), while the third activity is a new addition. A single licence can cover any combination of the above, so a restaurant can apply for a single licence to sell late night refreshments, serve alcohol and play music. Licensed entertainment includes both live music and recorded music, in addition to plays, films, indoor sport, boxing and dancing. The licence is issued by the local authority.

For music, a licence is only needed when there is an audience. No licence is needed for a private rehearsal. Even when there is an audience, there are many exceptions where a licence is not required. These include:

- church services, which are specifically exempt;
- secular concerts in church premises (see below);
- church garden fetes where profits are applied to church or charitable purposes;
- carol singing in the street or anywhere else, unless pre-arranged;
- ringing church bells;
- Morris dancing (which is given a specific exemption), folk dancing, wassailing and similar activities;

- private parties and anything in a private home, provided no charge is made to guests;

- performances in schools which are limited to pupils and parents and for which any charge made is only to cover costs and not make a surplus;

- on moving vehicles (such as a sing-song on a coach);

- spontaneous performance (such as when the rugby club start singing in the pub, or when guests sing *Happy Birthday* in a restaurant);

- incidental entertainment, such as juke boxes, televisions in pubs and jingles in amusement machines;

- rehearsal studios and broadcasting studios;

- testing or demonstrating an instrument in a music shop;

- performances by stand-up comics, story-tellers, magicians, clowns and children's entertainers, unless they include music.

"Church services" includes the ritual of any faith.

As originally drafted, the Licensing Act would have required a licence for secular concerts in church premises, which previously only applied to churches in London. The original argument was to ensure fairness between churches competing for custom with licensed concert halls. This requirement was dropped in the face of considerable protest that churches do not compete with concert halls.

A licence for entertainment usually *is* required in these circumstances:

- performing music which is neither part of a church service nor in church premises;

- singing carols in a railway station, shopping centre or elsewhere *by arrangement*;

- parties for which attendees are charged admission;

- performances in schools which are to be attended by people other than pupils and parents;

- performances in schools where a charge is made which is more than merely covering costs (even if just raising funds for the school);

- performances in church halls, village halls and the suchlike (though the licensing process is simpler);

- entertainment in sports clubs;

- a dress rehearsal to which members of the public are admitted;

- a disc jockey performing in a pub.

Where a licence is required, there are broadly three sets of circumstances determining the licensing arrangements:

- permanent premises (such as pubs, restaurants and sports halls);
- private clubs; and
- temporary event notice.

Permanent premises need a **premises licence**, and a named individual with a **personal licence**. Private clubs need a club premises certificate, which is less onerous, and do not need anyone with a personal licence.

Conditions may be attached to these licences, such as the hours for which music may be performed.

For pubs the old "two in a bar" rule is abolished. This rule said that up to two musicians (eg singer and pianist) could perform without a licence. Under the new rules, a pub now needs a licence for a single musician, but once it has that licence it can engage the Royal Philharmonic Orchestra.

A **temporary event notice** (TEN) applies to such events as festivals, fetes (if they need a licence) and conferences if they provide music, alcohol or late-night refreshments.

The event must:

- not exceed 96 hours (four days) duration;
- be limited to no more than 500 people present;
- not start within 24 hours of a previous licensed event finishing.

There is a limit of 12 events or 15 days' worth of TEN events for any one venue.

The person seeking the notice must:

- be at least 18 years old;
- not hold more than five licensed events a year (50 if the person holds a personal licence);
- not be associated with someone so as to circumvent the previous provision (such as getting your wife to apply for a TEN for a sixth event);
- apply at least ten days before the event (though the council may specify a longer period); and
- notify the police.

The council must acknowledge the application within one working day. Only the police may raise an objection to TEN, which they must do within 48 hours (two calendar days). The police may only object on grounds of crime and disorder, and may not use the licensing process to enforce the law in areas for which they have other powers. The council decides whether to uphold the police objection.

Many organists are unlikely ever to be involved in a licensing issue as church services and carol singing round the streets are specifically exempt. However it can be an issue if performing elsewhere.

An organist who is invited to sing carols in a supermarket or shopping centre should check that a premises licence or TEN is held. If there is no licence or TEN, the premises holder is more likely to be prosecuted than the musicians.

Carol singing

There are three legal issues and several practical issues in arranging carol singing. The three legal issues are:

- whether a licence is required;
- nuisance; and
- collecting money.

A **licence** under Licensing Act 2003 is not required for carol singing in the street or anywhere else unless it is by arrangement. So if carol singers simply turn up at a pub unannounced and sing carols, no licence is required. If they arrange with a publican in advance, a licence is required, though the pub premises licence will probably be sufficient. A special licence could be required to sing in a supermarket or shopping area by arrangement.

If a choir visits a school, hospital, old people's home or similar premises, no licence is required if:

- the singing is part of a religious service; or
- only residents and their relatives are present, and they do not pay to be present.

Nuisance is two different offences:

- the civil offence of private nuisance; and
- the criminal offence of public nuisance.

Both are common law offences. This means that there is no Act of Parliament outlawing them. They became offences because judges outlawed them in specific cases, and judges in subsequent cases are obliged to follow those precedents.

A nuisance is "an inconvenience materially interfering with the ordinary comfort physically of human existence, not merely according to elegant or dainty modes of living, but according to plain and sober, simple notions among the English people" *(Walter v Selfe [1851])*.

A **private nuisance** is a tort of wrongful disturbance or interference with a person's use or enjoyment of land. It is not a criminal offence, which means that the aggrieved person must bring proceedings himself and cannot use the police. Private nuisance may be remedied by damages or an injunction to stop the nuisance.

Public nuisance is a common law criminal offence of causing substantial annoyance to the subjects of the Crown by exposing to danger, or in other ways affecting injuriously, their lives, health, property or morals.

In practice, annoying one household is a private nuisance, while annoying a neighbourhood is a public nuisance.

The law expects people to tolerate a reasonable amount of noise depending on the location.

There is no nuisance just because someone does not think much of your singing or is an old misery. It is necessary to show that you are unreasonably preventing them from enjoying their property. In practice, this would have to be extreme for carol singing, such as staying for a long time in the same place and using amplified music.

You should note that there is no law against singing or playing instruments on pavements, traffic islands or even in the middle of the road, unless you **obstruct** the road to other road users, which is an offence under Highways Act 1980 s137. A resident cannot complain that you are obstructing a road unless you are stopping the free flow of pedestrians or vehicles. You can be guilty of obstruction if you attract a sufficiently large crowd that you block the highway, even though the singers themselves are not blocking the highway. The inconvenience must be to other road users, not to nearby residents. Someone blocking the highway may be arrested under Police and Criminal Evidence Act 1984 s25.

Using amplified instruments can cause problems as this is more likely to be construed as a nuisance than acoustic instruments. There is a practical problem in obtaining electricity. The permission of whoever pays the electricity bill must be obtained, as abstracting electricity without permission is a specific criminal offence under Theft Act 1968 s13. Many street lights have 13-amp power points in their base. Permission is needed from the local council to access these.

Collecting money

If you wish to collect money while carol-singing, you need a collecting licence under House to House Collections Act 1939. A licence may only be issued to collect money for a charitable purpose. (There are plans to amend this law.)

The licence is issued by a senior police officer. Although the law is quite clear, it seems that it is widely ignored with impunity. There have been instances of police stations unable to find the forms or even in knowing what you are talking about, so be patient and allow plenty of time.

The House to House Collections Regulations 1947 state that collectors must:

- be at least 16 years old;
- wear a badge identifying the person as a collector;
- carry a certificate signed by the collector and an officer of the charity.

If the carol singing is to raise funds for the church, it would seem that the certificate should be signed by the minister as the charity officer. All churches are charities.

Street collections which do not involve going from house to house, such as carol singing with collecting boxes in one place must comply with local authority regulations issued under Police, Factories &c (Miscellaneous Provisions) Act 1916. Contact your town hall for advice. It is doubtful they will be that bothered. Indeed you may find difficulty in finding anyone who knows what you are talking about.

If you attempt to collect money other than as allowed, you could be prosecuted for non-compliance with the relevant Act. There is a very remote chance of prosecution for begging under Vagrancy Act 1824 s3, but this Act is designed to avoid annoying the general public on the highway. There is no known case of carol singers being prosecuted. The court once held that striking workers seeking assistance from the public were not begging.

Practical issues

In addition to the legal issues, there are several practical issues to consider in planning carol singing:

- deciding the date, time and starting place;
- deciding the general route; and
- deciding where to end up.

There is no obligation to inform the police of your intended carol singing, though this is advisable if many people are involved. The police may tell you that your route is also that of a protest march, or that one of the roads will be closed that day.

The answer to the last question is usually a pub or someone's house for some refreshment.

You also need to provide words of carols. Even though everyone "knows" the carols, most people would struggle to sing two verses of even the most well-known carols. Also there are significantly different versions for carols such as *We Three Kings* and *As With Gladness*.

You may also wish to consider providing music for any instruments.

Arrange illumination, either by providing torches or lanterns, or by stopping at street lights. It is more effective to stop by a street lamp and sing carols together than it is for small groups to attempt to sing carols in front gardens.

Concerts in church

There is no law against holding concerts in church, even when tickets are sold with a view to making a profit.

Such a concert is outside the scope of certain exemptions for church services, which in particular means that:

- you must comply with the Licensing Act 2003;
- you must comply with fire regulations; and
- you may need a performing rights licence.

These implications are explained in other parts of this book.

For the Church of England, there is a specific canon F16 which requires that:

- "the words, music, and pictures are such as befit the House of God, are consonant with sound doctrine, and make for the edifying of the people";
- the minister must follow any general direction from the bishop;
- the minister is satisfied that regulatory requirements have been met and any necessary licences obtained.

The first of these three conditions asks more questions than it answers. In practice, a performance of purely secular music, such as a Beethoven symphony, rarely causes a problem. A Protestant church may object to a performance of a requiem mass or a work such as Elgar's *Dream of Gerontius* or any prayer to a saint, on the basis that the Catholic doctrine of these works does not conform to their Protestant views. In practice such issues are simply addressed by checking in advance with the minister.

It is also advisable to check with the minister if there is any objection to:

- siting of equipment, such as microphones on the altar;
- moving furniture;
- serving refreshments;
- serving alcohol;
- selling programmes;
- running a raffle;
- Sunday performances.

Organ maintenance

A pipe organ needs to be **tuned and maintained** at least once a year. It is common practice to keep a notebook by the organ in which faults are recorded. These typically include notes that do not sound, pipes going out of tune, and moving parts which do not operate properly. The organ tuner goes through the book, and notes that he has fixed the problem or records what needs to be done to do so (if the problem is serious). Some notes about electrical work are given in chapter 8.

Some organists may be able to do some of the more routine tasks themselves. Depending on your practical skills, this could include knowing where to replace fuses, tuning reed stops, removing ciphering pipes, reconnecting ducting, tuning pipes which have become significantly out of tune by something dropping on the sliders, and replacing labels.

Periodically, the organ needs a thorough clean, combined with inspection for such matters as water damage, wood rot, wood warp and animal infestation. Typically this is about every 30 years, but is less for organs in open spaces, dusty organs and those used frequently. For more enclosed and less used organs, a longer period may be acceptable.

You should always remember that an electrical blower needs maintenance, such as regular oiling and checking its bearings. Most pipe organs can benefit from a humidifier (sometimes called a rehumidifier). Wood can split or warp depending on temperature or humidity. There are many modern materials which avoid this problem. Relative humidity below 50% can cause problems for wood.

Excellent advice on looking after and replacing organs is contained in the booklet *Sounds Good* by John Norman and Jim Berrow (Church House Publishing).

Anything more than tuning or routine maintenance may require a **faculty** in the Church of England. A faculty applies to consecrated buildings, their contents and surrounding land and churchyards. A faculty is a licence or dispensation authorising works of alteration, including repairs, renovations, removals and additions to the fabric or contents of a church. A faculty *permits* work but does not require it. This is a church-based requirement and is in addition to any requirements under planning law. A faculty is granted by the Chancellor of the diocese. Faculties do not apply to cathedrals and some other places which are covered by the Care of Cathedrals Measure.

Faculty applications must be published, and contested applications are heard by a special consistory court, as may happen when opinion in a parish is divided. There have been contested cases over plans to replace a pipe organ with an electronic organ in *re St Mary's Lancaster [1980]* and *re St Martin's Ashton-upon-Mersey [1981]*. The organ is often the most expensive single item in the church. It is the responsibility of the minister and churchwardens to ensure that necessary faculties are obtained.

A faculty is needed for significant work to the organ, such as:

- installation of new organ or removal of old organ;
- replacement, removal or addition of pipes;
- relocation of the console;
- changes to the organ case; or
- replacement of the organ action.

If considering such work, you should first contact the Diocesan Advisory Committee (DAC) for your diocese. They will usually appoint an individual as specialist adviser on organs, often the cathedral organist or precentor. Discussing the matter with the adviser from the beginning will provide you with excellent advice as well as smoothing the passage for granting a faculty for whatever is agreed.

If your church is being **re-ordered**, such as having the furniture and fixtures moved, try to ensure that:

- the organ console is in the right place for the organist to hear a balanced sound;
- the console is no more than 12 metres (40 feet) from the pipes (unless using an electronic action, when the console will need to be about 3 metres (10 feet) from the pipes);
- there are clear sight lines from the organ console to the choir and all parts of the church where a service may be led;
- acoustics are considered, such as not drowning the church with carpet.

On the issue of church carpets, Exeter Diocesan Advisory Committee gives this excellent advice:

> Extensive or heavy carpeting can have a very dampening acoustic effect, hampering speech, singing and other music, as well as sound reinforcement for all of these. An unsympathetic, 'dead' acoustic will discourage congregational singing, by making people self-conscious about their efforts. Carpets, curtains and upholstered chairs absorb sound, unlike wooden floors, panelling or plastered walls, all of which reflect it. Have you consulted your organist or choir as to their concerns about carpet?

At a practical level, any building or maintenance work in the church may require protection for the organ from dust and water. It is possible that the blower housing may contain asbestos which needs specialist handling or removal.

Electronic organs

An electronic organ is as good as a pipe organ in the sense that Spam is as good as steak. The financial arguments for electronic organs are questionable.

Since 1990, the development of digital sound technology has considerably improved the quality of electronic organs to the point where some sound as good as recordings of pipe organs. However, the difference between pipe organs and electronic organs is that, at best, you are hearing a recording of an organ. This is like using a synthesiser for a flute, trumpet, guitar or other instrument.

The sound is rarely as good as a pipe organ, as it is not moving as much air. Much of the problem with modern electronic organs is not in the sound production but in its amplification. Rarely is an organ given enough power. This is not needed just to produce deafeningly loud sounds, but to give quality to quieter sounds. You need powerful amplification to get quality, particularly on low notes.

A more significant aspect is cost, as few churches consider the capital cost of the instrument. In a deanery, you will probably find several pipe organs over 100 years old but no electronic organs more than 25 years old. According to surveys published in the magazine *Organ Builder,* the average life of an electronic organ when replaced is 15 years (but many organs are then used again). The capital cost of buying four new organs every century is often overlooked.

Also repairs, when needed, can be more substantial. Amplifiers and loudspeakers can rarely be properly mended when they start to play up, and need replacing completely. When an electronic organ fails, it quickly becomes unplayable. A pipe organ remains playable with no loss of quality of sound even when it has developed faults. Unlike pipe organs, electronic organ parts cannot be easily fabricated. The best manufacturers guarantee to keep electronic parts available only for ten years.

It should also be remembered that electronic organs are much less attractive to the best church musicians.

If **offered** a piano or electronic organ, only accept if you really have a need for the item. Otherwise politely decline. A church is not a dumping ground for unwanted furniture. If an item has been donated to the church, it becomes church property which means the church may dispose of it when it wishes. If the donor is still a church member, it is diplomatic to discuss the disposal with the donor, who may like to suggest another recipient or even take the item back. But a church should not keep junk just to avoid offending a donor. In the Church of England, a faculty may be needed to remove an item even if no faculty was obtained to put it in.

Sound levels

In November 2001, the European Union agreed a directive on sound levels in the workplace. Under the rules of the European Union this would become law five years later in November 2006 (two years earlier for factories). Its proposal is a limit of 85 decibels without earplugs and 87 decibels with them over an eight-hour day. The sound level is measured over a week. There is a move to lower the level to 83 decibels. The previous rules set a limit of 90 decibels. Earplugs reduce sound by about 15 decibels but can distort the sound unless of a special type used by brass players and organ tuners.

Sound is a form of energy measured in **decibels**, where 120 decibels represents one watt of energy per square metre. Each 10 decibels increase means that the sound level has increased tenfold. Conversely each 10 decibels decrease means that the sound level has reduced to one tenth. So 100 decibels represents one hundredth of one watt per square metre. The figure of 0 decibels (10^{-12} watts/sq m) is the threshold of hearing, while 120 or 130 decibels is regarded as the threshold of pain, above which the ear can suffer damage. Prolonged exposure to sound as low as 75 decibels can also cause damage.

The following are examples of typical sound levels:

Decibels	Activity	Decibels	Activity
130	Artillery at close range Bagpipes or trumpet at max volume Firecrackers	60	Business office Normal conversation Quiet street
120	Amplified rock music Standing near a jet on take-off	55	Cough Horn playing mezzo forte
115	Chain saw	50	Restaurant Private office
110	Loud orchestral music heard in audience	40	Quiet room at home Humming of a fridge
100	Electric saw Orchestra playing fortissimo	30	Quiet bedroom
90	Bus or truck engine Noisy pub	20	Empty recording studio Soft whisper
80	Car engine City traffic noise	10	Empty soundproof room
70	Busy street Loud telephone bell or radio Helicopter overhead	0	Absolute silence

Musicians have asked for music to be exempt. Many works would therefore become unplayable, including the European Union's own anthem from the last movement of Beethoven's ninth symphony. In March 2002, musicians won.

Loud sounds, particularly trumpets and percussion, aggravate a condition known as **tinnitus** which gives a ringing in the ear. Some estimates are that one person in ten suffers from the condition.

Loud sound can damage the ear drum. Pete Townshend, guitarist in The Who, suffered. It has been estimated that 10% of Americans have suffered hearing loss. Once hearing has been lost, there are surgical techniques and hearing aids which can mitigate the effects but not cure them. The ear does not get used to loud sounds; those who think their ears have toughened up have suffered hearing loss.

Data Protection Act

Data held on living people is protected by Data Protection Act 1984 as amended by Data Protection Act 1998, effective from 1 March 2000.

The main provisions of the Act are that to hold personal data on living people:

- you must register with the Data Protection Registrar;
- data must be obtained fairly and lawfully;
- the data protection principles must be followed; and
- the person must have access to the file on them for payment of a fee of £10.

Under the 1998 Act, data now includes non-computerised data, such as a card index system. The data need not be particularly sensitive, so details of qualifications and telephone numbers can be within the scope of the Act.

The following (among others) do not come within the scope of the Acts:

- an attendance register;
- a payroll;
- normal correspondence;
- references;
- examinations;
- journalistic material.

Data on the realisation of the objects of a charity are registrable. This includes records for fund-raising or providing pastoral care.

It is unlikely that an organist will want to keep any protected data under the Act, but if he does, he must be registered either himself or through the church. Conversely, an organist cannot have secret files held on him, except in limited circumstances. A choir will normally be registered through the church and not separately.

Miscellaneous practical points

Every organist should:

- prepare so thoroughly that nothing can go wrong; and
- know what to do when things do go wrong.

These notes deal with some practical points of everyday organ playing.

An organist should know when and how to **play over** the hymns. Normally, the organist plays the first one or two lines unless it is an unfamiliar tune when playing the whole verse is justified. The organist should start the play-over with the first notes sung by the congregation, and not "lead in" from the last line. The congregation must not be in any doubt as to when to start singing.

There can be a problem in knowing when the **hymn announcement** has finished, as some ministers simply announce a hymn number while others may wish to speak about the hymn. If in any doubt, the organist should count to four after what appears to be the end of the announcement before starting to play. (Four seconds is the time that a pause becomes recognised as silence.) If a hymn announcement continues after the organist has started playing, the organist must continue playing to avoid disrupting the worship.

An organist should be able to **cover the action** by filling in during gaps such as when the offertory hymn finishes before the collection is brought up, or during short periods of moving round the church. The organist should not normally play when the action is itself part of the worship, such as lighting a Pascal candle or processing to and from reading the gospel. If in doubt, the organist should check with the minister.

Covering the action either means playing a short piece in the same key, such as from *Covering the Action* (published by Kevin Mayhew) or by **improvising**. Organists have a long tradition of working suitable popular themes into such improvisations. This is fine, provided it does not distract from the dignity of worship.

A service may be **disrupted** so that it cannot continue, such as by drunks at midnight Communion, or by hecklers or protesters. As soon as the organist realises that the service has been stopped, he should immediately play the organ loudly until told to stop by a minister or appropriate officer. A hymn in which the congregation can join is ideal. The churchwardens or similar officers can then deal with the trouble while denying the troublemakers the oxygen of publicity.

There is provision for **objecting in a wedding** to the marriage when the minister asks if there is any just cause or impediment against the marriage. Despite popular fiction, there has been no known successful challenge in over 200 years. However there is a procedure in that the minister, the couple and two witnesses must withdraw for the minister to decide whether the service may proceed. The organist should play quietly during this. It does not particularly matter what you play as no-one will be listening.

A **visiting organist** should arrive in plenty of time to familiarise himself with the organ and what is required of him in the service. The visiting organist needs a list of all items where organ music is required, exactly where these occur, and whether the item is announced. This includes knowing when to provide a note for a minister to lead responses, intercessions or litany. The visiting organist should also check in advance whether the console is locked and, if so, where the key is.

Music before the service should last about 5 to 15 minutes, after any **bells** have finished pealing. This may require liaison with bellringers, or even adjudication by the minister. In the Church of England, the minister has authority over bells under Canon F8. The purpose of this music is to set the tone for worship. This should be a matter of church policy.

Organ music should not be **interrupted**. It is good practice for there to be clear sightlines between the organist and minister, so the latter can nod when he is ready to speak, such as to start the service or to say bidding words at Communion. Similarly a churchwarden should not speak over music before the service to give out a notice, but should first ask the organist to pause the music. The organist should bring the piece to a quick conclusion, which is always possible within four bars. If someone does talk over the music, bring the music to a conclusion rather than stop mid-phrase, and tell the person how to behave in future. The final voluntary should not be interrupted.

Public address systems should not normally be used during music. It may be necessary to leave microphones and amplifiers switched on for those using hearing aids, but otherwise amplification disturbs the quality of music. Ministers should have their microphones turned off or turned down during hymns.

Recorded music should always be resisted. Worship means expressing the "worthship" of God. It is the offering of the people to God, and not a spectator sport. Those who want recorded music should be invited to replace sermons with recorded addresses, and flower arrangements with photographs. Indeed why bother to have a service at all, when you can simply play a video in an empty building?

What we have not covered

Although this book aims to be as comprehensive as possible, it is inevitable that some issues will arise which have not been addressed.

It is always a good idea to have some kind of professional support. Get to know other organists. Attend meetings organised by bodies such as the Guild of Church Musicians, Royal College of Organists, Royal School of Church Music and Incorporated Society of Musicians.

The cathedral organist is almost always supportive of the work done by church organists. His position at the top of the pile depends on the loyal service from many parish organ grinders to make up that pile.

The authors of this book are always interested in learning of novel problems and may be able to assist.

Above all, remember that all cathedral and church organists are working for the glory of God. We organists have a sacred trust to assist our Christian brothers and sisters in the worship of God. He is a loving Father who supports the work of all his children. Ultimately the church organist has access to the greatest adviser of all.

Appendix 1: Useful contacts

To contact the authors or publisher:

Robert Leach, 19 Chestnut Avenue, Ewell, Epsom, Surrey KT19 0SY.

020 8224 5695. E-mail: robert.leach1@btinternet.com

Bodies for church organists:

Guild of Church Musicians, St Katharine Cree, 86 Leadenhall Street, London EC3A 3DH. www.churchmusicians.org
General correspondence to: John Ewington, Hillbrow, Godstone Road, Blechingley, Surrey RH1 4PJ. 01883 743168
E-mail: JohnMusicsure@orbix.co.uk

Incorporated Society of Musicians, 10 Stratford Place, London W1C 1AA. www.ism.org. 020 7629 4413.
E-mail: membership@ism.org

Institute of British Organ Building, 13 Ryefields, Thurston, Bury St. Edmunds, Suffolk, IP31 3TD, United Kingdom.
01359 233433 e-mail: administrator@ibo.co.uk

Royal College of Organists, Millennium Point, Curzon Street, Birmingham B4 7XG www.rco.org.uk. 0121-331 7222.
E-mail: admin@rco.org.uk

The Royal School of Church Music, Cleveland Lodge, Westhumble, Dorking, Surrey RH5 6BW. www.rscm.com
01306 872800 E-mail: enquiries@rscm.com

(The school is due to relocate to Sarum College in 2006.)

Magazines for organists:

Choir and Organ, Orpheus Publications, Newsquest Specialist Media Ltd,
30 Cannon Street, London, EC4M 6YJ. www.choirandorgan.com *Subscriptions:* 020 8606 7301.
Editorial: 020 7618 3483.

RSCM publishes *CMQ*, and the Guild publishes *Laudate.*

Chapter 1 Good relations

Mediation service:

Bridge Builders, 14 Shepherds Hill, Highgate, London N6 5RQ. www.menno.org.uk 020 8340 8775

To trace hymns and worship songs:

Hymnquest Database, Stainer & Bell Ltd, 23 Gruneisen Road, London N13 1DZ. 020 8343 3303.
E-mail: hymnquest@stainer.co.uk

Chapter 4 Fees and budgets

British Institute of Organ Studies, (including British Organ Archive), Archives Department, Birmingham Public Libraries,
Central Library, Birmingham B3 3HQ. 0121 303 4217

Chapter 5 Copyright

Copyright licensing::

CCL Ltd, PO Box 1339, Eastbourne, East Sussex BN21 4YF 01323 417711. See also page xxx

Calamus Licence, Decani Music Ltd, Oak House, 70 High Street, Brandon, Suffolk IP27 0AU. 0845 456 8392.
www.decanimusic.co.uk, E-mail: sue@decanimusic.co.uk

MCPS-PRS Alliance (Mechanical Copyright Protection Society and Performing Right Society), Copyright House,
29-33 Berners Street, London W1T 3AB. www.mcps-prs-alliance.co.uk 020 7580 5544.

Chapter 6 Child protection

Churches' Child Protection Advisory Service (CCPAS), PO Box 133, Swanley, Kent BR8 7UQ. www.cpas.co.uk
0845 120 45 52, E-mail queries: info@ccpas.co.uk

Catholic Office for the Protection of Children and Vulnerable Adults (COPCA)

12 St Paul's Square, Birmingham, B3 1RB. 0121 233 1963

Chapter 8 Health and safety

General advice:

Ecclesiastical Insurance Group, Beaufort House, Brunswick Road, Gloucester GL1 1JZ. 01452 528533.
www.eigonline.co.uk. gbeigmkg@inmail.com

Health and Safety, HSE Books, PO Box 1999, Sudbury, Suffolk CO10 6FS. 01787 881165 www.hsebooks.co.uk
Purchase of safety equipment:

Churches Purchasing Scheme Ltd, Beaufort House, Brunswick Road, Gloucester GL1 1JZ. 0845 458 4584.
www.cpsonline.co.uk sales@cpsonline.co.uk

Chapter 9 Everything Else

Data protection helpline:

First contact 01625 545 745; e-mail mail@ico.gsi.gov.uk

Appendix 2: sources quoted

Canons of the Church of England

Books quoted

Scripture quoted

Index